PASTORAL THEOLOGY:
A REORIENTATION

PASTORAL THEOLOGY: A REORIENTATION

By

MARTIN THORNTON

Priest of the Oratory of the Good Shepherd

WIPF & STOCK · Eugene, Oregon

Wipf and Stock Publishers
199 W 8th Ave, Suite 3
Eugene, OR 97401

Pastoral Theology
A Reorientation
By Thornton, Martin
Copyright©1958 SPCK
ISBN 13: 978-1-60899-744-2
Publication date 5/14/2010
Previously published by SPCK, 1958

ACKNOWLEDGEMENTS

The author and publisher wish to make grateful acknowledgement to the following for permission to quote from published works:

Longmans, Green & Co. Ltd. (*The Vision of God* and *Some Principles of Moral Theology*, both by K. E. Kirk, and *Christ, the Christian and the Church*, by E. L. Mascall); Macmillan & Co. Ltd. (*The Nature of Metaphysical Thinking*, by Dorothy M. Emmet); Routledge and Kegan Paul Ltd. (*The Graces of Interior Prayer*, by A. Poulain); S.C.M. Press Ltd. (*The Intention of Jesus*, by J. Bowman); the Syndics of the University Press, Cambridge (*The Monastic Order in England*, by David Knowles, and *Philosophical Theology*, by F. R. Tennant).

CONTENTS

PREFACE

I have tried to make this book a connected whole, and I would prefer it—ideally—to be read as such; nevertheless some explanation as to the relation between its two main parts may be helpful.

The second part of the book deals with ascetical theology on an ordinary pastoral level, and it is in this subject that my particular interest lies. But I do not think it is possible to treat the prayer of an individual soul in isolation from other souls, or to treat private prayer in isolation from the corporate liturgy. There is, after all, no such thing as an individual Christian if that phrase means a soul divorced from the whole mystical Body, and I think that the failure to give full expression to this fact is the weak point in a good deal of modern ascetical thinking. Before we can guide the progress of a single soul we must clarify its relations with other souls in local environment—i.e., in a parish. Part One of the book deals with this complex of parochial inter-relations and thus becomes the necessary prologue to the main study in Part Two.

In Part One, I have attempted to propound and substantiate one particular system of parochial organization. I think this is a good system, even the best system, but I do not maintain that it is the only one. This system is briefly set out in the Introduction (Chapters 1 to 5), and if a particular reader is willing to accept it, he may find its exposition in Part One rather dull and superfluous—in which case he may prefer to omit it and proceed to Part Two. Conversely, the reader who rejects my introductory viewpoint—whose parish is perhaps working perfectly well by some other system—need not, I think, necessarily find Part Two wholly condemnable on that account.

I must confess, moreover, that although Part One is necessary and relevant to the complete thesis, it has led me rather far from my special interests. In fact I think it is ultimately a subject for a group of writers—at least a Biblical scholar, dogmatist, and historian—rather than for one. But as I firmly believe that one can only be a Christian by incorporation into Christ's Church, and that Christian prayer is prayer in and of that Body, the problem of "parochial" theology presents me with a responsibility that I can hardly evade.

M. T.

NOTE TO SECOND EDITION

I AM GRATEFUL to The Reverend Wilfrid Browning who, in an article in *Theology* (January 1958), accused me of teaching that "we may be counted members of the local Christian community not in virtue of our baptism, but only in virtue of certain notions we hold about the obligations of membership". Although I still doubt if the book as a whole can be made to support this view—which I most certainly do not hold—I think I am guilty of ambiguity in places. To my footnote on p. 167, I would add that to describe the "Remnant" as the local or microcosmic Body of Christ means that it is the creative pastoral agent, vicarious, evangelistic, and redemptive, of the whole organic parish. But this does not "expel" any baptized soul from the Mystical Body. Like all constructive criticism, this raises further questions, such as the ontological, as against the pastoral, status, of "indiscriminately" baptized non-Communicants. All this needs further study, but that such souls are irrevocably "incorporated into Christ" quite irrespective of their own subjective views or practices, I am in no doubt whatever.

Where possible I have tried to clarify this point in the text, and there are a few other minor corrections. Otherwise this edition is substantially the same as the first; even in the major point my attempt has been to clarify and not change the original meaning.

M. T.

INTRODUCTION

1

PASTORAL THEOLOGY

"THE GENIUS who could write a history of prayer would provide in so doing an exhaustive history of religion." This frequently quoted statement of Ménégoz implies that, ultimately, prayer and religion are the same. But although this is precisely the view to be accepted in this book, it is also a dangerous oversimplification as it stands. It is necessary to define, and in so doing introduce the plan of this thesis.

At its very simplest, religion is the relation between human souls and God: an intrinsic awareness of supernatural powers impinging upon our world and our life. It is "a response to reality beyond our minds" (Professor Dorothy Emmet)[1]; "a feeling for the infinite", "a feeling of absolute dependence" (Schleiermacher)[2]; "an emotion resting on a conviction of a harmony between ourselves and the universe at large" (McTaggart)[3]; "that which drives man forward in his quest for God" (Dr Matthews).[4] Such descriptive phrases all point to something primary, and therefore strictly indefinable; and all point to the fact that religion begins with a total human experience, a mental response, feeling, emotion, conviction or urge. In due course an attempt will be made to unravel the tangled mass of controversy which surrounds religious experience; meanwhile Archbishop Temple's sublimely sensible tenet that religious experience is "but the special way in which the whole of life is experienced by a religious man" is worth remembering.[5] Thus religion and experience both imply life,

[1] *The Nature of Metaphysical Thinking*, p. 4.
[2] *Reden: 2nd Address.*
[3] *Some Dogmas of Religion*, p. 3.
[4] *God in Christian Thought and Experience*, p. 5.
[5] *Christus Veritas*, pp. 37 ff.; *Nature, Man and God*, p. 384 ff.

and together they spell "spiritual" life; all of which adds up to the fundamental concept of activity, or process.

This is most important because it means that the word "religion" is in essence verbal, and when we speak of a man's "religion" we really mean a man engaged in religious activity. This distinction is necessary, for unless it is understood, a man's religion becomes some static "thing" which he "owns", like a book or a wrist-watch; or a system of external views which he happens to hold at the moment. As a man's love for his wife is an active experience, a continuous process, a total response, so is his religion, and any other interpretation of this word draws us into the old "faculty psychology" against which Dr F. R. Tennant argues so strongly and convincingly.[1] But if, following Tennant, we deny existence to the will apart from an agent willing, to the conscience apart from the activity of moral consciousness, or to love except as agents loving; so we would deny any real meaning to the word religion except as an agent "religioning"; a soul, not as a faculty, but as a sacramental personality absorbed in religion-as-activity.[2] For the dissonant verb "to religion" we would substitute "to pray", and it is in this sense that religion and Prayer become synonyms. Written with an initial capital—Prayer—we have a generic term for any process or activity qualified by a living relation between human souls and God. It not only embraces all the usual divisions of prayer—adoration, confession, thanksgiving, supplication; meditative, contemplative, and vocal; liturgical and private, etc., but all such works, arts, and moral acts which truly spring from our communion with God. Prayer, quite simply, is the total experience of a "religious man". *Labore est orare* is either religious sublimity or Pelagian nonsense, depending on whether or not we start with a religious man; thus the whole pastoral function is concerned with the nurture of religious men—in other words with Prayer.

I have been careful to speak of a *total* experience in order to do justice to the fullness of personality, and to avoid the popular view of experience, and especially religious experience,

[1] *Philosophical Theology*, Vol. I, pp. 17–18.
[2] "There is no such thing as 'the will'—it is but a word; there is only a subject that wills": ibid., p. 131.

as largely a matter of feeling. However proportions may vary, all religious experience, and religious activity or Prayer, comprises conative and cognitive elements. As Dr Matthews is so keen to stress, experience cannot be dissociated from intellect, thence religion, upon reflection, issues in its own science which we call theology.[1]

Christianity began with the active response of men to God revealed in Christ; with the active religious experience of a group—*communis consensus fidelium*—which through the centuries has crystallized into a systematic theology. Dr Tennant clarifies these distinctions by seeing religion as conative and pre-rational, psychic (ψ); and theology as its later cognitive, psychological (ps) exposition. Religion takes the flash-photograph, theology prints and develops the film.[2] By translating these definitions into personal terms, we come to his invaluable pastoral distinctions between faith as conative and volitional, and belief as intellectual. As theology is a science, so belief is scientific; we *believe* in the logic of a mathematical formula—three times two equals six—which though potentially useful knowledge is in itself static and uncreative. To *have faith* is the much more potent power, applicable to the conative quest for experiment and research. The dynamic of religion is summed up in James Ward's great phrase, "conative-faith-venture".[3]

But it is clear that the relation here involved is one of interaction, for if religion issues in theology, then theology in turn is adaptable to the furtherance of religion. Now the doctrinal synthesis which evolves out of the manifold divisions of theology is usually called dogma; "those propositions whose acceptance or rejection by any person would alter his *religious* position".[4] So because of this religion-theology interaction we may qualify dogmatics, as we do mathematics, by the adjectives "pure" and "applied". As the work of the

[1] *God in Christian Thought and Experience*, pp. 89 ff.

[2] *Philosophical Theology*, Vol. I, p. 40.

[3] Cf. Alvarez de Paz on "Spirits": "A spirit . . . is that invisible element by which man is incited interiorly to do some human act", "a spirit is an internal impulse by which man feels himself urged to do something". Quoted by Guibert, *The Theology of the Spiritual Life*, p. 131.

[4] McTaggart, *Some Dogmas of Religion*, p. 2.

pure mathematician is taken over by engineers and applied to
the practical business of bridge building, so dogmatic theology
is to be applied to the everyday experience of souls to the
furtherance of faith and religion. Recalling Ménégoz, applied
dogmatic becomes the art and science of Christian Prayer,
normally if somewhat loosely known as ascetical theology.
All this continues to stress activity, movement, and progress
in the spiritual life of the soul, but spiritual progress, like
religious experience, presents us with another mass of misconception which we must attempt to elucidate in due course.[1]
Suffice it to say that the only valid yardstick by which spiritual
progress may be measured is *moral* theology; to divorce
ascetic from dogma and then to measure progress in terms of
devotional fervour or quasi-mystical feeling is to embark on
an intricate voyage with an inaccurate compass and the
wrong map.

We conclude from this that ascetical theology, with moral
theology as its correlate, is the true core of pastoral practice,
and in view of the extraordinary range of subjects which
creep in under the head of pastoral theology, this needs stating
very clearly and very firmly.

A general criticism with far-reaching consequences to this
inquiry must now be levelled against much present day
ascetical thinking. Whether the art and science of Prayer are
approached through philosophy, psychology, and epistemology, or whether they are studied in the classical systems of the
Christian Saints, modern emphasis inclines towards an isolated
individualism. This position is untenable because modern
philosophy, and especially moral philosophy, is placing more
and more stress on social and environmental factors, while the
ascetical schemes of Christian tradition are all firmly embedded
in rigid corporate order.[2] One cannot just lift an Ignatian
formula out of the Society of Jesus and apply it to Mrs Jones
as an individual; it is quite impossible to think of St Teresa's
ascetic without any reference to the Carmelite Order in sixteenth-century Spain. Christianity is so essentially social that

[1] Chapter 13 below.
[2] In support of this criticism see E. L. Mascall, *Christ, The Christian
and the Church*, pp. 142 ff. and 146 ff.

its applied dogmatic must issue in a *corporate* ascetic as well as a science of individual prayer-process. If SS. Ignatius and Teresa are to be of any real use to us, not only their teachings but their Orders must be adapted to twentieth-century local conditions. If, say, the Ignatian formulae are to be creative they must be made applicable to Mrs Jones *as a member of St Peter's parish*. Ascetics become sub-divisible into the personal and the corporate—which may well be called "parochial theology"—so pastoral theology may now be defined as applied dogmatics (or ascetical theology) divisible into both personal and corporate aspects, with moral theology as the one test of progress. Thus the essential work of pastoral priesthood is ascetical direction, with moral theology as a test and parochial theology as a setting.

2

2

ASCETICAL DIRECTION

PREJUDICE and misconception have given a slightly un-
pleasant flavour to the words "ascetical direction", and so
they need to be explained as clearly as possible. It is no accident that the word ἄσκησις—exercise, or effort—was adopted
by the Church from its specialized meaning in Greek culture of
athletic training. From this it is a short step to describe the
Egyptian fathers as the "athletes of God". If we keep this
analogy in mind we shall not go very far wrong, for ascetic will
appear as the necessary exercise, training, and discipline
demanded in the creative development of Prayer. It is but the
spiritual equivalent to the effort needed to become proficient
in carpentry, cricket, piano-playing, or any other human art.

Further, this analogy makes clear the meaning of "direction", which may now be translated "coaching". "Ascetical
direction" (or more commonly "spiritual direction") is simply
coaching in prayer. It has nothing whatever to do with
Manichaeism, unhealthy austerities, or tyrannical priestcraft.
It is no more nor less than what Dr Kirk calls "the work of a
priest in fostering spiritual progress".[1] But here two distinctions must be noted, for their confusion has been and still is the
cause of ambiguity in pastoral thought. The first is that
ascetical *direction*—coaching—differs from religious *teaching*.
Strictly, to teach cricket means to give classroom instruction
on the rules, strategy, and possibly moral implications of the
game, while coaching is the practical development of technique and correction of faults in matches and net-practice.
I suggest that a person who is told to kneel upright and recite

[1] *Some Principles of Moral Theology*, pp. 202 ff. Cf. Joseph de Guibert,
The Theology of the Spiritual Life, Cap. 1, paras. 3–6. A. Goodier,
Ascetical and Mystical Theology, pp. 3–5.

an office while directing all his energies—eyes, emotions, intellect, and will—in praise of the transcendent Father, then to adore and receive the Eucharistic Christ, and then to make a meditation prepared for by *Veni Creator Spiritus*; I suggest that such a soul is being coached in Trinitarian religion. Committing the Creed to memory, or a series of lectures on the Holy Trinity, are very different things, in fact mere teaching. Our analogy amply illustrates the impossibility of teaching, explaining, or understanding a crisp off-drive through the covers for four; but we may still so coach a young player in batting technique that he eventually *does* it. The distinction is still that between pure dogma and applied dogma or ascetic; between theology and religion, belief and faith: it is obviously of very great pastoral importance, and we are not helped by the general ambiguity of these words. Both Gore and Bicknell, for example, point out that the New Testament "teachers" are those of special prophetic gifts, guiding the faithful in the ways of God, as opposed to academic preachers like Scribe and Pharisee. If we look closely at our Lord himself as a teacher we find him ever trying to induce creative religion by telling people what to *do*. His demand is for "faith, fasting, and prayer" rather than knowledge; even at the institution of the Sacrament upon which his Church depends for its very existence he gave no explanation, no theology, no liturgical instruction: simply "*do this* . . .". His teaching is in fact what we would now call direction.

With Dr Matthews we must never forget that some intellectual element enters all religious experience. Ascetical direction is not obscurantism seeking to eliminate reason or explanation from the practice of Prayer. But it does uphold the possibility that an illiterate ploughboy may be more truly religious than a divinity student, and that knowledge, though a useful *part* of direction as a whole, is never self-sufficient. "Teaching the faith" then, is a contradiction: only belief can be taught, whereas faith arises and deepens through direction.[1]

[1] "Intellect and reason, unless the personal foundations have been pruned, are not enough. The deepening of individual spirituality is the first essential, and only when that harmony has been secured can the reason be employed. We must be humble enough, is Keble's outstanding

The second distinction to be made clear is that between
ascetical direction and *moral* guidance. The relation here, as
we have seen, is one of practice and test of progress, the actual
voyage and the map. In the case of, say, drunkenness, moral
guidance would consist of an exposition of gluttony, as sin,
exhortation to the positive virtue of temperance, with possibly
an appeal to social and family responsibility. Ascetic would
attempt the direct development of Prayer and faith by
spiritual exercise and use of sacramental channels of grace.
The one aims at the eradication of bad fruit, the other at the
creation of the good tree. In practice the two will overlap, but
the distinction is pastorally important in that it issues in the
vital difference between ascetical Rule and moral rules. Rule,
in the singular, is an integral ascetical system like the Prayer
Book scheme of Office, Eucharist, and private prayer,[1] or the
Regula of St Benedict; a comprehensive system aiming at
wholeness, or better holiness, of life in Christ. Moral rules, in
the plural, imply a list of ethical tenets, which may have
nothing to do with religion at all. Of course, this does not make
ascetic antinomian; self-examination, confession, and the
strengthening of moral volition by Prayer and grace, all play
their part in one integrated ascetical Rule. Against Pelagius
and all extreme humanism the contention is that we do not
embrace religion primarily to improve our morals, but rather
undertake the moral struggle in order to improve our Prayer.
However interdependent the two may become, the end of man
is not purity of heart but the vision of God. The best way to
attain the former is by aiming purposefully at the latter.[2]

These distinctions, clearly seen, go a long way to remove
any bias against ascetical direction in general.   From the lay
point of view it becomes pastoral care taken seriously, mutual
love in and for the Body of Christ, a simple definite desire on
the part of the shepherd to *be* a shepherd; in the best professional sense of the word. Within Anglicanism, direction

moral, to be content with probabilities." Kenneth Ingram, *John
Keble*, p. 49.
  [1] Chapters 18, 19, and 20 below.
  [2] Cf. K. E. Kirk: "Self-discipline is meaningless to a Christian except
as an instrument to develop the life of prayer." *The Vision of God*, p. 190.

must always be empirical, it cannot be dogmatic.[1] But direction, guidance, or coaching, in anything, presupposes an authority freely given to the professional. We consult the mechanic about our car, the doctor about our health, and the solicitor about our legal affairs; which would be futile if we did not mean to follow their professional counsel. So the priest is impotent without a similar freely given authority, but—and this is the point—he has neither use nor need for any other authority. This is of the greatest importance in an age which tends to see priests either as nice kind encyclopaedic seers or as licensed busybodies; an age when they are either avoided or consulted on all subjects except their own. The priest has no authority, knowledge, or right to advise on education, choice of career, political theory, legal affairs, or even the practical aspects of matrimony. His vocation, indeed, should make him less concerned with "human problems" than doctor, solicitor, or garage hand, while his professional integrity should set him well apart from public affairs. The priest's one legitimate approach to these things is such personal direction in Prayer that individual decisions have the greatest chance of being guided by the Holy Ghost. Moral guidance is permissible— just as a doctor may warn against excessive smoking—but in each case the ruling factor is professional—ascetical or medical—rather than directly ethical. The priest as director should eliminate rather than encourage the idea of one who cannot mind his own business. Lord Melbourne's notorious remark, "Things have come to a pretty pass when religion is allowed to invade the sphere of private life", rightly inter- preted, contains more solid sense than is sometimes supposed. If this seems exaggerated, it must be realized that the Christian ideal makes no such rigid distinction between sacred and secular; thus all possible things may be discussed as of ascetical import. I merely insist that the best way to sanctify the whole of a life is to concentrate on ascetic, and to advise on private affairs divorced from ascetic is only to widen the gulf between religion and life.[2]

[1] *Vide* Francis Underhill, *The Christian Life* (ed. O. Hardman), Vol. II, pp. 126–7.

[2] See Supplementary Note 1, below.

The objection from the priest's viewpoint derives from a certain pomposity about the phrase "direction of souls" and from the needlessly narrow sense in which it is wont to be used. The foregoing definitions distinguish in kind between direction and teaching, preaching or exhortation: but there is no implication as to quality or degree. It is so often held that whereas anyone can teach or preach, direction is a vague esoteric term applicable only to very saintly priests and very "advanced" souls. But surely when a child is shown how to kneel before the altar and pose the hands to receive the sacred Host, he is being directed and not merely taught? Whatever the difference in degree, the Bible story disciplined by image, intellect, and will is the same in kind as counsel given to a pure Contemplative; net-practice still means coaching, whether the batsman be rabbit or County player. And further, the capable coach is not necessarily an expert performer. Direction in Prayer demands vocation, Orders, and acquired knowledge rather than a sort of "holy brilliance".

A useful working distinction is that direction, being empirical, is a working partnership between two souls, whereas teaching suggests a one-way lecture or sermon. But we have seen that such individual ascetic is incomplete without its corporate complement; however brilliant the individual athlete, creative performance comes only within a team. This is the problem of "parochial theology", to which we must now turn.[1]

[1] See further, Supplementary Note 1, below.

3

CURE OF SOULS

IF MODERN ASCETIC is concerned overmuch with the individual member to the neglect of the unity of the Body, the position is not improved by a presupposition that this personal subject is an "advanced" soul: one who seems to accept without question all the implications of direction, Rule, penance, discipline, and duty. Most ascetical writers are careful to avoid, or try to avoid, the charge that they are writing for an exclusive spiritual clique—"the Faith in all its fullness is for *all* people"—yet in the light of pastoral facts this becomes little more than a saving phrase. The rank and file of our parishes do not queue up at the Rectory door for spiritual counsel; and the attitude of the ascetical Saints does not suggest that they should. The teaching of St Ignatius Loyola was bluntly *not* for all, but for members of the Society of Jesus, Carmelite spirituality grew in and for Carmelite Order, and the Prayer experiments of the Franciscans are directed at the needs of the friars minor. Even the domestic-secular emphasis of Salesian systems presupposes the fairly rigid order of Madame Chamoisy's household; to argue that this, as non-monastic, is directly applicable to the suburban families of Huddersfield, is a little naïve.

Parochial theology is concerned with giving some sort of unity to the parish body without which its individual members cannot really exist; while facing the facts of modern society, it seeks to reduce a prevalent confusion to some ordered pattern. As one would expect from this, many modern parishes will contain much real devotion, deep Prayer, sound knowledge and a host of other good things; but they will tend to lack shape and form, which real creativity demands. Thus the problem of parochial theology begins with the problem of cure of souls, and the ambiguity of this term itself supports the validity of our criticism. It is significant that we must spend some time in finding out what so common a phrase really means.

When a priest is instituted to a parish he is said to acquire "cure of" or "care for" souls, he accepts a stewardship and he undertakes a responsibility. The first difficulty arises when, assuming a responsibility *to* God, we ask precisely whom the priest is responsible *for*. Superficially there seem to be two possible answers. (1) The priest with cure of souls is directly responsible to God for the spiritual well-being of each and every individual soul within his parish; or (2) he is responsible only for the flock of Christ, for the members of his parish church at any given time. It is argued that despite the duty of evangelism, no one can be held responsible for the unresponsive, for those of other religious persuasion, or even of other Christian denominations.

Both theories are unsatisfactory. The first, if consistently applied, would lead to such a lowering of Christian standards as to admit as many as possible to the fold consistent with the existence of a Church at all. The emphasis is numerical, membership is nominal; which inevitably means convention, respectability, Pelagianism, apathy, and spiritual sterility. The sole pastoral function is ostensibly evangelism, which is so frequently reduced to mere "recruitment". Such an approach finds little room for ascetic, creative Prayer, or objective worship. More serious still is what might be called the futurist element inherent in such an outlook; its only ideal is a population of one-hundred-per-cent churchpeople. This means that every activity and every detail looks forward to an ideal never to be achieved; the parish, as such, never worships, intercedes, or appears before the throne of God.[1] All human worship is inadequate, but parochially speaking we are to suggest that it can be, and indeed must be, complete. The Father's House on earth is necessarily sin-stained, leaky,

[1] A discussion on "realized eschatology" would be outside the scope of this book, but it might be pointed out that if there is any truth in such a doctrine, this "futurist" element becomes even more serious.

ramshackle, jerry-built, and generally inadequate to his transcendent glory; but it can still be in a real sense whole. The parochial system under review never gets beyond the ideal blue-print, its house only exists in an hypothetical future. Ironically, a scheme of things aiming at complete, literal, individual representation of all souls in the Divine stream, ends with no Church at all. And no good purpose is achieved by imputing Christian hope to what is only impracticable nonsense. The world may end to-morrow, and although the priestly plea before Christ's judgement seat must be "guilty", there may yet be a more worthy defence than "I have not had time to begin". This theory may be called *multitudinism*; an ugly and unwieldy word, by no means inappropriate.

The second position, that pastoral priesthood's responsibility ends with the Christian element at any given time, is more obviously unsatisfactory, yet it has the unqualified pastoral advantage of facing facts. Before the multitudinist priest has been instituted a day he is forced to make reservations; Jews, Baptists, Papists, and Hindus if there are any, are best left alone, the heathen nonagenarian and the lunatic boy are unconvertible: one such case and his system, as system, collapses. This second theory is unshaken and untroubled by such contingencies, for which reason it becomes a policy of purposeful exclusion, and we are down to a complacent satisfaction with the "nice little nucleus". Here is plain dualism, for an exclusive spiritual élite, whatever the depth of its devotion and purity of its Prayer, is just not a parish. If we are rid of recruitment, we have left no place for true evangelism.

It will be argued that we are looking at extremes and that a simple compromise—a little of both—will solve the problem. The reply is that, granting an element of truth to both theories, a simple compromise leads to even more muddle and even less system. Parochial theology does not seek a list of good ideas but an overall pattern; pastoral shape, form, and design. The very fact that the first ideal is generally held, and that it degenerates into the second position in practice, only supports our main contention. It also backs the initial criticism of modern ascetic; books clearly written for an exclusive spiritual élite are not pastorally justified by saving phrases saying that facts ought to be other than they are.

But there is a further and very important criticism applicable to both the foregoing or any compromise between them. "Cure of souls" and "parish" are wont to be used interchangeably, whereas it seems more reasonable to construe them as the two parts of a sacramental whole. Cure of souls, as here discussed, implies a *function*, while a parish is, in some sense at least, a *place*. Whatever system we adopt, the elimination of this latter leaves us with human souls—people—not only isolated from others but as disembodied spirits floating in mid air. The doctrines of Creation and Incarnation can only attach a good deal of importance to bodies, and if Christian Prayer is the expression of the whole personality, then it cannot be dissociated from environment. Later in this book it will be explained in some detail how sense-experience, "contemplative harmony in place",[1] and the sacramental aspect of Prayer generally, all take their rightful place on the ascetical map. But in the simplest possible terms, faith issues in works, Prayer is expressed sacramentally, sin finds its outward sign in the cruel and the ugly, adoring faith in love and beauty; the slothful drunkard is not going to grow many flowers. But for the moment it is enough to stress that any worthy parochial theology must take some account of the ascetical significance of things and places, as moral theology must take account of society in environment.[2]

It will be seen that the main problem here posed is no particularly new one. It is in fact the old dichotomy of humanism and rigorism, the old problem of the "double standard" and the "two lives". In past ages the practical application of one or other of these conflicting ideals, or at least a decided stress on one side, has been dictated by circumstances. Very generally the Church has been either persecuted and rigorist or favoured and formal: it has been despised, small, exclusive, disciplined, and creative, or popular, multitudinous, liberal, and more or less impotent. It is pertinent that our own age is not so easily classified; there is fierce persecution on one side of the globe

[1] Chapter 14 below, but see also pp. 97–8 n.
[2] But see my note on the word "Sacramental", p. 106.

and a not uncomfortable apathy on the other, while in this island the Church of Christ is neither persecuted nor especially popular. We have neither martyr nor multitude.

To summarize the problem in its simplest terms, we must conclude that God the Creator and Father of *all*, who sent his Son into the world to die for the sins of *all*, cannot possibly be concerned with less than *all*; neither can his Militant Church, nor his parish priest. The initial multitudinist ideal is inviolable, and the most liberal humanism seems the proper approach.

Yet if there is a grain of meaning in the Cross and Passion, if victory means suffering and sacrifice, there seems to be need for Rule, discipline, struggle, and penitence; which as every parish priest knows in fact, applies only to the few. Rigour is not popular.

Discounting the chaos of compromise, can parochial theology suggest a working synthesis? Might we achieve, in practice, disciplined direction, zealous Prayer, sacrificial living, in more than an esoteric clique? Can we direct pastoral practice wholly God-ward without turning our backs on the masses to whom such an ideal is as yet unmeaning? Or can we embrace and serve the multitudes without plumbing the depths of multitudinism? More domestically, is it possible to achieve disciplined pattern, form, and shape in our parishes without offending hard won Anglican liberties? Can the paradox be resolved? Is humanist-rigour nonsense or supreme?

There appears to be considerable hope if he who died for all converted so few; if he who loved Magdalene cleansed the temple with the lash.

4

THE PARISH AS AN ORGANISM

THE THEORIES which were discussed, and rejected, in the last chapter are both concerned with the *numerical* in one sense or another. Both are conceived in terms of the sum of isolated units. But once we introduce the idea of society in environment, interest in the numerical sum is supplanted by an emphasis on the unity of the Body; body implies space— or pastorally, place. The one hope of solving our problem appears to lie in the elimination of numerical thinking altogether, and in seeing parish-plus-cure-of-souls as a sacramental whole—that is, as an integrated organism.

In dogma, the one Church is the organic body of all the faithful; body and members, vine and branches, shepherd and flock. So in philosophy we think of individuals comprising a racial solidarity. But when these pure sciences are applied in practice, pastorally, or in ethics, sociology, or politics, we are faced with the need of a middle, local term. The theoretical brotherhood of mankind becomes divided into smaller brotherhoods—nations, races, and families—before political theory means anything in practice. The monism of a thinker like F. H. Bradley needs the introduction of a local environmental factor before it makes ethical sense; "my station and its duties". So the transition from pure dogma to applied dogma, or pastoral ascetic, necessitates an equivalent middle term; the local church or parish as organism. The Catholic Church of dogma becomes not only the body of all faithful people but of all faithful parishes; or of all faithful people in local society, local environment, local worship, and local love. Without the middle term this supreme moral fruit of Christian Prayer is left out of account. One cannot love a theological formula, and one cannot love one's neighbour in the abstract. In fact one can only love a *neighbour*, especially since Christian love, rather than mere emotionalism, is a volitional virtue demanding discipline and sacrifice.

The Catholic Church is the body, not the sum, of all the faithful; an organic whole comprising parishes as organic wholes comprising souls as organic wholes: which is only saying that the vine consists of branches which consist of cells. And the relation between the Catholic and parochial organism is seen to be one of recapitulation or microcosm: ideas constantly recurring in Christian theology. The concept is implied in the doctrine of the Trinity, in Christology, and in Atonement. St Paul addresses the local churches with "Ye *are* the Body of Christ"—no mere portion of it, still less a group of individuals within it, but the complete Body in microcosm. "The local church would be regarded by S. Paul not as one element of a Catholic confederacy but as the local representative of the one divine and Catholic society."[1] And if this applies to Ephesus and Corinth, it applies equally to Little Puddlecombe parish and St Barnabas, Barchester.

The recapitulation of all in Christ, extended to the Church wherein all share in Christ, is the theme of St Irenaeus. St Cyprian writes: "The episcopate is one; it is the whole in which each enjoys full possession. The Church is likewise one, though she be spread abroad, and multiplies with the increase of her progeny: even as the sun has rays many and one light. . . ."[2] As in a myriad local places *the* sun is out, so in those places is *the* Church.[3]

This pastoral-parochial concept becomes synthesized in the dual doctrine of the Body of Christ; the Church is the Body of

[1] Gore, *The Epistle to the Ephesians*, appended note E.

[2] *De Catholicae Ecclesiae Unitate*, para. 5.

[3] Strictly, of course, the local pastoral unit is not the parish but the diocese, just as the proper minister of the Eucharist is not the priest but the bishop. A return to primitive organization would make theological justification easier on this point, but if.the modern bishop in his large diocese delegates authority to his parish priests, then the theological pastoral unit must share in this delegation. In this respect my thesis appears to support the plea for more bishops and smaller sees. See further E. L. Mascall, *Corpus Christi*, pp. 13, 14, and 19, 20.

Christ because it feeds on his Eucharistic Body and Blood. The consecrated elements are Christ to the communicant; wholly and completely Christ, divide them into ten thousand fragments and each is *the* Body and Blood of Christ. So the parish is the Catholic Church in microcosm. This Church, moreover, is threefold. The holy concourse in paradise and in heaven does not split itself up into insular parties of patrons-per-parish. If the whole Body is complete at every altar, the whole communion of saints are in attendance at every altar. As the Lady Julian saw all creation in a hazel-nut, so her hazel-nut comes to universal size. When parochialism is organic and when ye *are* the Body of Christ, it is the antithesis of narrow because it is, in place, the Catholic Church. There is but one Bread, so each altar is microcosmic of the Throne of the Lamb in heaven. There is one Church and one Body, so that the work of each server, each organist, each verger, each good lady who arranges the flowers is of Catholic significance *because* it is truly parochial. This is why the Church's Office, said by two souls in the village church on Monday night, is an infinitely tremendous thing; the "special" service with its teeming congregation is trivial by comparison.

We are now in a position to examine the personnel of our parish-plus-cure-of-souls without idealism and without evading the facts. And we find a heterogeneous society bound together, however variedly, by life in common place. The organism and the implications of place will vary considerably as between garden-city and ancient hamlet, dormitory suburb and self-contained farming village; and the term "parish" must obviously be widened to include schools, ships, prisons, hospitals, and so on.[1] Yet in all cases, as in all society, there is a certain corporate proximity, a locality to which all but disembodied spirits are bound. The parish has become a totality, an organism, a *thing*, within which exists a population, and this population, from whatever viewpoint we regard it, is generally divisible into three strata. Religion in parishes, cricket in schools, politics in nations or any other subject in any other unit, consists of first, the accomplished, the leaders, first eleven, ruling body, or other zealous minority; secondly,

[1] See Supplementary Note 2, below.

enthusiastic supporters, learners, or the generally "up and coming"; and thirdly, the rest, spectators, the apathetic or the antagonistic. It is of special interest to note how this grouping so constantly recurs throughout religious history. Judaism thought in terms of the world, the chosen race, and the faithful remnant within it; the early Church centres around the Twelve, proselytes, and again the world outside; and later Monachism is to distinguish between choir, *conversi* and seculars.

Plainly, our parishes contain the few really faithful, the occasional "churchgoer", and everyone else; parochial theology seeks a comprehensive pattern of relations between these three strata. What I have called multitudinism fails to face the facts, pretending that its parish is a uniform mass.

The policy of exclusion, were it to extend its purview beyond the little nucleus to a few groping souls, faces facts but evades its responsibility. We have but a segment isolated from the main parochial body.

The parish seen as organism, elaborated into what I propose to describe as the Remnant Concept, arranges its three strata as concentric circles in which power from the centre pervades the whole. "The fact remains that the human race is not the Christian Church, even although the Church is meant for all men and claims them all, and although there is no man who is altogether excluded from the Church's redemptive life, which, like a river in flood, overflows its formal boundaries and irrigates the surrounding land."[1] Parochial theology must give practical expression to this theological fact.

[1] E. L. Mascall, *Corpus Christi*, p. 12.

5

THE REMNANT HYPOTHESIS

It must be insisted that the "Remnant" is a highly technical term with roots embedded in Hebrew prophecy and—as will appear later in this book—branches spreading through the Christian tradition.[1] The principle is held and the term used successively by Elisha, Amos, Micah, First Isaiah, Zephaniah, Jeremiah, Ezekiel, Zechariah, Joel, and Ezra; reaching its fullest consummation and clearest exposition in the Deutero-Isaiah. This insistence is needed because in plain English the word has an "exclusive" sound and a numerical import, both of which we have rejected. Furthermore, the term is a popular one in pastoral discussion, where it is apt to be used with many shades of meaning, none very clearly defined. But the most cursory glance at the Second Isaiah brings to light four connected points which should suffice for initial definition.

(1) Monotheism is never more clearly set forth than by this prophet. Yahweh is majestically transcendent yet majestically personal; he is the Father-creator of all things whose ultimate concern can be limited to nothing less than *all*: all nations, ages, and even creeds. But

(2) Israel is *his chosen race*, the peculiar people, the elect, the priestly caste; set over against the Gentile world. Yet through sin and apostasy, its mission and even salvation is delegated to, and depends upon, the faithful Remnant, and the *faithful* Remnant is typified by purity in worship and loyalty in faith:

[1] In claiming Old Testament parentage and a general orthodoxy for the "remnant" concept, I do not of course feel tied to any particular expression of it in detailed practice—living religion involves change and adaptation from age to age. I do not suggest that the modern English parish should slavishly copy Isaiah! and I do not think this is inconsistent with normal theological development.

religious or ascetical, rather than directly ethical, qualities.
Thus

(3) the salvation of the world depends upon the faith of
Israel the chosen instrument, which in turn revolves around
the faithful Remnant. So we are faced with the tremendous
implications of

(4) the vicarious principle; epitomized in the Servant poems
and prophetic of the Cross.

The Remnant, far from being an amputated segment—the
clique detached from the whole—is at the centre of the parochial organism and of power extending beyond it. It is the very
heart which recapitulates and serves the whole; the heart
of the Body of Christ in microcosm, and its relation to its
environment is the relation between Christ and the twelve, to
their world. This palpitating heart pumps the blood of life to all
the body as leaven leavens the lump or salt savours the whole.

Strange as this may seem in its context, it is pertinent to
notice how reasonable it sounds in almost any other context.
A "good cricket school" is not one wherein all pupils are good
at cricket nor even one where all play cricket, but one whose
first eleven wins most of its matches. A law-abiding country is
not one in which all the citizens are lawyers, judges, or
policemen, but one with efficient police and judicial systems
pervading the whole. A football club with dwindling gates and
lack of support is one with its first team at the bottom of the
league. It will rectify matters far sooner by improving its
team and winning some matches than by appeals for support,
and issuing recruitment propaganda. Young men do not
become doctors, architects, and engineers, nor do young
women offer themselves as nurses, teachers, wives, and mothers
as the result of appeals or lectures, or being told that it is the
respectable thing to do. These choices imply vocation, gifts,
interest, the desire to be trained and become proficient in
the service of others. But we have stopped thinking of religion
in terms of training and proficiency for the service of others.
Multitudinism has reduced Christianity to a conventional
mediocrity, in which the hard things, and consequently the
inspiring things, have no place.[1]

[1] See Supplementary Note 4, below.

Once religion is held really to mean something, once it is seen as specific activity with its relevant arts and sciences, then a Christian parish ceases to be the dream—or nightmare —of a hundred-per-cent nominal, conventional "church-people", but rather becomes a virile organism pervaded by the power of the Remnant's Prayer. It is a parochial organism with a good first eleven: coached, disciplined, trained, and bound together as a representative team. The school match is won or lost directly by its selected players, yet because a school is a unity there is a real sense in which it is won or lost simply by "the school". After a game between twenty-two players, untold thousands declare that "we" have won and thousands more that "we" have lost. A parish of a thousand souls, under multitudinist policy, is not really a parish at all if only nine hundred and ninety-nine are present at the altar; yet a parish of ten thousand souls is truly before God, both organically and so individually, if the Remnant of three recite the Church's Office. It is interesting that whereas Sunday services are thought of in terms of numbers, an element of the vicarious is often imputed to the weekday Office of the priest. Yet Anglican theology insists that the creative channel of Grace in the world is not the priesthood but the Church; thus there is a most vital distinction between priest alone and priest plus Remnant of one. There is no such particular distinction between priest plus one, and priest plus two, sixty, or six thousand. Those who are worried over lack of support might substitute ascetic for arithmetic. There is nothing so contagious as holiness, nothing more pervasive than Prayer. This is precisely what the traditional Church means by evangelism and what distinguishes it from recruitment.

But it must be emphasized that in all these analogies, schools, nations, and football clubs generally *are* recognized as organic in a way that parishes are not. People do in fact train to play *for* the school or club, they do suffer discipline and hardship to fight *for* their country. Yet normally they do not worship *for* their parish. They may pray for others as simple intercession, a few may even intercede for the parish as a whole, but it is not the vicarious *for*—on behalf of, as representative of, or even bluntly instead of—which implies duty and responsibility. Clearly all this demands not only ascetical direction, discipline, and sacrifice, but corporate Rule, for only this can bind people, streets, fields, houses, and the whole social structure into organic unity. The Remnant concept is more than the "nice little nucleus" backed by a comfortable theory. True representation, real vicariousness, the whole process of Christ's redemption of creation by the redeemed in him, is to be ascetically achieved.

Dogmatically and ontologically the Church *is* one. A pastoral system is false when it fails to give practical expression to this fact. Similarly "It is not, however, merely the human part of the created order that receives redemption and makes its true self-offering to God by joining 'with angels and arch-angels' in the heavenly worship. The whole material realm is involved, for man is 'nature's priest'."[1] "Not only man, but the universe, will be transfigured and glorified, and in this transfiguration the great mystery of the Resurrection of the Body will be brought about."[2] There is a further falsity in any pastoral system which fails to take due account of places and things.

Our task is twofold. First we must examine the Remnant hypothesis in the light of theology and history, then we must seek to apply it in terms of creative ascetical Rule.

[1] E. L. Mascall, *Christ, the Christian, and the Church*, p. 164.
[2] Ibid., p. 148.

PART ONE

"PAROCHIAL THEOLOGY"

6

THE EXAMPLE OF OUR LORD
JESUS CHRIST

ASCETIC suggests that meditative prayer is the most creative approach to the Gospel story, for such prayer confronts us not so much with isolated sayings, miracles, and parables to be taught and studied, but with the living Christ to be known and adored. A man does not know and love his wife because she says certain things, does certain things, and behaves in a particular way; he loves her because of his continuous living relationship with her as a *person*, a life-pattern which embraces and synthesizes all these things and millions more. Christianity *is* Christ. The Church is the Body of Christ: Church and sacraments are the extension of the Incarnation and Atonement. So the life and function of the Church must follow the same pattern, the same overall principles, that are to be found in the earthly life of Jesus.

We believe in a God of order, so we cannot believe that the pastoral life of his only begotten Son was a shapeless mixture of teachings, miracles, stories, and works; sublime as all these are, they must be set within a purposeful life-pattern. If we are to avoid Apollinarianism we cannot dissociate our Lord's life from historical and environmental factors to which Man is bound.

So we note in passing that the will of the Father of all is that his only Son should be born into that particular religious ethos which thinks in terms of the "chosen race", the promised land, the Messianic concept, and racial solidarity demanding objective atonement; in short, those ideas and tenets which go to make up Remnant theology. There may or may not have been alternative methods of world redemption in the Divine mind, a simple fiat or a second flood; but to the Christian such speculation is both meaningless and objectionable. The fact is that atonement is achieved by the vicarious sacrifice of God incarnate, and that its benefits are perpetuated through a Church which began with Twelve. In fact the price of the sins of all the world, the sin of solid humanity, was paid by the God-Man who recapitulated that total humanity within himself and carried it to the Cross. And that whole life, beginning in the stable, led purposefully to the Cross, and beyond it to the Resurrection and Ascension. Every minute, every word, every detail of that life is significant to this overriding purpose. It follows that that life must conform to some all-pervading plan.

What elements then, and in what proportions, enter into our Lord's atoning life as a pastoral design? What is his integral plan? If the Remnant Body, his Remnant Church is to relive his life, extend his work and fulfil his function, what is their first function, and second, and third, and how do they all fit together and take *shape*? By what *form* can our Lord's life be relived by the Remnant Church in its essential wholeness or, better, holiness?

We might begin by remembering that the Nativity itself was hardly of a multitudinist order: the picture of St Mary and St Joseph, followed by a few shepherds, seers, and three local lords of the manor, all assembled in an underground stable, does not suggest trumpet fanfares or an appeal to the masses. It augurs ill for widespread conversions by divine fiat. If anything is a parochial microcosm of the whole universe it is contained by four walls in Bethlehem. And then the thirty years of near obscurity until the Baptism in Jordan—we know little or nothing about fifteen-sixteenths of this life. This very fact is of an immense significance. The teaching of Jesus regarded as divine sayings isolated from the personal Christ cannot avoid an Apollinarianism which is incompatible with meditative prayer, and conversely, which is only eradicated by meditative prayer. That is why the religious significance of our Lord's infancy is missed by the intellectual and ennobled by the Little Flower.

But the real significance of our Lord's life in relation to his baptism is contained in Luke 2. 40. There need be no lament

that this is our only glimpse of Jesus' boyhood: it is all we
are told because it is all we need to know. The dangerous
speculative meditations of apocryphal New Testament
writings are unnecessary; it is safer, and in the end more constructive, to assume that little is recorded of this period because
there was nothing very startling to record. What we do know
is that the Christ on the Cross was the Lamb without blemish,
and that this sinless sacrifice atoned for the sin of the whole
world. What St Luke tells us is that Jesus spent his life
growing up, developing, progressing, bodily, mentally—and
in spirit.[1] He came *into the world,* his mission was to and his
sacrifice for, the whole world; which necessitated a perfect
contemplative harmony with it too: and a perfect union with
both God and Man *in place.* He was truly the Second Adam
not only by restoring our access to Eden but by bringing an
Eden back into Bethlehem. *Cur Deus Homo?* Because no
divine fiat would restore the human world, it had to be
embraced and lifted on to the Cross within the loving heart
of Jesus. Contemplative union, contemplative harmony, in
perfection, can be interpreted to mean love—and you cannot
love from a distance. This love is no vapid emotion, but an
ascetical achievement which is epitomized in the Temptation
narratives.

Here we have the whole system of later Christian classification, a forty-day retreat, fasting and mortification, recollection
of the Father in stabilized place, the capital sins and all the
rest. But this is truly an *ascetical* epitome; the Lord's life was
of constant and perfect union with the Father, with and in
his world. He alone prayed without ceasing, he alone was
never distracted, he alone achieved perfect recollection.
Furthermore—and this seems to have been forgotten from
Eusebius of Caesarea until the seventeenth-century French
Oratorians—Jesus alone is the perfect worshipper of the
Father. The *whole* life of Christ was one of unbroken adoration,

[1] Incidentally this disposes once and for all of all the "spiritual
hierarchies" in the wrong sense. His prayer was always what we should
classify as perfect contemplative union with the Father, and yet we can
still speak of "spiritual progress" through infancy, childhood, and boyhood. For true and false views of "spiritual progress" see Chapter 13 below.

but because it was spent *in* the world of humankind it was an adoration which burst forth into every aspect of life and carried the whole world with it. His perpetual adoration is as vicarious as his defeat of sin in the wilderness, and a great deal of confusion would be avoided if all his pastoral activities were seen against this background. His preaching, teaching, healings, absolutions, and miracles are all meaningless if they are isolated from adoration. This is so often forgotten because of its very constancy. The end of man is the Vision of God, and the purpose of man is the glory of God. If Christian life in the Christian Church which is his Body is to have any form, shape, and creative plan, its whole power is summed in its adoration. Pastoral practice is made ridiculous by the idea that Jesus "taught the disciples to pray"—occasionally, that he frequented the mountainous solitude to pray; occasionally, that he prayed in Gethsemane; once, that he worshipped in the synagogue—every Sabbath. No wonder prayer is an individual appendage to static religion if we omit thirty years of growth in place and growth in community from the life of the Saviour.

Further, Christ *is* the Saviour of the *whole world,* and it is important to realize that apart from a few square miles in the Middle East, he did not bother to look at it. Here is the ultimate answer to "narrow" parochialism: in the prayer and worship of Jesus the environs of Bethlehem *is* the world, his little social group is both his cure of souls and the microcosm of humanity of all ages, creeds, and classes. In his first thirty years of perfect obedience, prayer, and adoring worship, all infancy, all childhood, all humanity, and all creation are recapitulated. Bethlehem is the epitome of every parish and every home; all is sanctified in him whose own sanctification is "for their sakes".[1]

Against this constant background of perfect adoration of the Father coupled with a recapitulation of all places and all men through Contemplative union and Contemplative Love, we may proceed to examine the ministry of our Lord in more detail. Having discovered frame and outline, we can attempt to bring out the features of the pattern.

[1] John 17. 19.

The problem of our Lord's baptism is controversial. How can John minister baptism "unto repentance" to one without sin? Professor J. W. Bowman has coupled our Lord's baptism with his sacrificial death, and has pointed out a pattern formed by a forty days' fast at both the beginning and end of his ministry—hence the Church's Lenten tradition. This scheme has the advantage of seeing Jesus' life as a whole and of searching for some form pervading that whole. But whatever the answer to this baptismal paradox, it can only follow the suggestion here, that both baptism and death—and consequently the whole life—are essentially vicarious. Our Lord's baptism unto repentance, like his death, is for the sins, not of himself, but of all others.

Professor Bowman continues with a remarkably illuminating commentary on St Mark 1. 10, 11 [1] (Luke 3. 22; Matt. 3. 17): "And straightway coming up out of the water, he saw the heavens opened, and the spirit like a dove descending upon him: And there came a voice from heaven, saying, Thou art my beloved son, in whom I am well pleased." Bowman couples these words with Psalm 2. 7 and Isaiah 42. 1 which may be said to contain the Messianic coronation formula and what is here called the ordination formula of Deutero-Isaiah's Suffering Servant. Our Lord's ministry begins with a self-assumption of these two recurrent Hebrew concepts, which is of much interest if we are to glean a pastoral pattern from our Lord's life-example, because nowhere in Old Testament literature is creative suffering of a vicarious nature so clearly set forth as in the Servant poems, and nowhere is it less pronounced than in the national Messiah—the conquering avenger of Israel. Dr Guillaume says "the characteristics of God's chosen servant are that he is quiet and restrained; no loud proclamations herald his activity", that is, no conquering hero of popular Judaism—nor is it a quest for a "good congregation". Further, "judgement" in Isaiah 42. 1 ("he shall bring forth judgement to the Gentiles") is interpreted as "the knowledge of how to worship", hence (Dr Guillaume's italics) "*religion*". Then in verse 4, "He shall not fail nor be discouraged, till he have set judgement in the earth: and the

[1] *The Intention of Jesus*, pp. 33 ff.

isles shall wait his law"—"The prophet sees the heathen world longing for knowledge of the true God"—law: not the Mosaic law but the earlier and literal meaning of *torah*, i.e. (again Dr Guillaume's italics), "*direction*".

Now the Servant of Isaiah is clearly the Messiah of the Remnant *through* whom all the nations will be blessed, and whatever the technical interpretation of Isaiah as "prophetic", it is clearly this concept that our Lord chose, embraced, and applied to himself. The old problem of whether the Servant is prophetic of a person or the personification of a tribe is irrelevant once we accept the vicarious Remnant in its fullness, and accept St Paul's "Second Adam" or the "recapitulation" of Irenaeus. In Remnant theology the Suffering Servant motif can only finally apply to both the person of Christ and the Remnant which is his extended Body.

So however we interpret either the Servant stories as "prophetic" or the voice at John's baptism of Christ, he himself sees his active ministry under the dual designation "Suffering Servant, Messiah of the Remnant", and this becomes by literal translation through Greek to English: "Crucified Saviour, Lord of the Church".[1] This indeed is a startling discovery of Bowman's, and it becomes more startling still when we widen it to include the whole religious ethos of first-century Judaism.

The world into which Jesus was born was, like our own, made up of divergent streams of tradition issuing into a complex of religious themes, policies, and parties; and exactly how like our own some of these prove to be. For if any doubt remains that our Lord took upon himself a synthesis of these two great prophetic personalities, Suffering Servant, Messiah of the Remnant, it is dispelled as soon as we consider what he rejected. The actual word Jesus used in speaking of his Body—the Church—is that which in his native tongue means Remnant. "Thou art Peter and upon this rock will I build my Remnant-Church."[2] But that is not the meaning in the context of most pastoral practice to-day; for the

---

[1] *The Intention of Jesus*, p. 76.

[2] Note also that "Church" itself, ἐκκλησία, implies not a vague numerical mass but a religious society *assembled for worship*.

multitudinist idea we must begin not with the Messiah of the
Remnant but the Messiah of popular Pharisaism, and for the
intellectual emphasis we must turn to the Sadducees; for a
"nice little nucleus" there are the apocalyptists: and if one
thing is plain to all it is that Jesus was not any of these.

Professor Bowman concludes from his thesis that *the intention of Jesus* is to perpetuate his atoning work by his foundation of a Church which is the new Remnant rather than the
New Israel. From this viewpoint his whole life and ministry
is planned, and his method and outlook evolve from his
conscious adoption of the *prophetic* strand in Hebrew spirituality. Truly, he would have the living religion of the prophets,
and poured nothing but scorn on the legalism, ritualism, and
shallow convention of Pharisee and Sadducee. He assuredly
coupled the fruits of true religion with a morality associated—
albeit often exaggerated—with the prophets, and doubtless he
found the exotic visions of the apocalyptists rather ridiculous.

But for whatever reason, Professor Bowman appears to have
made one most serious omission. No doubt these sects and
schools of first-century Judaism tend to overlap, as do
Churches and denominations in our own day, but the whole
line of priesthood must still justify specific mention. And
Jesus' chosen synthesis was not only of the two prophetic
types of Remnant Messiah or Servant Messiah, but these
together with his supreme High Priesthood. Throughout the
New Testament he is the Paschal Lamb and the sacrificial
Priest in one; a comparison between the words he used at the
Last Supper and the institutions in Exodus 24 leaves no
possible doubt on the point. This is important, because if the
prophetic element means religion-as-activity or prayer as
living power, priesthood implies a stabilized liturgical system
as central to it. It means acceptance of the covenant relation
in the ideal however it may be transformed and purified:
"This is my Blood of the new *Covenant* . . .", and covenant
relation needs a priesthood which leads not into ritual
legalism but Rule. Priest-plus-prophet spells synthesis of
stability and evangelism, ordered discipline and spiritual
freedom, corporate worship in place and "private" prayer.[1]

[1] I.e., "The Rule of the Church", Chaps. 18–20 below.

So Jesus makes atonement for sin on the Cross. His sacrifice is acceptable and efficacious because he is both Man and God, sinless yet at one with the solidarity of sinners. He is the true mediator because of his constant adoration of the Father from, in, and with, the world. But this objective redemption is to be perpetuated through the ages until the end. Of the conflicting values and ideals within his religious ethos, he chooses the priestly and prophetic strands. What pastoral pattern arises out of this choice?

Our Lord's pastoral plan, as every page of the Gospels plainly tells, is based upon his calling, training, and direction of the Twelve. This is his constant consideration. Should it be doubted, one or two rather blunt quotations put the question beyond dispute:

". . . So Jesus Christ set Himself to give humanity a fresh start from a new centre, and that centre Himself. To do this He withdraws from the many upon the few. To the multitude He speaks in parables, 'that seeing they may not see, and hearing they may not understand'. Only a few whom He sees capable of earnest self-sacrifice, of perseverance, of enlightenment, are gradually initiated into His secrets. These are the disciples. These He trains with slow and patient care to appreciate His person. From the most ready of these He elicits, after a time, by solemn questioning, a formal confession of His Messiahship—a formal confession that He, the Son of Man, is also the Christ, the Son of the living God (Matt. xvi, 16). This through recognition of His claim gives Him something to depend upon. He has got down to the rock; He can begin to build. . . . This gives us the clue to His method. . . . Indeed the more we study the Gospels the more clearly we shall recognize that Christ did not cast His Gospel loose upon the world—the world which was so incapable of appreciating it; that would have been indeed to cast His pearls before swine; but He directed all His efforts to making a home for it, and that by organizing a band of men called 'out of the world' and consecrated into a holy unity, who were destined to draw others in time after them out of all ages and nations (see Jn. xvii).

On this 'little flock' He fixed all His hopes. He prayed not for the world, but for those whom God had given Him out of the world."[1]

Little comment is necessary here, but two small points might be noted for future reference. First the underlying emphasis on ascetical direction is summed up in the account of St Peter's confession in Matthew 16. 16. What a masterpiece of directional technique this is! There is no direct "do you believe or do you not?", but neither is there to be any compromise. Peter is given all the help possible, all the warmth of true pastoral humanism, he is given time, and he is given the spiritual support of the surrounding eleven. But still there is no nonsense, in the midst of this supreme love, this divine pastoral cure: the total answer is demanded, the complete surrender alone would suffice. Secondly, this Twelve, this extended Body of Christ, the first parochial Christian Remnant, "were destined to *draw* others in time after them"— "I, if I be lifted up . . . will *draw* all men unto me." (John 12. 32.) The implication in both cases is of a magnetic spiritual power flowing from Christ's Body into the world. To draw is the antithesis of to drag, or to push, or to cajole, it implies some activity to be drawn *to*, not a static goal to be pushed *at*. And the seat of this hypnotic power is the Cross; only "if I be lifted up". The power of the Body of Christ is creative suffering and creative love, which to us means ascetical discipline, in Christ, by the Holy Ghost.

Again, in Bishop Gore's words; "The crowds press upon Jesus, the merciful and wonderful healer: but He appears to be as far as possible from wishing to make a multitude of converts on easy terms, He seems on the contrary to be even repellent. On the whole it is evident that His aim is not present success or numbers of adherents, but the preparation of a solid nucleus of men and women so absolutely committed to the service of the kingdom that they have cast all self regard and all prudence to the winds; and from these He asks an absolute faith, and a complete detachment—the attention of their whole minds and the loyalty of their whole hearts,

[1] Gore, *The Church and the Ministry*, pp. 32-3.

without any regard to their traditional prejudices or their personal or family interests."[1]

But none of this is "exclusive" policy. This withdrawal onto the few is to save the multitudes who were to crucify him; this preoccupation with the Remnant of Twelve is but the forging of an instrument to save the whole. "Pity, infinite pity, He gave the crowds—but Himself he never gave; He could not commit Himself to them. His work, His mission, His purpose on earth—how could they receive it? How could they understand it? . . . How could He build on that loose and shifting rubble, on that blind movement of the crowd, so vague and undetermined?"[2]

Professor Manson raises an extremely suggestive point by analysing the audiences to which the "teaching of Jesus" was directed. He concludes that something like seven-tenths of our Lord's sayings, as recorded in the gospels, was given privately to the Twelve. Recognizing how slight the gospels are as a chronicle of two or three years' active ministry, and further, that public speeches are more likely to be remembered and recorded than the most private conversation, we may safely conclude that the vast preponderance of Christ's "public" ministry is concerned with the private direction of the Apostles.

Such mathematics are admittedly a crude way of interpreting the New Testament. Yet Professor Manson's meaning is clear enough. Jesus the teacher, healer, preacher, wonder-worker, ethicist, and so on would be better described by that deeper composite name for all these things: director of souls —and largely of twelve souls.

It remains to look at our Lord's personal dealings with others, and seek some particular approach, some pastoral technique which would help us to follow him in practice.

His general manner to his larger audiences is described by Bowman as "winsome"[3]—"and all bare him witness, and wondered at the gracious words which proceeded out of his

[1] "The Teaching of Our Lord Jesus Christ", in *A New Commentary on Holy Scripture*, p. 285.

[2] Scott-Holland, *Creed and Character*, p. 34.

[3] *The Intention of Jesus*, p. 85 ff.

mouth" (Luke 4. 22), "Never man so spake" (John 7. 46).
This is pastoral appeal in the truest sense: God is love and
God incarnate attracts through love. Here a warm humanism
bursts forth on all who come within range of a radiant personality. This is the Incarnate beauty of God's love to all men.
Gore goes so far as to call this manner of teaching "homely",
with its parables, stories, and proverbs of a divine simplicity.
But this "winsomeness" has the inevitable effect of dividing
Jesus' audience into two distinct and generally disparate
parts: those who have "ears to hear" and those who have not.
In the first group the "winsome" aspect remains, but it is
complemented by stern demand; the humanist approach
implies the most extreme rigour on acceptance. In the second
group the "winsome" attitude remains for a time just
"winsome", the issuing demand for *all* becomes infuriating.
The pearl is a pearl indeed but its price is great. It would
appear that Our Lord is humanist to the masses, rigorist to
the disciples; and this is no paradox but the first principle of
parochial direction. If the faith in people did not "attract"
there would be no "conversion" as we know it, but if it did
not repel there would be no progress in faith. There seems to
be justification for the rule of a warm humanism towards
the babes in Christ—the middle stratum of parochial society;
rigour applies and must apply to the creative Remnant. So
the humanist rigorist paradox is resolved in what has lately
been called Christ's twofold invitation of "final succour and
absolute demand"[1]. The paradox is resolved because it takes
little imagination to see these as thesis and antithesis of the
synthesis called love. Pastoral direction is a courtship, and
courtship begins with an offering, yet its consummation is
fulfilled only with demand. This is surely the very core of
Christian monogamy: not its moral or social or educational
advantages, but that the peak of love on any plane is that
which gives and demands absolutely, which both offers and
receives all.

In approaching our Lord as *healer* two preliminaries must
be borne in mind. He accepted the somewhat naïve scientific
theories of the first century; whether or not he knew better is

[1] H. H. Farmer, *The World and God*, pp. 24 ff.

4

debatable, but it is certain that his concern was for religion, which did not depend upon the scientific or theoretical. Secondly and arising from this, he accepted a close relation between disease and sin, which is but the natural corollary to Jewish sacramentalism. Body and soul are interrelated, and this view of physical suffering is nearer the truth than we usually admit, if the vicariousness implied in the solidarity of the race has any meaning at all. Thus to the Jew the healing of the body is the outward counterpart of the healing of the soul. The Gospels in general and St Mark in particular stress the healing power of Christ over the sick *soul*. "Go in peace, thy sins are forgiven", is the obvious remark to make after the healing of bodily disease. So Jesus the healer emerges from the Gospel pages not as a mere miracle-monger as some would believe, but again as physician of the soul. And his patients? They were invariably the faithful, or what we should now call penitents. In like manner life and death, to the first-century Jew, are *spiritual* analogies, and the raising the dead miracles may be interpreted in similar terms. Lazarus and Jairus' daughter are given *spiritual* life—these things are no longer wonders but sacraments of grace. This is sometimes suggested on the grounds of our Lord's repeated demands for secrecy after healing miracles of all kinds: "And . . . . strictly charged him . . . See thou say nothing to any man: but go . . . show thyself to the priest" (Mark 1. 43, 44); "and he straightly charged them that they should not make him known." It is certain that Christ never would be the spectacular wonder-worker, but is it over-stretching the point to suggest that this was simply the necessary seal of secrecy, which must apply to all private direction and especially to the confessional? " . . . and by his authority committed unto me, I absolve thee . . . Go in peace . . ."—and do not breathe a word to anyone? Our approach to the Gospel story is transformed if we consider how much of our Lord's direction of the Twelve was "under the seal", buried for ever.[1]

[1] It is significant that of late years, much publicity and thought have been given to the question of "spiritual healing" by the Church. In the light of this last paragraph two comments might usefully be made. The first is that, much as we owe to such organizations as the Guild of St

By so saying we have virtually answered the question arising from Jesus' work as miracle worker—but it might be added that first-century Palestine knew nothing of quasi-scientific laws of nature in the modern sense. It is now generally conceded that his signs were not publicity stunts, but it is not always appreciated just how esoteric most of these miracles were. If there are no laws to be broken, there can be no conjuring tricks to amaze. But, religiously, what did these signs portend? What was the meaning behind them? Obviously something much subtler than demonstrations of divine power, otherwise why did the Jews continue to shriek for signs, and why did our Lord so constantly refuse to give them? The signs become not only acted parables but acted direction which the faithful alone could hope to understand. Feeding the multitude, for example, reviewed from our own experience is clearly Eucharistic, but what could it have meant to the disciples before the Last Supper, and before Emmaus? It was the subtlest initiation into principles that the Twelve not unnaturally failed to perceive. They were not meant to— the Eucharist is still a secret reserved for the faithful alone. This centre of all Christian life, this supreme channel of Grace, is as esoteric a rite as ever there was; to which admission is to be hard won. The Eucharist, as will be shown in the next part of this inquiry, is the centre of a disciplined Rule, the pillar of Prayer in all its vastness. To allow souls to communicate indiscriminately and irregularly is very unfair to *them*.

We conclude that the example of Jesus gives us a clear pastoral pattern which may be summarized in four points:

(1) The true extension of the Body of Christ is his Remnant Church. Its all-embracing aim is simply to *be* the Body of Christ as an instrument surrendered to the dictates of his Spirit. This implies

Raphael, the first requisite to any such service as theirs is parochial theology. Christ's healing power flows not through the priesthood but through his local Body the Church, and without the Remnant we are all impotent. If this is not realized, spiritual healing becomes but an additional item in a pastoral jumble. Secondly, the lack of spiritual healing in the modern Church is only the lack of spiritual direction in different form. And if we are truly to follow Christ in the matter, the latter art is the prior one.

(2) vicarious responsibility and common Rule which only serves the world by aiming at constant adoration of the Father, whilst in union with an organic parochial whole.

(3) Nine-tenths of the work of pastoral priesthood, seeking to bring all to Christ, is the training and direction of the Remnant.

(4) Such Rule can only issue in works—in the widest possible sense: growing flowers, painting pictures, bringing up children, feeding the multitudes with broken bread and washing their feet. All this, flowing from the faith of the Remnant into every corner of parochial organism, is the only true "Church work."

7

SOME GOSPEL STORIES

CHRISTIANITY is Christ. It is religion, which means an active quest for Christ, it is Prayer seeking encounter and living relation with Christ. The Gospel, however inadequate as a theological system, biography, or ethical treatise, is nevertheless perfect and complete since it serves to introduce us to this Person, this living and glorified Son of God. And the most enlightening of all methods of following him in pastoral practice—as is the case with any expert in any sphere—is not only to read about him or study his theories, but to watch him at work. And that, we claim, is what the New Testament is for. Living religion, as an active encounter with Christ and in Christ, demands ascetic, and ascetically the Gospels form, pre-eminently, a devotional manual; they are the source of meditative prayer.

If, therefore, we use these stories in substantiation of a venture of faith in a particular parochial theology, we make no apology for using them meditatively, because it is the only way we can use them consistently. If such treatment should seem objectionable, this chapter can be regarded as a meditative interlude and given any value the reader likes. But it should be added that these meditations seem not wholly out of place in the general context, their conclusions do not appear to be theologically disreputable, and they are not necessarily the writer's personal interpretations.

John 15. 1–8 ff. The Vine and the Branches

This is obviously parallel to "the Body of Christ" analogy, and need not be set out in full, but it adds certain points of interest to us here. The vine is a traditional symbol of the

Jewish race, but it has needed pruning, pruning back to the Remnant in order that it may bear fruit. (Judas Iscariot has been suffered until now but he was expelled in the upper room —the Eucharist at least must be celebrated by the faithful only; wherever the multitudes are admitted it is not here.)

The Church, the Body of Christ, is the Vine—there are plenty of other trees, but the work of the Vine is to bear fruit, fruit is grapes and grapes contain pips, seeds, and eventually perhaps more vines, churches, from the parent stock. This is evangelization, but it is a lengthy, complex, and almost subsidiary process, not an immediate one. But fruit depends on purging, pruning, and cleansing: these words suggest penance, mortification, and humility. (Humility, because this follows the feet washing in the upper room.) This fruit-bearing process is also one of growth, and is strongly ascetical. "This is my commandment, that ye love one another, as I have loved you" (v. 12), states an ascetical fact springing from mutual feet washing, penance, and mortification; that is Rule, in Christ.

But the Remnant is to experience both joy and suffering (vv. 11, 12, 13) almost side by side: "final succour and absolute demand". And this is also suggestive of the Church's periodicity of festival and fast. Both joy and sorrow, in Christ, in his Body, are creative, but they imply the Church's Rule: Easter is meaningless without Lent, and only the Remnant can or will keep Lent.

There is a difficulty in giving the second stratum a place in the Body analogy. The Vine suggests leaves. The Vine is Christ, the Remnant Twelve are branches, permanently joined. Are not the ordinary churchgoers then, the spiritual second eleven, like the leaves? These come and go, grow and fall off, they are truly part of the Vine, and yet the Vine is as complete without leaves in winter as with them in summer. The parish grows and worships in winter and summer, whether the spectators are there or not; but when they are, they are truly part of the parish, with a special part to play. "Without me ye can do nothing" (v. 5). Does this confirm the view that the Remnant members alone are creative and vicarious, that the second stratum are good Christians

individually but of no spiritual value to the rest of the parish?
The branches must be in the Vine, not merely connected.
Vine and branches are one, Christ and the Twelve are one,
priest and Remnant are one; the parish priest is impotent
alone, and the creativity of the Remnant—its *power*—is at
objective worship when all face God; so soon as the priest
turns round to "teach" there is a dichotomy, a dualism, a
man-man encounter instead of a God-man encounter. We
might have numerous individual suckers springing up around
the root and connected with the root underground—these are
in touch with the life of the parent vine, with Christ, not in
Christ: suckers do not bear many grapes. (Are suckers part of
the vine? Are non-apostolic denominations part of the Church
Catholic?)[1]

The two great omissions from the Body and the Vine
analogies are firstly the personal element and secondly the
necessary "otherness" or transcendence of God. We can argue
from the duality in unity of all experience (see Chapter 14
below) that we are both *in* Christ yet always necessarily other
from him. "Encounter" suggests a unity of subject and object,
God is both immanent and transcendent. If we are not very
careful both Body and Vine suggest immanentalism, almost
pantheism, and if we applaud Dr Relton's boldness in suggesting that Jesus Christ is somehow incomplete without his
Body the Church, we are bound to add that Dr Relton would
strongly insist on a transcendent otherness in the Incarnate
Lord, whereby he ever remains apart from all creatures.[2]
Jesus Christ in his extended Body is still the perfect worshipper
of the Father, while his Body the Church can still worship God
in him. These difficulties are diminished by:

John 10. 1–18. The Good Shepherd

The concept of the Remnant is perfectly contained in this
trilogy: the Body of Christ and his members, Vine and
branches, Shepherd and flock. Apart from the personal and
transcendent elements mentioned above there is little to
add, since the Remnant implications of pastoral practice
are obvious. We might merely say that this essential

[1] See Supplementary Note 5, below.　　[2] *Cross and Altar*, p. 81 ff.

duality-in-unity is extended to the priest-lay elements within the parochial Remnant. A flock without a Shepherd is tragic, a Shepherd without a flock is ridiculous. Here we have one Church localized in a parish, yet in another sense priesthood is specifically pastoral, and so set apart from the world, even from the Remnant members in the capacity of director of souls. This work necessitates, as we have seen, a detachment or lack of concern for personal problems and private circumstances (see above, pp. 11 ff). Priest and layman remain brothers in Christ, they form one Church which is the Body of one Christ, but in a special way priestly functions spring directly from the High Priesthood of Jesus: sacramentally the priest "feeds my sheep", "feeds my lambs". This is fully stressed in this Johannine passage, priesthood must be authorized by Christ, it must flow from the Good Shepherd, not the hireling.

The Good Shepherd owns the sheep and leads them to pasture. This the hireling cannot do. Pasture suggests place: only authorized priesthood can be parochial, in place, only authorized, ordained priesthood can hold cure of souls under the chief pastors and bishops of the flock. Thence flock and pasture suggest a close-knit group, in place; leading and tending suggest ascetical direction of a humanistic kind and this complements the rigour of pruning, cleansing, and purging of the vine. Jesus seeks diligently for a *lost* sheep, that is a stray who rightly belongs to the integrated flock; but there is a distinction between lost sheep and goats.

"And other sheep I have, which are not of this fold: them also I must bring, and they shall hear my voice; and there shall be one fold and one shepherd" (v. 16). Here is necessary eschatology, it remains the shepherd's job to tend *his* flock, to die for them if need be, not to round up the goats. They "shall hear my voice" and "I . . . am known of mine" (v. 14). Christianity is Christ, "I" and "thou" in personal encounter, which is achieved by ascetical endeavour, necessarily including mental prayer. Christianity is not "I will command" or "I will teach" or "I will exhort" but "*I am known*". "To know"—γνώσκειν, γνώσκω—is the most intimate relation of all: "How can this be seeing I know not a man." So spiritually

to know is the consummation of to love, priestly love is consummated not in "teaching" but in the most intimate relations in ascetical practice—direction and the confessional. The
analogy undergoes some transformation with the modern
stress on commercial breeding, arsenical sheep dip, and the
general stupidity of sheep: with our pride, sentimentality, and
lack of discipline perhaps it is just as well.

And we can sum up the relation in a Church which is both
Body of Christ and spouse of Christ; that is the duality of love,
Christ and Remnant, husband and wife, but the "twain are
one flesh" and this is "a great mystery but I speak of Christ
and his Church". Indeed, it is the most glorious of all
mysteries. Christ is God transcendent, and George, Mary,
Henry, and Fr John are finite and sinful. The work of this
Remnant is the worship of God, yet the twain are one flesh
one Church—one local microcosm of the whole Catholic
Church in which is God because it is his spouse.

Mark 2. 3–12 ff. (Matt. 9. 2–8; Luke 5. 18–26).
The Sick of the Palsy

Our Blessed Lord was preaching to the multitudes who had
gathered round the house where he was staying because this
was "noised". The huge audience happened to be there and
Christ condescended to speak—the big congregation was not
his idea.

Four strong men, strong in body and strong in faith, the
Remnant, bear the paralytic towards the Christ. They go to
tremendous trouble—even to the extent of demolishing half
the roof—to get this man at the feet of Christ. The multitudes
are a nuisance, they get in the way, but once the man is
lowered to the Lord, he immediately stops talking to the
crowds. Sin and sickness are very closely identified here, and
our Lord's absolution comes first, then secondly comes the
practical cure of the palsy. The answer to most human
problems is the confessional.

We know nothing of the faith of the paralytic, though the
sin-sickness identity suggests that it is weak or non-existent;
so the faith, as well as its corollary works, of the four strong
men, is vicarious. This man only reaches to Christ because of

the Remnant, he would never have got there in any other way
—certainly not by asking the multitudes, who would not even
make way for him. Here conversion and the faith of the Remnant are coincidental.

The first necessity for parochial evangelism is four strong
men: the Remnant who work together, to Rule and in
harmony. You cannot carry a stretcher any other way, you
must all be in step; and the greater the obstacles—like
crowds—and the more difficult the route—like mounting a
ladder—then the more a team must work together by discipline. And you must be quite sure where you are going—
towards Christ, objectively; not towards parochial "success"
but towards the Vision of God. The most direct route to
Christ is the worship of the Church, especially the Eucharist.
The paralytic seems to be one of those souls at the beginning
of a process of conversion, otherwise why did the four pick
him out? Or possibly he was a friend gained in normal social
contact. (Our Lord later *has a meal* with publicans and sinners.)
In these days, with such a man—on the edge of conversion—
the pastoral difficulty is to prevent him going to church
indiscriminately: certain services might put him off for good.
If he can be invited to share the Eucharist with the Remnant,
four strong men, our Blessed Lord will do the rest. The trouble
with the multitudinist congregation is that it consists of one
fairly strong man struggling with hundreds of paralytics.
The strongest priest can do nothing without the Remnant.
You cannot carry a stretcher by yourself.

When this encounter is over, our Lord goes back to the
multitudes. At least, he goes off alone and they follow, and
he condescends again (v. 13). It is interesting to read on,
regardless of historical chronology. Jesus has given the
crowds a long session of teaching, but he does not ask for
supporters from among them: he calls Matthew with two
words: here is the difference between teaching and direction.
Then he eats with all the publicans and sinners: contemplative
union, harmony, with *man*, with the world, in social intercourse. St Luke (v. 29) says this is St Matthew's idea. The
Lord says "Follow me", and St Matthew says "All right,
come to dinner." Then come fast and festival again in the

beautiful bridegroom metaphor. This is Renan's "idyllic" period; the Lord and the Twelve at St Matthew's dinner party: High Priest and Remnant on feast days, social intercourse, love in Christ. It does not sound much like a parish tea, because it is real and not artificial: just a dinner-party, no one has any axe to grind.

Matthew 15. 21–32 (Mark 7. 24–30). The Canaanite Woman

The Canaanite woman crosses the border; she makes some real personal effort to reach the Christ—and all on behalf of her daughter. The Christ completely ignores her, the disciples beg him to get rid of her. "She crieth after us" is more accurately "she calls after us in between the tears." Jesus wept himself for Lazarus, he shared the tears of Martha and Magdalene: feminine tears and feminine sympathy. Now they are all very callous and hard-hearted: the Twelve had been trained very well indeed.

The Suffering Servant in Isaiah preached to the Gentiles. This is the one great reservation Jesus made as he accepted the rôle of the Servant Messiah. Isaiah is inconsistent because the Messiah of the Remnant is contradictory to a world-wide mission—in the immediate recruiting sense. Jesus Christ's pastoral plan is the most rigid of all parochial theologies; he is sent to the lost sheep only of the house of Israel, that is his "Cure of Souls", and he only seriously concerns himself with the Remnant of Israel: Twelve in all. He cannot be bothered with Canaanites because his work is to save the whole world. He restricts nine-tenths of his ministry to twelve Hebrews because it is the only way to redeem all the Americans.

This woman is very faithful, very clever, and very persistent —they are beautifully strong feminine tears, like Magdalene's; she argues with Christ. It is almost a battle of wits, and the Incarnate Son of God gets the worse of it, or so it seems if we consider the words. This is the sort of thing some parish priests might find infuriating. An affront, perhaps, to their dignity. Divine Humility simply gives in, he condescends, he stretches a point, he breaks his Rule (perhaps this story inspired St Benedict's great tenet that Rule is a means to an end, never an end in itself). Jesus kept a Rule by discipline, but not like the Pharisee's rules; it was a vital ascetical principle which has distinguished Puritan and Catholic ever since.

He accepts the woman's worship, the fruit and hallmark of the true faith. But he heals the little girl from a distance, without word or touch, which is unusual, it is not sacramental because the woman is not of the chosen race, the Remnant. We can serve anyone in pastoral practice but we must be careful with the sacraments. Even faith is no qualification for the Remnant without baptism and loyalty. "A hearty welcome to you all"? No, "Private, members only", is nearer to the Lord's ideal.

Then the Lord went off and sat down alone on a mountain top (v. 29) without the disciples. The multitudes arrive again and he heals many of them without any question. He is attractively humanist to the crowds, having treated this single woman with extreme rigour, *because* "her faith was great". He paid her by far the greater compliment despite rough words. Because we love the Remnant in Christ, we must keep them up to the mark: we can afford to be kind to the crowds. To these latter we are very nice ("Charming gentleman, the vicar"); to the Remnant we are father-in-God, we are "known" to the true flock ("Charmed, Mrs Jones"—or "Go in peace dear daughter and pray for me a sinner").

This story is followed by:

Matthew, 15. 32–8 (Mark 6. 34–44; 8. 1–10; Luke 9. 10–18; John 6. 5—15). The Feeding of the Multitudes

to which we have briefly referred. It is Eucharistic and symbolical but it is not the institution of the Eucharist; that took place only in the upper room with the eleven; Judas Iscariot was excluded first. The Canaanite woman was excluded from sacramental ministrations because she was not "confirmed", yet the five thousand seem a mixed lot. The Twelve are quite bewildered by all this. Is it a symbolic prophecy to be referred to after Emmaus? Not quite because some believed, not because of signs, but because they did eat of the bread and were filled. On the other hand the operative, consecrating, pastoral, and parochial phrase is omitted, "This is My Body".

Perhaps there is a rightful place before the altar for all the crowds on great feasts? So long as they do not get in the way on ferials? And also there has to be some sort of *order*. They are arranged in fifties and hundreds—parishes (6. 39–40); and of course the Remnant Twelve *serve* the crowds. Poor Andrew: "But what are they among so many?" What is *he* among so many? Alone, nothing; with the eleven as the Body of Christ, everything.

They are then the Remnant Church, the leaven, the slow subtle power of the spirit which will pervade, and convert, the whole human lump; the salt, the subtle, soluble flavour. You do not need much of it but it must not have lost its savour— if it has, a ton is as useless as a pinch. What are *we* among so many? It depends on our savour, our worship; on whether we are a little boy's lunch or the Body of Christ: they are both the same *size*. (Luke 13. 18–21; Mark 9. 50.) A grain of mustard seed is smaller still but it produces mighty works; only indirectly and incidentally does it produce a great deal more mustard seed.

Mark 7. 31–7. The Healing of the Deaf and Dumb Man

Again *they* bring the man to the Lord, he is quite dependent upon the faith and strength of the Church. *They* act vicariously both by faith and in practice. Here the man is taken aside from the multitudes to be healed, absolved and charged with the seal of secrecy. The important point of this story is that everything in it is sacramental and directive. It is singularly useless to preach to the deaf, but this lack of teaching does not hinder direction; the result is "ears to hear", and those who have not such spiritual ears—"let him *not* hear". Direction and absolution—private things—give grace.

Mark 5. 1–20 (Matt. 8. 28–34; Luke 8. 26–39). The Gadarene Demoniacs

This man was a roaring, raving maniac, "possessed with a legion of devils". Who is the subject of vv. 5–7? Who cried out and worshipped and acknowledged the Incarnate Godhead? The man or the devils, or both in concert? Devils would hardly worship even if they acknowledged "Jesus, son of the most high God ". Insanity, even in this foaming at the mouth stage, is no obstacle to religious faith; so it cannot be intellectual, it cannot depend on teaching. Beneath or beyond the mind and intelligence is what Spinoza calls *conatus*. This is one of the primary elements in experience—conation—this is the seat of religion-as-activity. You can no more teach belief to lunatics than to the deaf and dumb, but can they be directed? Our Lord could direct them. If we can it must depend on prayer on a higher plane than the intellectual, but which can still influence the lower, or more fundamental, plane of conation. Multitudinism has to give up the lunatic boy, the Remnant does not. Christ's whole ministry is framed by the Remnant, which is why he gave up no one; not even the proud Pharisees who were in a worse condition, in some ways, than the deaf and demented. It is better to be mad than proud.

Commentators are all bewildered by the pigs. All we know is that our Lord would not cast pearls before them—perhaps he did not like such a multitude of them? Or perhaps St Mark has got it wrong.

After the cure, absolution, direction, religious activity, spiritual combat; the man wants to follow the Lord with the Twelve (v. 18). Christ would not allow this. The Twelve were chosen, elected, predestined; it was "members only". Instead, he told him to go home and "tell them how great things the Lord hath done for thee . . .". This is quite contrary to our Lord's usual practice of demanding secrecy. This man becomes a sort of free-lance missionary, on the Lord's commission, but it is incidental and unusual. St Francis of Assisi, Wyclif and the Lollards, the friars, Whitefield and the Wesleys all follow the pattern. Wandering preachers, evangelists, missionaries in the usual if inexact sense; all these have their place in the divine economy, but they are incidental and exceptional, not the norm. The Salvation Army to-day can be served and embraced by the Remnant, along with all other souls without exception—in a vital sense they have the Lord's approval, but these are neither the Church nor are they doing the work of the Church. There need be no argument between the Church and other Christian denominations once it is recognized that the Remnant embraces all in one of its three

strata, and that their functions are different. Only the
Remnant can embrace all because it is the efficient Body
localized in place.[1] Stability in prayer is the Rule of the
Church, nomadic preaching an occasionally permitted variation.

Mark 9. 15–18 (Matt. 21. 12–17; Luke 19. 45–6; John 2. 13–18). The Cleansing of the Temple

Nothing is quite so obvious as a whip: "Members only." A
whip gives something more than a hint that one is not welcome.
"My house shall be called of all nations the house of prayer."
The temple was not quite parallel with Christian church
fabrics; these latter are meeting-places, and various things are
permitted in them—the hosannas of the children are quite in
order—but their primary function is prayer and worship,
which applies equally well to the church buildings or the
Church as the Body of Christ (which analogy is stressed again
in John 2. 21, "But he spake of the temple of his Body"). But
Jesus' object is to rid worship of the element of selfish gain,
and this seems to apply to spiritual things too—the church
building is not the place for quasi-mystical experiences of a
eudaemonistic kind. There is a necessary place in ascetical
Rule for subjective elements, but the worship of the corporate
Church is mainly objective, it is where the Body assembles to
give first and get second. Therefore if it is not for raising
money neither is it for teaching—a house of Prayer is neither
a market nor a lecture theatre. Should we allow special
appeals for missions and so on? They are a good cause, but
so were the lambs and doves. Is this the right place for
Sunday-school? Business in the vestry and children's songs
seem to be more in keeping with either.

"Out of the mouths of babes and sucklings thou hast
perfected praise" (Matt. 21. 16). It is conation versus intellect
again; how old, how grown up is a soul? How advanced in the
real ascetical sense? "Become as a little child . . ." Aged
sanctity and children are both ascetically "simple", we are
sin-torn and complex. The old ladies and the children have a
vital part to play in the Remnant. How can we measure their

[1] See Supplementary Note 5, below.

spiritual power? How can we split them up into "children's services", youth, men, mothers, women, and aged, and pretend this is anything to do with the *one* Church?

Mark 6. 1–4 (Matt. 13. 54–6; Luke 4. 22; John 6. 42).
The Carpenter's Son

"Whence hath this man this wisdom, and these mighty works?" (Matt. 13. 54.) Ask the Curé d'Ars, who "learned all his theology on his knees". "Is not this the Carpenter's Son? is not his mother called Mary?" Professor Turner tells us that the pagans Celsus and Libanius mocked at the carpenter, and if manual labour was not exactly scorned by the Jews it was considered beneath a Rabbi's dignity. Jesus had worked regularly at his trade. But during his first thirty years or so he lived in a perfect relation with the Father, perfect Prayer, Prayer without ceasing; but also in perfect pastoral harmony with the world. He was Son of God, he was also Son of Mary, thence Son of Man, all men, mankind, humanity. He carried the whole world onto the Cross and lifted the whole world up to heaven. He held the whole world in his holy hand like Julian of Norwich's hazel-nut: all this by contemplative union, by perfect loving empathy, thence *harmony*. So he was supreme High Priest, Mediator, Advocate with the Father. He had to know both sides perfectly, God's side and Man's side, so he was perfect pastoral High Priest in a perfect pastoral relation with all men because he was perfect carpenter. All this he achieved not by organizing campaigns, but by making barn doors: this is parish work in perfection.

St Paul made tents, St Bernard carried corn (rather badly), St Luke was a doctor, the Holy Mother, according to the apocryphal gospels, made vestments, and St Dunstan was a coppersmith. This is Christian work, the fruits of faith, of sacramental significance, like painting and music and poetry, like the monks who built cathedrals. Craftsmanship is sacramental, and if it is beneath our dignity we refute the divine artisan, we have no part with the fishermen. This is parish work, *pastoral* work, if it is done within an ascetical Rule, in recollection.

Mark 14. 66–72 (Matt. 26. 57–75; Luke 22. 54–63;
John 18. 15–27) John 20. 24–9. The Sins of the Saints:
Peter's Denial and Thomas' Doubt

At Caesarea Philippi St Peter made a supreme venture of
faith; on his confession Jesus Christ inaugurated his Church
which is to be his Body. St Peter was surrounded by the
apostles. After Pentecost St Peter's traditional characteristic
was *boldness*; as head of a local Christian community he was
afraid of nothing. St Peter followed Jesus into the house of
Caiaphas in company with "another disciple [who was]
known unto the high priest" (John 18. 15) and then St Peter
was left *alone* (v. 16). Alone he was as frightened as a kitten
because a little maid looked at him. The confession was made
on behalf of the Twelve, surrounded by the Twelve, supported
by the Twelve; the denials came when he was alone.

We have not many Peters in our parishes. Even if we had,
they would be useless alone, individually, in isolation from
the localized Body. A "good congregation" of a thousand
individual Peters would be sterile and useless, it would have no
chance at all against a little pagan servant girl. Six disciples,
of far less sanctity than St Peter, under common Rule,
discipline and love, may conquer the world because they are
the Body of Christ. The "sins of the saints" is no contradiction;
all saints are sinners, and from now on through history we
find saints falling when they are *alone*. This is logical, because
a saint cannot really be alone, he cannot be an individual
apart from the Remnant Body localized in place. Christ was
tempted alone by Satan, and his conquest was therefore the
more supreme and the more vicarious, but he does not ask us
to fight Satan alone because he knows we would not have a
chance: his body must always have several members, and these
are strong in him, in his united Body. The arms of a boxer are
useless if they are out of harmony with his feet. Satan is very
fond of "good congregations"; he is scared of the Remnant
because it is the Body of his conqueror.

St Thomas doubted the Resurrection, not because he was
not a saint, but because when the risen and glorified Lord
appeared in the midst of his Church, St Thomas was not there.

5

Where was he? Perhaps he was worshipping God in a quiet walk through the country lanes, or making beautiful meditations, or enjoying smooth religious experiences. But he ought to have been in the Church; there he would have been better off even had he been thoroughly bored. When he did get back to the regular routine of worship it was made easy for him, but "blessed are they that have not seen, and yet have believed" (v. 29). It is more blessed to venture in prayer, to struggle by Rule, to submit to ascetical discipline, and to be bored, than to sit back comfortably on a "firm faith". Religious experiences of the mystical kind are signs of weakness not sanctity, sweets of encouragement dropped by Christ to his babes; like being allowed to feel the Blessed Wounds of the Crucified Lord. If we are arid and bored and tired of it all, we are making progress because Christ is paying us a tremendous compliment —he is leaving us to follow him without any rewards, without having to follow a carrot dangling before us as an incentive to move. But we cannot get far alone; we have to be supported and loved by the Remnant.

No one would stand wet through and shivering in the middle of a football field all alone, but even if we are ten goals down we can carry on quite easily if we are part of a team, if we are surrounded by a team: and it is even worth while.

John 17. The High Priestly Prayer

This chapter contains the sum of pastoral theology; and is itself summed up in verse 19, which alone supplies enough meditative material for very many months. This is the core of priesthood, the pastoral heart of the Body of Christ. The Remnant as his Body, its pattern of life as the pattern of his, is ratified once 'and for all in verses 11, 18. And this Remnant, set right over against the world, is chosen, predestined, elected (verses 2, 6, 9, 12, 14). But they are not exclusive; the prayer is addressed to the Father of all, yet this is not multitudinism because all is arranged in order; prayer is made for three distinct strata: three concentric circles, a pattern which embraces all, but which remains a pattern. Prayer, intercessory and vicarious, is firstly "for those whom thou hast given me" (v. 9), secondly for "them also which shall believe on me through their word" (v. 20), thirdly and vicariously for all the world eternally:

"*And for their sakes I sanctify Myself*" (v. 19).

Sanctity itself is vicarious, therefore the whole of religion is vicarious. Sanctity ends with the Vision of God (v. 3), but only after a long progressive struggle. If "they are one as we are" (v. 11), if we are a Remnant not a "congregation", then every particle of common Rule is "for their sakes", every communion, meditation, office, and act of recollection, every confession, prayer, penance, fast, festival, examination and exercise, is "for their sakes"; every "private" prayer is "for their sakes", so that there is no such thing as "individual" prayer. We cannot save our own souls without saving others, and if we try, exclusively, to save our own souls we lose all. Religion is activity which issues in works, which are another sort of activity. The two go together but religion is prior, and therefore more creative: pastoral priesthood reciting the Office of the Body on Monday morning is doing infinitely more for its neighbours than the Good Samaritan ever did by works.

Morality is not the same as sanctification, but moral theology is a test of progress towards sanctity. Temptation is not conquered by theology and ethical theory. If I sin perhaps God will forgive, but sin is "original"—it concerns *them* as much as ʃprayer does; only adversely. But who are *they*? All other people? Yes, indirectly, but this is pastorally meaningless. The members of the congregation? Yes, but they are individuals, so they can look after themselves. The Twelve? The Remnant? The "middle" term? George, John, Andrew, Peter, Magdalene, Sally, Teresa, and Jane? "For *their* sakes" get thee hence, Satan.

Pastoral priesthood must one day appear before the judgement seat of Christ: not for itself but "for their sakes". It must make a continual Eucharistic plea, it must give account of its stewardship—it is in charge of a parochial vineyard, it has cure of souls, and a soul is neither an opportunity nor a "success" but a responsibility. So how are we to plead? For the multitudes we have tried to win and many we have given up—Mohammedans, Jews, and the lunatic boy? We have tried the impossible and failed. For the exclusive few? We have played safe, buried our talent in a napkin. For the parish as organism? Our plea before the judgement seat is "guilty" in any case; our Eucharistic petition is always "have mercy", but "Here O Christ Jesus is my parish, not them but it, regard not our sins but the faith of thy Church: the sin-torn struggle of this your local Body in this place. Never mind this good man and that bad one, never mind this Remnant nor the hordes outside, but in thy divine mercy have compassion on *it*, on *us* who are *it*: here in this all Holy offering, this oblation of Bread and Wine, this which is to be your Body and your Blood. Here is not me and a few stragglers at the back, not me even in union with a solid Remnant at the back, but because of them, here is the parish, the organic whole, the cure complete: accept O Lord not me, not us, not all the others, but *it*. Alternately accept me for their sakes and accept them for my sake and accept us for thy sake. Amen."

8

THE APOSTOLIC CHURCH: THEOLOGY

THE APOSTLES are the seed of the Church and the Church is truly Apostolic which grows out of that seed. The plant is the seed in a developed form as the man is the infant in a developed form: they are organically one, however much the embryo and the evolved organism may appear to differ. It is sometimes suggested that Catholic authority is based upon the twofold strands of the Scriptures and the primitive tradition of the Church. But these are in fact one and the same thing. The one constant theme of the Gospel story—as background to the Birth, Death, and Resurrection of Jesus Christ—is his direction of the Twelve; and we can safely assume that the vast proportion of this was either secret or given in such fashion that it could not be recorded: the very fact of fellowship with the Lord is possibly the greatest influence of all. So it is not surprising that the primitive Church is governed by little stereotyped detail. This is simply to say that our Lord's dealings with the Twelve were *religious*. He implanted faith, developed prayer, and at Pentecost sent the Holy Ghost to guide, direct, and govern. Organization, method, and theology evolved from this religious organism: *consensus communis fidelium*. So we can believe that the Twelve as Remnant organism have the authority of Christ's direction, and what they *did* in the Spirit is the fruit of that direction. And this cannot be radically different from the pattern of our Lord's own life. If we could find an historical correspondence between the pastoral form of our Lord's ministry and that adopted by his Church, then we might humbly claim that the Remnant concept as parochial theology stands on firm ground.

Dr Bicknell, amongst others, warns us that we miss the

real point of the Acts of the Apostles unless we realize that its central character is not St Peter or St Paul, but Jesus Christ. If St Luke's gospel describes "what he began to do and teach" in his earthly ministry, the Acts describe what he continued to do and teach through his Church inspired by the Spirit whom he sent. It is inconceivable that the two should be at variance; certainly the primitive Church entertained no such possibility. We find it at Jerusalem under St James as a tight little body of disciples engaged in prayer and worship (Acts 2. 42, 46–7), stabilized under the influence of all that is implied by κοινωνία. It is still a sect of Judaism and is still connected with the temple worship, and thus we see the Remnant in transition from the old Israel and the new; the old covenant and the new. Dr Bicknell points out the significant fact that ἐκκλησία, as this sect came to be called, is the Greek translation of the Hebrew word meaning Israel "*assembled for worship*". Thus a "*missionary Church*" is really a contradiction if it implies nomadic evangelism alone—there cannot be a wandering assembly. That it is in the truer sense, in our Lord's sense, a stabilized body of missionary *power* is quite another matter. The Church is missionary in precisely the same sense as her Lord, who in saving the whole world, wandered little more than twenty miles from his birthplace.

But after a year or so the Jerusalem Church broke up. The sect within Judaism was religious, therefore it had to advance, and such advance meant unpopularity. It broke up through extraneous circumstances, and its growth led to complications of a social and political nature for which the Apostles seemed quite unprepared. The very idea of growth in numbers seems hardly to have been considered; if it had, the need for further organization would surely have been foreseen. The solution was the appointment of the seven (Acts 6. 1–7), which may be regarded as an innovation sanctioned by the Spirit to meet a particular contingency.

Such providential crises are necessary acts of God, as circumstances demand deviation from normal practice. Apart from such exceptional acts of Christ within his Body, we are wise to pay respect to established tradition. We may believe that another such crisis led to the conversion of St

Paul. The Damascus Road experience represents a unique, specific act of Christ. Circumstances demand a direct, in the narrower sense, missionary approach to the Gentile world— a startling innovation so far as the Church's normal life is concerned. St Paul becomes the archetype of a completely new sort of missionary, the archetype of St Francis, St Gregory, St Augustine of Canterbury, St Martin, Wyclif, the Wesleys perhaps, and our modern pioneers. From now on, this type of ministry, this *method* of evangelism, is to be regarded as a deviation sanctioned by Christ; but complementary to, and dependent upon, the local church, stabilized in place, bound in brotherhood, adoring the Father; whichever remains the norm. Misplaced missionary zeal which exalts the deviation and forgets the prior purpose is a constant danger to the Church's life.[1]

The one distinctive feature of any reaction against tradition is the claim to exceptional, personal, spiritual experience; which is a notoriously dangerous claim to make, and upon which to act. The only possible test for Christ's true call and true sanction of unorthodox deviation from established practice is the orthodoxy of the fruits of that deviation. It is significant that in the examples of the missionary vocation mentioned above, St Paul and the Catholic Saints pass the test, Wyclif does not, and the Wesleys' work is still very much in the balance. St Paul and, for example, St Francis, pass the test because the fruits of their deviation revert to type; both, despite themselves, produced not followers, but stabilized local communities. St Paul founded Churches, while the modern Franciscans are possibly nearer to the ideal of St Benedict than they are to St Francis: the friars who rebelled against the monks have now become monks themselves. Deviations truly sanctioned by Christ issue in Remnant Churches; those not so sanctioned issue in schism.

But St Paul accepts the Remnant concept as whole-heartedly as anyone. It is he who gave us the Body of Christ doctrine, who saw the pastoral fact of predestination in some sense or other, who knew by the most personal of personal experience that conversion was not a matter of intellectual

[1] See Supplementary Note 6, below.

argument, doctrinal teaching, or evangelistic emotion, and who knew above all that there was no justification in works however many good congregations emerged out of them. His letters are not only pastoral but essentially parochial, they deal with ascetical and moral theology, with Church *order*, and with the relations between the Church and the world. His overwhelming concern is for the "care" or "cure", "of all the Churches", for the integrity and purity of the local ἐκκλησία —"the church assembled for worship". His references to numerical expansion are minimal and incidental, and it is always "the Lord who gives the increase".

Not surprisingly, therefore, the influence of this religious genius within the Apostolic band begins to pervade the whole; which is in itself Remnant theology. The missionary tours begin as St Paul sets off to Cyprus in company with St Barnabas, but they go "being sent forth by the spirit" (Acts 13. 4), that is, under a direct consciousness of God's guiding hand; this journey is the fruit of prayer.

But if St Paul is unique among the Apostles we must not forget that the Apostles are unique in themselves. This is very important, since we are apt to speak of the "Apostolic Church" rather loosely. The phrase usually means, quite correctly, the Church which has descended in living evolution from the Apostles; that is the living organism, the Body of Christ, which was born with the Apostles. But in another sense the Apostolic Church may mean the primitive Church of the Apostles' lifetime, and this, though the same organism as that of which we claim membership, has unique characteristics. We might say that if the Gospel story is chapter one of our Lord's life and the Acts of the Apostles is chapter two of that same life, then the sub-Apostolic age is the *beginning* of a third chapter, which still goes on.

The Apostolic Church at Jerusalem is, as we have seen, true to type; circumstances, providence, divine guidance caused a missionary deviation sanctioned by the Lord of the Body; this created local churches ruled by bishops—the successors to the Apostles, who never accepted and possibly never considered the idea of appointing any more Apostles. The transition from the Apostolate to the Episcopate is still an academic battleground, but the fact of the transition remains, and the fundamental distinction in function, or rather method, also remains. The one is the unbridled authority who may choose to abide or roam at will, the latter is bound to a place. The Apostle has no geographical ties, the bishop cannot exist without a diocese; literally ἀπόστολος is one who is sent, a messenger, and a messenger travels; ἐπίσκοπος is an overseer, an elder or one who stays still and looks, or looks after, a group. Here in embryo is the future pattern of the Church; the germ which is to develop into the ascetical tenet of stability.[1] The self-contained adoring, worshipping, Prayerful group, is to become not only the Church's norm but the Church's missionary norm. All glory to God that his providential love calls men like Paul, Francis, and the Wesleys as occasion demands; while shepherd and flock, vine and branches, the Body of Christ in the precincts of Bethlehem, in Gethsemane, on Calvary—ever recapitulated in Jerusalem, Antioch, Rome, Canterbury, New York, and Little Puddlecombe—the Body of Christ in microcosm, localized in place, localized in bread and wine, priest and Remnant, in Prayer and in place: this remains the pastoral norm of missionary power.

In the first century we find local stability in the Antiochene community of St Ignatius: "Wheresoever the bishop appears, there let the people be, even as wheresoever Christ Jesus is, there is the Catholic Church—*ubi episcopus, ibi ecclesia*."[2] Half a century later the Remnant concept is expressed by the writer of *The Epistle to Diognetus*: ". . . what the soul is to the body Christians are in the world. The soul is spread through all the members of the body; so are Christians through all the cities of the world. The soul dwells in the body, and yet it is not of the body; so Christians dwell in the world yet they are not of the world. The soul, itself invisible, is detained in a body which is visible; so Christians are recognized as being in the world, but their religious life remains invisible."[3] We have here those fundamental pastoral principles upon which we are claiming to build a systematic

---

[1] See E. L. Mascall, *Corpus Christi*, pp. 13–14.

[2] *Epistle to the Smyrnaeans*.—But see my note on p. 19, above.

[3] *The Epistle to Diognetus*, Cap. vi.

parochial pattern: sacramentalism, the distinction yet inter-relation between the Church and the world, thence vicarious-ness; the worldly-otherworldly, or worldly-ascetic relation:[1] and, especially, *"their religious life remains invisible"*—the leaven that leavens the lump works without a lot of noise.

At the turn of the second century the Remnant Church remains; "We are a body formed by our joint cognizance of religion, by the unity of discipline, by the bond of hope. . . . 'See,' say they 'how they love each other' . . . we come to-gether in a meeting and a congregation before God, as though we would in one body sue Him by our prayers. This violence is pleasing to God. We pray also for emperors, for their minis-ters and the powers, for the condition of the world, for the quiet of all things, for the delaying of the end . . . we feed our faith, raise our hopes, establish our confidence, nor do we the less strengthen our discipline by inculcating precepts."[2]

Again, worship in stability, the close knit bond of love, vicarious prayer for all the world, ascetical discipline—the same Body of Christ in the world, yet set apart from it, is the parochial pattern which grew and converted because it cared little about conversion. But this very growth, together with extraneous circumstances, led to difficulties. From the experience common to this Church of churches evolves theology; and the rigorist versus humanist problem arises with the alternation of persecution and popularity. We have plunged into what has come to be known as the "problem of discipline". The Church exists as the Body of Christ, but further questions arise, because, as one would expect, the formulative period of dogmatic is equally the formulative period of parochial theology; and the same questions face us still. The basic pattern and function of the Church is estab-lished but it is necessary to ask who belongs to it and how a particular person comes to belong to it. Translated into theo-logical terms these are problems first of predestination and

---

[1] "Christians are not distinguished from the rest of mankind by country, speech or custom . . . or use a different language, or practise a peculiar life . . . but their citizenship is in heaven." *The Epistle to Diognetus*, see Cap. v.

[2] Tertullian, *Apology*, Cap. xxxix.

election, and secondly, of conversion. We must now pay some attention to these controversial themes.

The baptismal controversy of the third century initiated the rigorist-humanist struggle in an acute form. The question of the *lapsi* after the Decian persecution brought the whole problem to a head, and finally the conversion of Constantine in A.D. 313 confirmed a humanist victory. This turbulent period naturally provided a forcing-ground for controversy; two distinct views, or rather another view, of the nature and function of the Church arose, and the vicarious Remnant began to resemble an exclusive sect. Extreme rigorism issued in the doctrines of the Church as the society of ἅγιοι—the saintly band; vicariousness fell into the background, the Church was the ark of salvation, and damnation lay outside. The humanist element began to see the Church as a kind of educative society, a liberal compromise on the failure of its members. Despite the mediating hand of St Cyprian, the latter won the day; the masses flowed into the Church and multitudinism was born. But the rigorist ideal did not die with this Church of the popular crowds, and if its discipline was discounted in everyday religion, its penitential theory remained to be feared. Within the Church was *ipso facto* final salvation, outside was final damnation, and the seeds of "double election" in St Augustine and Calvin were sown. But this theory is, ironically, the fruit of multitudinist liberalism itself, since it grows from the ambiguity between faith and belief, between religion and theology. "Salvation" and "damnation" are static, Christianity is no longer a living Person but a state—there is no struggle and no progress.

Predestination and election are themes which run throughout the whole length of the New Testament, and this is because they run throughout the whole length of the Old Testament. The "chosen race" motif is saturated with predestinarianism, which is far earlier than any idea of individual immortality. The Christian Church is veritably based upon the idea of resurrection, and it is not surprising that in an age of intellectual confusion these two concepts should become mixed. But St Paul, be it remembered, is a Hebrew of the Hebrews, to whom divine election is neither ultimate nor personal. Thus "the elect" are not individual people but the Corporate Body, the individual is elected, predestined, into the Corporate Body only. The problem is clarified if we stop thinking of what we may be elected to and consider what we are elected for. Then predestination becomes, as it was to Isaiah and the Twelve against St Augustine and Calvin, vocational; we are called into the Church, which implies not final salvation but a job. Neither does the apparent absence of such vocation to Church membership imply damnation; it obviously cannot when we see this calling, this job as vicarious, as spiritual work on behalf of those who are—for the present—outside.

When predestination and election are seen in this sense, and orthodoxy is upheld against both Calvin and those who would deny any such doctrine at all, then two points emerge of special pastoral interest. Firstly, we have an explanation of pastoral facts which does justice to the Christian idea of God. In any one of our parishes some are Christians and some are not, and if we can allow any element of blame in our consideration of the latter, we most certainly cannot allow equality of blame. Nor can we restrict blame to non-Christian souls without bringing a vicarious culpability upon the shoulders of the Church. This view of a much disputed doctrine does justice to the Christian idea of God because, secondly, such election to his Church as his chosen may imply a compliment, a blessing as well as a demand, but it has nothing whatever to do with final salvation—a state which the Saints of the Church would be the last to claim. Vocation to the Remnant Church is always and in all cases the call to St Matthew, "Follow me": never mind where to, or even why. The tremendous truth involved is that, as Gore puts it: "The purposes of God are not exhausted by His Church . . . God is not bound by His own ordinances—but we are!"[1] No other view is consonant with the divine transcendence, and so far from being derogatory to the Church, it exalts the majesty of the Church's God. The point is made in majestic language by Baron Von Hügel: "God is stupendously rich reality, the alone boundlessly rich reality. . . . Our prayer will lack the deepest awe and widest expansion, if we do not find

[1] *Unity and Orders*, p. 22.

room within it for this fact concerning God. We will thus retain a strong sense that not even Jesus Christ and His redemption exhaust God. Christian prayer, indeed Christian theology, are thus not soteriology, practical or theoretical . . . hence the most fundamental need, duty, honour and happiness of man, is not petition, nor even contrition, nor again even thanksgiving; these three kinds of prayer which, indeed, must never disappear out of our spiritual lives; but *adoration*."[1]

This doctrine of election goes some way to solve the pastoral difficulties of conversion. Plainly the two are connected. All the intricate examples and definitions of conversion which we find in religious and psychological thought fall very roughly under three main heads: (*a*) the type exemplified by violent experience like the Damascus Road; (*b*) the slow psychological or ascetic process; and (*c*) that which is typified by the idea of surrender.[2] Obviously these are not mutually exclusive, and elements of them all may be found in a particular case: (*a*) and (*b*) are commonly held to be the same but for the duration factor, and (*c*) forms an essential aspect of Christian conversion if Christianity *is* Christ and sin is rebellion rather than surrender to him. The two qualities with which conversion is not mainly concerned are the intellectual and the emotional; neither "teaching" nor hortatory preaching are likely to serve in bringing it about. We are dealing with the first stirrings of *religion* rather than with theology and ethics; we are concerned not with intellect or moral consciousness but with conation, volition, spirit, the subliminal, noumenal—the pre-rational element in human consciousness or subconsciousness.

This has been said often enough before,[3] and it leaves us, pastorally, in the air. But the discussion becomes more pertinent when we consider our main conclusions regarding predestination and election. Conversion now becomes initiation to a job, and a job which has no peculiar interest in recruitment.

[1] *Essays and Addresses*, Series II, pp. 218, 224.
[2] See especially Gore, *Epistle to the Romans*, Vol. I, p. 17 ff.
[3] See especially W. James, *Varieties of Religious Experience*, and A. C. Bouquet, *Religious Experience*.

Rightly interpreted the three classes of conversion given above all imply process: the second by its very nature, the first because "love at first sight" is consummated only by marriage—or in ascetical terms, by union with God, and "surrender" as an "active" ascetical term is a positive, volitional venture rather than a negative quiescence. This means that conversion, like election, has very little to do with soteriology; and any static view of conversion, as expressed by such a phrase as "I am saved", becomes self-condemned. When thus seen, as a mainly *vocational* concept, conversion— however wrapped in quasi-mystical or quasi-psychological jargon—becomes normal, reasonable, and slightly uninteresting. Conversion is simply the vocational experience of desiring membership of the laity by baptism, just as vocation in a narrower sense is the same experience of desiring ordination to priesthood: that is, the original urge, conative desire, or volition to do a particular piece of work in the Body of Christ. This is a valuable parallel, because if the Body of Christ doctrine is true, then it must *be* a parallel, and there can only be one organic body with one fundamental work to perform. But pastoral practice of a multitudinist order now becomes an impossible contradiction. It is generally agreed that to force men to become priests, to exhort and canvass for the priesthood—let alone for other religious under vows—is extremely undesirable: why should vocation to baptism or confirmation —or even marriage—be so very different? Truly we always want enough priests, enough religious, enough couples being married, enough doctors, nurses, policemen or what you will; but something is wrong with any of these callings if they need recruiting propaganda. Vocation to the medical profession and conversion to the Body of Christ are of comparable origin; but a doctor would not regard the fostering of such vocation in others as his main work.[1] The direct agency of conversion is the fruit of the work of the profession; in religion it is worship and works rather than preaching and exhortation. In religion certainly, in most other things possibly, such agency on a conative or noumenal level can only be spiritual: the original converting force can only be religious activity, or

[1] See Supplementary Note 4, below.

Prayer—and this is logic rather than piety. The personal agency can only be the Holy Ghost in his relation not with individual "evangelists" but with the worshipping Church. The only positive method of attaining conversions is epitomized in the worshipping Remnant that forgets all about trying to convert.[1] It is important to be reminded here that the New Testament word "spirit" means not so much "immaterial" or the transcendent, but activity or power. "Spiritual" religion confirms our coupling this word with activity, making religion-as-activity-equals-Prayer a matter of spiritual power pervading all things, and so of vicarious significance. Thus is the Spirit likened to mighty winds and tongues of fire (John 3. 8) inspiring and flowing through the corporate Body of Christ at Pentecost.

If we are rid of the exaggerated soteriology and extravagant emotionalism which surrounds conversion, we are ready for a further idea of the ever practical St Paul: that of *diversity of gifts* in the *unity of the Body*.[2] The very fact of χαρίσματα stresses the idea of election, the initial recognition of which is a further aid in our understanding of conversion. This is especially true when we find faith, religion-as-activity in personal form, listed among the gifts. Gifts of personal spirituality are diverse—that is the whole burden of the first half of this chapter. Thus the Remnant member retains his individuality only so long as he gives his developing gift to the common discipline of the Remnant and thence to the parochial organism. In ascetical terms this means that private prayer really *is* and always must remain private and individual—the reformers' vital contribution is their insistence that the core of religion is encounter with God as personal—but such private prayer will not develop unless it is set within a framework of discipline and objective worship in common. Nor has

[1] That is by playing our part as well as possible as members of the Church—the instrument through which God acts upon the world. Cf. E. L. Mascall: "Being a Christian is an ontological fact resulting from an act of God." "The Christian is a Man to whom something has happened." But we can believe that Christ calls men *into* his Body, *through* the instrumentality of that Body fulfilling its essential function of worship. *Christ, the Christian and the Church*, p. 77.

[2] 1 Cor. 12.

the individual any transmitting agent, or pervading instrument in himself; private prayer, whatever its quality and potential spiritual power, is sterile without the Body, the Church, or the Remnant organism. So in another sense Christian private prayer is always of corporate significance—"for their sakes I sanctify myself."

In this way, personal gifts of prayer, acceptable and creative to the purposes of the divine donor, do not in themselves qualify for Remnant membership. The qualification for baptism, or ordination, or for the Church or Remnant, is still conversion, but this implies the conative or volitional urge to serve Christ *within his Body*. Thus, the door is immediately opened to the "babe in Christ"; it is opened as wide as need be to the faithful who, called by the Lord, are zealous to serve the Body of the parish organism by submission to Rule, by surrender to the common discipline of the Remnant. The same door opens less easily to the advanced individualist. Therefore all ideas of conversion which revolve around the emotional, the purely moral, or the intellectual, are to be distrusted. Any sort of campaign of recruitment along individualist lines is similarly to be discouraged; not because it is invalid or such conversions are necessarily false, but because, pastorally, they are useless. A willingness to surrender to common discipline alone has power. Any kind of prayer, works, or evangelism which is divorced from the corporate Rule which expresses the life of the Body of Christ is in no fundamental sense Christian.

Professor Bowman quotes Manson as saying, "In the doctrine of the Remnant a decisive step is taken towards the individualizing of religion; and this religious individualism modifies in one essential matter the idea of a people of God . . . membership in a nation came by accident of birth; in the Remnant it is a matter of deliberate choice by the individual." Multitudinism obviously assumes something much nearer to primitive Judaism—religion by birth. And the "deliberate choice" of individuals as qualification for Remnant membership insists with the Church that conversion is a question of *will*. "Now, it ought to be obvious that the *universalization* of the idea of man's religious relation to God of necessity follows its *individualization*. Take away from religion its national and racial basis, make of it a matter of an individual relationship achieved between God and man, and obviously the religion is well on its way to becoming a universal faith."[1] This assuredly is what St Paul means by "diversity of gifts among individual members of one Body". Within the Church the individual and the corporate are complementary and indissociable, which explains why the Church Catholic, in virtue of its very Catholicity, is also the Church Local; rather than a narrow insularity, true parochialism alone leads to true universalism.

Justification by faith is only completed by sanctification *in* Christ, that is "in the Body". So faith here becomes the gift of conversion, the urge to live to the Rule of the Church, the venture of faith which assures sanctification after a long struggle in and by this corporate Rule. Initial faith justifies through a "deliberate choice" to struggle towards sanctification in the Church, but if a person is so to enter the Church, then that Church must be in *local* manifestation. As the difficulties of election are diminished by our asking "election to what?", so the difficulties of the Pauline conception of faith are diminished by our asking "faith in what?" The answer is, "in Christ"; but here we must be extremely careful with the comma: "faith in,—Christ" is very different from "faith,— 'in Christ'". To St Paul, this always means in the Body or as a member of the Church, and if faith to St Paul means religious activity then justification by faith is as much vocational and as little soteriological as election and conversion. Thus although faith is listed as a gift of the spirit, implying all these things, it is nevertheless but an item in such a list of complementary gifts.[2] All these are of value within the corporate Church, none are of value outside it, and faith is chosen as the gift giving justification because it alone demands membership of the Body. Faith alone precedes sanctification, again, in Christ, which issues in the single immediate goal to which all the Epistles move; the ultimate aim of Christian ascetic, which is not personal contemplative union as is too frequently supposed, but *corporate* adoration.[3]

---

[1] *The Intention of Jesus*, pp. 70–1.   [2] 1 Cor. 12. 8, 9, 10.

[3] See further E. L. Mascall, *Christ, the Christian and the Church*, pp. 218 ff.; K. E. Kirk, *The Vision of God*, pp. 22, 44.

6

Any rejection of this doctrine ultimately leads into Pelagianism, and it must suffice to look very briefly at its pastoral repercussions. The worship of the Remnant in the midst of its proper supporters—hearers, proselytes, the second stratum —may look very similar to any other congregation, but one is the corporate worship of a parish, the other is a number of people "going to church". This latter is justifying works, against which St Paul's tremendous doctrine is directed. Yet rightful place must be found for the concept of duty. We must seek a distinction between works as justification and the duty of Rule. If attendance at the Eucharist on particular days is a justifying work then we are no further on than the Pharisee; if it is the duty of Rule, we have an ascetical principle aiming at sanctification "for their sakes". The one returns to a misplaced soteriology—works for salvation; the other is directly concerned with corporate adoration which is both the purpose of the mystical Body and the means of its existence. Rule is means to an end which fulfils its function only when all idea of personal justification or merit is jettisoned; a discipline necessary for a *job*, in Christ, to the Glory of the Father, on behalf of others. It is as necessary to the spiritual Body as the whole system of training is to a football team, whose aim is not to keep rules but score goals. By rejecting works and embracing Rule we are throwing over Pelagius for St Benedict; but the distinction is not without subtlety.

Pelagianism arises as soon as evangelism, in the sense of recruitment, is regarded as the main work of either priesthood or corporate parish. This again is an extremely delicate position, since sanctification in and through corporate worship is the most spiritually contagious thing there is. It is in fact the method of true evangelism laid down by the pattern of our Lord's incarnate life and followed by his Church ever since, but it follows only when a life of adoration is accepted as the one ultimate aim. In pastoral thought a very delicate twist is sufficient to reduce the most sublime common worship to a justifying work. We face a subtle kind of multitudinist-exclusion compromise when it is suggested that worship— even all we mean by Prayer—is only of value as the ascetical *means* of evangelism. Our *motive* for adoring worship of God in

Christ becomes recruitment to his Church[1]; which, like so many Pelagian ramifications, sounds wonderfully well so long as we do not listen too hard. As St Bernard said long ago, the only motive for the adoration of God is God himself. This is most serious when, as sometimes happens in modern practice, the zealous Churchman is used for evangelistic purposes as specific pastoral method; evangelism becomes the *raison d'être* of his conversion, his gifts, and his election; evangelism becomes his specific religious-activity, either at the expense of real religious activity—which means Prayer or nothing—or worse still, backed by worship as a mere means to evangelistic works. To-day's Sunday-school teacher is sometimes told that he will have no good influence on the children unless he worships regularly. This is true enough, but the Office and the Eucharist are not mere means to the edification of the Sunday school!

Through Rule, the overflow of spiritual power into the world is a necessary, unalterable, and fundamental part of the divine plan. Once assured of this we can forget about converts until they arrive; which in God's good time they must. It is plain enough that diverse gifts produce diverse works, through which spirituality impinges upon the world. The gift of evangelism—the true missionary vocation—is one in parity with many. Missionary *attrait* is a gift in precisely the same way as music, poetry, financial ability, the knack of arranging flowers, or laundering altar linen are gifts; all these are, in a *fundamental* sense, equal; for the value of each lies in its contribution to the work of the whole Church. It is as sensible to assume that all people should receive and exercise the missionary gift as the one supreme work flowing from Prayer, as that all should be proficient in washing the linen or playing the organ. The duty of a Christian poet is to be a poet. If Michelangelo had stopped painting to preach the world would be poorer and converts fewer.

But it follows that whatever the value of the works of, say, a Christian painter, he is justified not by these but by his faith; he takes the long road to sanctification only through his Prayerful share of the benefits of Christ's Passion. The

[1] See Supplementary Note 6, below.

modern situation demands an answer to the question of what happens to the works—really *good* works—of those outside, or possibly loosely attached to, the Church. What of the multifarious Church work undertaken by those whose faith seems, to put it charitably, dormant? Our parishes are full of people who seem to have no vocation to the Christian life of Prayer but will "do anything for the Church"— give their money,[1] run the youth club, tidy the churchyard or keep the accounts. Such work is necessary to the parish, but it is certainly not the fruit of faith. The rather grim Anglican Article XIII suggests that all this has "the nature of sin", presumably to be rejected as "unclean"; three-quarters of our practical organization is condemned as heretical. Against so rigid a view, most commentators argue that it is un-charitable and eliminates Christian hope, yet it may be wise to keep our heresies in mind rather more than we do. The real point, however, is that the Remnant concept offers an adequate solution. As soon as the parish is an organic whole, it is either justified, or not, sanctified, or not, by the faith and worship of the Remnant at its heart. All works, whether personally performed by heathen, pagan, agnostic, or atheist, become works of the parish; all are justified by the faith of the parish, recapitulated in the Remnant.

[1] See Supplementary Note 3, below.

9

THE MIDDLE AGES: MONASTICISM

"AGAIN and again in the history of God's people the many have fallen away, and only a 'remnant' have been saved to be the heirs of the promise (Rom. 9. 27–29; 11. 4–5). So it is with the incoming of the Gentiles. God always intended it, and again and again foretold it (Rom. 9. 25; 10. 19–20; 15. 9–12)."[1] With the conversion of Constantine the Church became established both by law and popular acclaim. Christianity became the religion of the Empire, which is rather different from the Empire becoming Christian. The leaning was towards the most liberal humanism, and, as is to be expected, the Church became secularized almost to extinction. The apostolic answer was monasticism—the Remnant which was to be indissociable from the Christian ethos throughout the full thousand years of the Middle Ages. As we survey the history of the Church from the fifth century to the sixteenth this monastic mountain can hardly be overlooked: this fact either condemns its whole structure during three parts of its history, or it goes a long way to justify the Remnant hypothesis.

But the Church is a living organism that grows, and monasticism, as the medieval Remnant, shows an historical development which approaches nearer to our postulated parochial Remnant as it develops. The parochial Remnant is no mere substitute for monachism—certainly not the diluted edition of it sometimes suggested by an over-romantic reading of medieval history—but rather its natural and rightful successor. The salient point here is that medieval ascetic is

[1] H. L. Gouge, "The Theology of St Paul", in *A New Commentary on Holy Scripture*, p. 416.

based upon, and is rooted in, monastic *Order*; out of which evolves modern ascetical *science*. Conversely, the existence of this body of science, plus other factors, renders practical monastic order less and less necessary to a life of creative Prayer. As in the fourteenth century learning depended largely upon ordered residence in an enclosed university, so to-day such things as printing, radio, and modern transport tend to take the pursuit of knowledge into more personal and domestic environments.

Four periods of monastic history are especially relevant in illustrating these claims: (1) The ascetical experiments of the Desert Fathers. (2) The development under St Basil and St Benedict. (3) The Cistercian reform of St Bernard. (4) The sublime story of St Gilbert of Sempringham, which is of unparalleled significance to any parochial theology.

(1) *The Desert Fathers* have become notorious for what is miscalled their "extreme asceticism". There is little doubt that they were influenced by a Manichaeism of some kind, or of various kinds, and by this they were carried to a distorted flesh-spirit dichotomy. Hideous stories, some authentic and many fictitious, have been spread about them, but the underlying motives of these early eremitic champions are as vital and as sound as the New Testament. However erroneous the chosen methods, the aims are clear enough, which to St Anthony were "the visions of the Holy Ones"—communion with the Saints and the Vision of God; to Origen, Methodius, and Macedonius, the Vision of God.[1] The method of this attainment is ascetical discipline of an essentially heroic order. These were the original "athletes of God" from whom monastic order and a purified, systematic ascetical theology were to spring. One thing particularly noteworthy about this period is the lack of any kind of numerical interest and the inevitable increase in converts. The Christian could remain within the persecuted Church and accept martyrdom; then in the words of Tertullian "the blood of the martyrs is the seed of the Church". Or he could accept the different kind of heroic death of the desert; and the crowds flocked to the desert after him.

[1] See Kirk, *The Vision of God*, pp. 174-95.

But the one constant falsity of the eremetical ideal was its inevitable individualism, against which some of the Fathers themselves had more than hinted. The Abbot Lucius could say: "Unless thou first amend thy life going to and fro amongst men, thou shalt not avail to amend it dwelling alone. If thou seest a young man ascending up to heaven by his own will, catch him by the foot and throw him down, for it is not expedient for him." Caught in a veritable maelstrom of circumstances, errors and absurdities are inevitable, but the desert remains as a kind of ascetical laboratory, a research station of spirituality. In Cassian's *Collationes* we have the first systematic treatise on what we are calling "direction". If only the modern pastoral world would be guided by both the strength and weakness of the desert experiment, it would substitute rigour, heroism, ascetic, and Rule for its over-intellectualized teaching, and it would also see the futility of eliminating the corporate organism of the Church by an individualism greater than some of the Egyptian fathers'.

The Remnant concept is rooted in the vicarious principle, the great omission in so much early asceticism, yet Origen could say: "Some of those who are possessed of greater merit are ordained to suffer with others for the adorning of the state of the world, and for the discharge of duty to creatures of a lower grade, in order that by this means they themselves may be participators in the endurance of the Creator",[1] and ". . . one just man, dying a voluntary death for the common good, might be the means of removing wicked spirits, which are the cause of many natural evils."[2] This sounds a little strange to modern ears, but so does the essentially Christian idea of vicarious suffering; we can barely believe that such was entirely wanting among the Saints of the desert. Whatever the vicissitudes of its history, here is the seed which is to find its consummation in the complete vicariousness of St Teresa's foundations some thirteen centuries later: in what Fr Bruno calls "the Apostolate by contemplation".[3]

Whatever the state of the Egyptian and Syriac seed-beds, they did, by organized planting and selection, eventually

[1] *De Principiis*, 11, ix, 7.   [2] *Contra Celsum*, 1, xxxi.
[3] *St John of the Cross*, p. 66.

produce the field. The importance to us is that amongst all the complexity of the third and fourth centuries, intellectual, social, political, and practical, the Church chose, or was led to —it matters little—monastic order: that is, an organization embodying Remnant principles. Henceforward all the emphasis is on stability in worship against nomadic preaching, the bishop in his diocese is backed by the abbot even more firmly rooted in place; and whatever the vicissitudes of monastic life, whatever its intellectual, artistic, architectural, and agricultural fruits, all pay homage to the primacy of prayer as the central human activity. And whatever the glamour of a St Francis or a St Martin, it is corporate worship in place as the supreme fruit of ascetical discipline and common Rule which remains the unquestioned converting power for a thousand years. This simply *is* the Christian life because it alone relives the life of Christ as the perfect worshipper of the Father. This *is* the Christian life because it is concerned with the order and true efficiency of the Body of Christ. This Church is a living and growing organism whose theology had evolved during the controversies of the second, third, and fourth centuries. But this Church would have died had there been no parallel *religious* movement, and this is the great contribution of the desert. The first hermits might have "applied" theology or they might have discounted it—which would have led into error—but either way they ventured faith in ascetical practice and Prayer-experiment; theirs was the initial plunge into spiritual research. By monasticism the Church was to lead the world into cultural, industrial, and social development, as the sacramental overflow of its adoration. The overwhelming value of the Desert Fathers is that they made quite sure of first things coming first, even if they erred in leaving out second and third things altogether.

(2) *St Basil and St Benedict.* Dr Kirk writes: "The fourth, fifth and sixth centuries of our era witnessed a remarkable series of efforts to bring the monastic life into closer kinship with the secular. It is difficult to exaggerate the courage and the conviction of a Church which thus set out to use the weapons of discipline, not to repress open wickedness, but to prevent those who were universally regarded as most saintly

from becoming righteous overmuch."[1] We are immersed in the technical problem of "the two lives" which any Remnant theory is bound to face sooner or later. But a vital point so often missed is that "the two lives" *is* a problem and has been accepted as such from the earliest days. Superficially, early monasticism is not other- but anti-worldly. Such an element occurs in the dualism created by the Desert Fathers, and it recurs throughout monastic history. But it is always a problem and not an accepted ideal. Even in the early days of the desert the flight was not so much *from* the world as *to* God, not the negative flight of popular idea but a positive ascetical race. And by the simplest sacramentalism inherent in an Incarnational religion, flight towards God cannot possibly be "selfish" or without significance to the world. At least from the time of St Basil a close relation between the cloister and the world has ever been the monastic aim.

Constantine's worldliness was countered by the exaggerated exclusiveness of the Egyptian desert. Here are "the two lives" in direct opposition. The problem now is to bridge this gulf, somehow break down this "double standard" and find a synthesis between the cloister and the world. Once again, this is the accepted problem, synthesis and not duality is the clearly foreseen ideal.

Pachomius had substituted work, ordinary worldly work for the exaggerated austerities that Manichaeism pronounced as the necessary means to the Vision: contemplation and work became partners rather than foes—a long step forward. In the East St Basil reduced the numbers of the cenobite organization to something nearer a close-knit family: the *local* corporate ideal is here expressed, not only in love within the family but in service to the world outside.[2] St Basil brought his monks to the environs of the large cities, work became skilled, and if there was still little trace of a spiritual vicariousness, service to the world of a practical nature became the keynote of his order. The aim is still the Vision, not service, but its means of attainment have passed from self-annihilation to an active surrender of the will and so to a contemplative-active synthesis. St Basil's great contribution to this

[1] *The Vision of God*, p. 257.　　[2] See Supplementary Note 2, below.

process is the synthesizing of "the two lives"—the counsels are no longer monastic but Christian: "The law which bids us love God more than father, mother or self, more than wife or children, is as binding in wedlock as in celibacy."[1] Poverty, chastity, obedience is the basis of all Christian progress, and if we still have the "two lives" they are no longer "standards"; they are types rather than degrees of Christian spirituality. St Basil adopts what Dr Kirk calls "the valid theory"[2] of the two lives, where monastic and secular have the same fundamental ascetical basis; they vary according to vocation and possibly in degree of progress towards the Vision, but they are the same in kind.

Despite the change from East to West, St Benedict is the true heir of St Basil; his aim is clearly the extension of the cloister-world relation. Monastic Rule is to be purged of all egocentricity, it is to serve the world through community, and significantly St Benedict seeks a greater geographical isolation from secular centres in order to attain it. Work and service go hand in hand as Prayer becomes idealized in corporate worship rather than individual Contemplation. It is significant that the controversies of this era centre around the *relations* between Contemplation and works of mercy, the service of God and the service of man, but not a word is said about the duty of evangelism as such: not because this is disregarded, but because it is an inevitable result of that quest for sanctity which is the central theme of the controversy itself. The religious life is vocational, it is the call to a job, and that job is now summed up in seven letters in one of the supremely great phrases in the whole vast story of the Christian Church—St Benedict's Rule revolving around the Mass and the Sevenfold office is *opus Dei*, the work of God. *Pastoral practice needs a daily reminder that it still is.* Thus St Benedict, in Dr Kirk's words again, ". . . adumbrated, if he did not actually reach, a condition of things in which the distinction between the monk and the world had been reduced to the smallest possible dimensions compatible with its existence at all. Within the limits prescribed by the theory of the double standard he succeeded in all but abolishing the

[1] *The Vision of God*, p. 264 ff.   [2] Ibid., p. 243 ff.

double standard itself."[1] What is especially if obviously
pertinent is that St Benedict is here succeeding in abolishing
any rigid distinction—in his age—between monasticism and
the Remnant. This quotation from Dr Kirk's book is as good
an illustration of the Remnant as any.

At least the underlying ideal is the same in both cases: the
Christian Remnant rubbing shoulders with the world, engaged
in similar work, indulging in similar pursuits, yet in the true
sense other-worldly and distinct because of ascetical discipline
and common Rule. In both cases we see society as a sacramental whole, with its distinctively spiritual and secular-
material aspects conjoined by intimate mutual inter-relations.

In so brief a comparative study as this it is necessary to
remember the essential differences which exist, not as between
monastic and secular, but between the medieval and modern
ages. We must remember that monastic and secular farming
estates were very close in general organization; the Benedictine
religious mission follows closely on the Roman method of
colonization. Discipline, by vow or otherwise, regimentation of
personnel, often, indeed, celibacy, are practical necessities in
all these cases. Throughout the greater part of the Middle
Ages the monastery was the sole resort of scholarship, art,
and science, as well as religion. Nor should we forget the great
diversity of monasticism itself: the self-contained enclosure of
Monte Cassino, the semi-eremetical experiments of later
Carthusians, Cistercian farm-management, and peculiar
mixed foundations like the Fontevrault of Robert of Arbrissel,
even the anchorite ideal, even Sempringham and Little
Gidding. These are all wont to be grouped together under the
one head. This changing and experimental diversity itself
supports Remnant parochialism, and we must beware of that
rather casual romanticism which is apt to see medieval
monachism as very much more austere, pure, other-worldly,
and rigid than it really was.

(3) *St Bernard and the Cistercian Reform.* Our conclusions so
far are confirmed as we glance at the circumstances which led
to the Cistercian reform in the twelfth century. St Benedict's
policy was to relate his order with secular life; the *Rule* says

[1] Ibid., p. 274.

little about vicarious spirituality as such, but there could be no other relation. Monte Cassino was ideally self-supporting and strictly isolated, except for the provisions made for journeys and the entertainment of visitors. But as the order developed and expanded, the vicarious principle comes more to the fore; the dualism created by the flight to the desert gives way to the Remnant proper as Benedictinism reaches its purest maturity.

"Throughout the Middle Ages the monks were regarded by their lay contemporaries as the intercessors for the rest of society, divided against those who gave it a livelihood by toil or defended it by force of arms. The monasteries therefore were not endowed solely as shrines of adoration or houses of charity, but as houses of public prayer, and when, in the perfected self-conscious feudal state, labour service and military service were imposed and assessed as necessary functions of different classes, the monks were regarded as executing an equally indispensable social service of intercession. Lands consequently given to them 'in fee alms' carried with them 'in tenure by divine service' the obligation of *quid pro quo* every whit as real as that which derived from the gift of an honour or the assignment of a knight's fee."[1] Coupled with the content and emphases of the Benedictine Rule we may surmise that this prayer *for* the world was of vicarious rather than direct intercessory implication.

But if the admitted aim of St Basil and St Benedict is to find a balance between monastic and secular, it has proved an even more difficult task to maintain such a relation when achieved. Monastic history shows a monotonously recurring cycle of reform and decline; reform tending towards otherworldly isolation, the Egyptian flight, even escapism, thence a drawing nearer to the world which only degenerates into complete secularization. St Bernard's Clairvaux is typical of this reforming movement in its swing towards extreme austerity. Traditionally, Cistercian policy is simply a return from a luxurious laziness to the purity and simplicity of the Benedictine Rule. In fact St Bernard goes far beyond it to an austerity not wholly free from Puritanism. This is particularly

[1] David Knowles, *The Monastic Order in England*, p. 684.

interesting because although, on the surface, it seems but one more example of the traditional historical cycle, it is also an historical paradox. And the problem presented is well worth a little attention because of its particular relevance to parochial theology of a very practical kind. *Le mieux est l'ennemi du bien* is St Bernard's cry of reforming zeal, and yet the Benedictine Rule to which he points is essentially a policy of *compromise*; and this paradox is central to the theme of this present study. I would side with St Bernard with all my heart if he is attacking idleness, luxury, and complacency, it is St Bernard who gives a noble battle cry: "My brothers, in matters spiritual, not to long for progress is to fail"—and no one knows better than St Bernard that progress in Prayer cannot stop short of the Vision of God: "Be ye therefore perfect" is the only possible Christian standard. But in pastoral practice, in the humanist-rigorist conflict, in practical policy, whether parochial or monastic, does compromise, the *via media*, necessarily imply mediocrity? St Bernard seems to say yes, St Benedict says no; and it is to St Benedict that St Bernard himself is appealing. The paradox is in fact embodied in the great Cistercian himself. Although "obscurantist" is an exaggerated epithet for him, his conflict with Abelard makes him the reverse of a rationalist. As Dean Rashdall has said, "To men like St Bernard the *Summa theologica* of S. Thomas, with its full statement of objections and free discussion of difficulties, would have seemed as shocking an exhibition of human pride and intellectual self sufficiency as the *Theologia* of Abelard." What we now know as ascetical theology is only beginning to develop,[1] which confronts us with an unanswerable question. If St Bernard, as champion of living religion, objected to the Abelardian *Theologia* and would doubtless have objected to the Thomist *Summa* as proud rationalizing, then what would he have made of a close reasoned system of *ascetic* such as the Ignatian Exercises? The answer must be a matter of speculation, of seeing St Bernard in terms of his life and its fruits, of seeking this spiritual genius not only in his letters and sermons, but in Clairvaux itself. And it is very certain that whatever the

[1] See above, pp. 75 ff.

answer to our unanswerable question, he would champion the idea of *ascetic* against to-day's intellectualism: St Bernard above all others directed rather than taught. His influence on the world of his age is unparalleled, his power of conversion miraculous, what we may call his pastoral and parochial success is astounding. What therefore is his method and policy?

If St Bernard's answer to contemporary laxity is the uncouth isolation of Clairvaux, a reformed Benedictinism so austere that one sometimes wonders if it has anything to do with St Benedict at all, one would expect an "invalid" double standard of an almost Calvinistic predestinarian kind; a rigid distinction between the cloister and the world with no very great interest in the latter. It would have been hardly surprising had St Bernard sided with the Desert Fathers and left the world altogether. Instead he virtually ruled it! Even if a merely intercessory duty was accepted by the Cistercian houses, we would expect little idea of any actual union—sacramental contagion with secular life; least of all would we expect any formulated policy of monastic-secular linkage of an accepted Remnant kind. We would in fact expect to find a monasticism so exalted, so ideal, so pure, and so austere, so contemplative and almost breathlessly holy, that our modern parochial Remnant sinks into a weak watery oblivion by comparison. Strangely, we find precisely the reverse.

One would expect St Bernard's seemingly "invalid" double standard to issue in its usual corollary that sanctification is a question of divine fiat—election, almost, to the Cistercian habit. Yet despite anti-rationalism no one is more consistently concerned with the ascetical life of *progress* than St Bernard. Even if he would have little sympathy with such elaborate progressive schemes as the *Exercises* or *The Interior Castle* or *The Ascent of Mount Carmel*; even had he dismissed these as rationalizing—it is nevertheless he himself who is being rationalized. He would assuredly emphasize the practice of prayer against the theory of prayer, but does his own genius for love and direction blind his eyes to the value of these schemes for the less gifted majority? Given St Bernard as personal director we could well do without the Carmelites; so it is significant that the modern Trappists see his true spiritual heir in St Thérèse of Lisieux, who almost because of her exalted holiness gives practically nothing to pastoral ascetic. Yet paradoxically *De Diligendo Deo* is concerned with spiritual graduations, and if this sublime little treatise has none of the intricate details of the sixteenth century, its central theme is spiritual progress; and—what is especially pertinent and unexpected—it begins on a very lowly plane. The first two degrees, "the love of self for self" and "the love of God for what he gives", are of a kind that St Teresa or St John of the Cross would hardly give time to, unless as the objects of invective. St Bernard deals with them coolly and not uncharitably. In his hands the first degree is "natural", a fundamentally worthy thing not so very far from the "cool self-love" of Bishop Butler. It is indeed the *first* degree of a road "that winds uphill all the way, yea, to the very end", but it is a necessary first degree of pastoral practice—it is very nearly the beginning of a "natural" or sub-Christian ascetic; and the last possible place where one would look for that is Clairvaux! The paradox begins to resolve itself in the humanist-rigorist relation which is the secret of all direction. His rigorism is the practical application of a faith which seeks the Vision of God for himself and his spiritual children, his mortification and penances are always pastoral and never penal, and he follows St Benedict to the letter in seeing Rule as a means to one end only, and never an end in itself.

And yet if overflowing love for all men is the keynote of humanism, then St Bernard was the greatest humanist of all. Where did love so indiscriminately lavished on monk, lay-man, saint, and sinner alike come from? From an unceasing *ascetical* attack on Apollinarianism, from shifting the emphasis from a theological Christ to a religious Christ, by a practised awareness of the personal presence of Jesus in his sacred and glorified *humanity*. St Bernard surely discovered, or redis-covered, the pastoral primacy of meditative prayer. However much he would have been shocked by the cold Ignatian classi-fications, this is the only first step to meditation as such. St Bernard's occasional outbursts of quite chaotic theology are the constant butt of scholarly criticism, which is not unjustified. Yet so many attacks on his "irrational allegory" in scriptural interpretation spring simply from a failure to realize that he is a director not a teacher; that he is religious rather than theological. He supports the present contention that the Scriptures form a devotional manual and not a doctrinal treatise. His concern for himself and his children is not biblical exegesis but encounter with the living Christ. He claims neither to teach nor to preach in that sense—his sermons are meditations to be criticized not in terms of an isolated academic but by their fruits in terms of living religion.

In that remarkable play called *Green Pastures*, Jesus Christ is portrayed as a South American Negro. It would take no very extensive historical research to prove that he was nothing of the kind, but it would be abstractive history. Ascetically and meditatively Jesus the Incarnation of Godhead is both historical Person and recapitulated Humanity,[1] and what then? How often is Jesus, as meditative presence, a bronzed Englishman with a strong Yorkshire accent? And who dare destroy religion by trying to deny it? The curious importance of this discussion is that St Bernard—whether he be called unorthodox, irrational, or obscurantist—is concerned with an ascetic which is not only pastoral but intensely modern.

What could be more directly vicarious than the so well-known sermon on Canticles 4. 2, or St Bernard's direction to the brother who had "lost his faith" to "go and communicate in *my* faith"? But speculation gives place to reason as we come to judge Bernard not only by his words but by his work, by his especial creation—Clairvaux itself. The achievements of the later Cistercians carry the Remnant to the very heart of the twentieth century, and this by a remarkable series of experiments springing from the reform. These are (*a*) their policy regarding secular work; (*b*) liturgical reform; (*c*) the institution of *conversi*; and (*d*) the development of the grange system.

(*a*) To St Benedict "idleness is the enemy of the soul", and

---

[1] On the doctrine of the incorporation of all humanity into the human nature of Christ, see E. L. Mascall, *Christ, the Christian and the Church*, p. 109 ff.

so manual labour is a guard against idleness; a negative safe-guard. By strict enclosure at Monte Cassino this work issued in craftsmanship of all sorts, but nothing presupposes an end outside the monastery walls. The trades therefore are domestic: cooking, shoe-making, laundering, gardening, tailoring, building and so on. The great Cistercian experiment, whether dictated by policy or circumstances, is to switch all the emphasis onto agriculture. We can speculate as to whether this is still a mere "guard against idleness" or whether some contemplative and meditative value of a positive kind is associated with this kind of work; whether the tillage of the soil is merely a respite from prayer or a part of prayer. What could not be plainer is that St Benedict's domestic trades are replaced by a constant social and professional contact with the secular world. You cannot *farm* within abbey walls; by farming you cannot be, in the practical sense, enclosed. We still have the distinction of monastic discipline and vow between monk and peasant, but they are to meet shoulder to shoulder in the bond of a common trade. What-ever the motive, work to the Cistercian meant agriculture, and work to the Cistercian was important. Whether by acci-dent or design the abbey walls fell as flat as Jericho's and monks poured on to the land; not, be it noted, to preach but to *work*.

(b) That this work is no mere negative support of an isolable prayer routine is strongly suggested by the liturgical reforms which at first sight seem so extraordinarily inconsistent with a reformed monachism. Later medieval accretions to the Benedictine Rule had certainly made it unwieldy and formal. But the Cistercian simplification cut away more than had been added. The accretions crept in as manual labour was reduced, and the Cistercians did not hesitate to make time for farm work, nor to place agriculture on so lofty a plane that the harvest might take precedence over the Office. Labour had advanced from St Benedict's negative stop-gap to a corollary to spiritual exercises, perhaps even a method of meditative prayer.[1] Further provisions of a vicarious nature were made for a proportion of monks always to be in choir, when work

[1] See below, pp. 242–4.

7

demanded the energies of the others. Clearly this proportion represented both the monk-absentees and the organic community at large. All this presents us with two conclusions of vital significance to Remnant theology. Firstly, *opus Dei* is still the work of God and the first duty of man. This is the *raison d'être* of the whole Order, the aim to which all other human energies are to be directed. But work in the world, as well as claustral meditation, is part and parcel of such direction. The Cistercians are taking more seriously than ever the anti-formalist injunction "Rule is a means to an end", a necessary means to an ultimate end; but never an end in itself.

The life of the spirit becomes sacramental and integrated. The Remnant and the rest are still clearly distinguished in virtue of Rule, but any cloister-world or contemplative-active dichotomy has quite gone. All life is to be adoring, all life and all things give glory to God, but only when the core of life is ascetical Rule, and this is because Christianity is a power which overflows from Rule. The distinct Puritan element in the earlier reform grows into a full sacramentalism; whether by accident or design, thatched hurdles and mud huts give place to the Gothic glories of Fountains, Waverley, and Rievaulx. Ascetically, all this is traceable to Cistercian emphasis on the divine *humanity* of Jesus Christ. But finally this Order degenerates with other Orders. The reason is surely that wittingly or otherwise the Cistercians are in the vanguard of a vast transitional movement from monastic Order to ascetical system. They fail because they are bold enough to modify the former before the latter is established. And they fail, incidentally, when they grow too large.

(c) These two points crystallize into the policy of substituting *conversi* for serf labour. Serf labour had been employed in vast quantities on the Benedictine estates as a normal and necessary procedure. The original Cistercian statutes forbade it, but the estate remained and the emphasis was still upon agriculture as a quasi-religious duty. Whatever the Benedictine theory and whatever the ideals of its founder, their contact with secular life on their estates had produced, in fact, a double standard of an exaggerated and invalid kind.

The gulf between the mitred abbot, his proud prior, and monastic seniors, and the serf-peasants farming the abbey lands was as wide as possible. The Cistercian answer to the problem of this double standard was spectacular in its originality; they curtly inaugurated a *triple* standard. They had indeed gone some way in a more orthodox direction by bringing back the duty of manual work into the fundamental Rule, but this did not provide nearly enough labour to staff the huge agricultural enterprise which had grown. Serf labour they would not allow. Pseudo-monks who had swarmed into a comfortable Benedictinism from an uncomfortable secular life they would not allow either. They did recruit the peasantry of a more than nominally Christian, but less than vocationally monastic, kind. These were *conversi*, lay brothers, peasant-monks; under Rule which was very simple and admittedly humanist. So we have the original choir-monks, whose job was *opus Dei*, the work of God in Prayer and praise, with farm labour as an essential part of it; and then the *conversi*, whose vocation was admittedly agriculture but with Prayer as its natural corollary. This was a monasticism in the closest contact with the surrounding secular populace through the mediation of *conversi*.

This situation virtually solves three problems of parochial theology of a Remnant type. Firstly, the inauguration of a *triple* standard implies a multiple standard, and consequently spiritual progress through infinite stages and degrees. This is the "valid" theory of the two lives worked out in practice so as to eliminate the original difficulties of monastic-secular dualism. Here we have a plain admission of pronounced vocation in some and little vocation in others, but the pervading idea of progress from any point to the Vision of God makes any rigid standard unmeaning. On the one hand the only Christian standard is perfection, on the other there are progressive standards of infinite multiplicity. But all the while a pastoral distinction exists between the Remnant bound by Rule and the crowds.

The second conclusion is that the Cistercian solution solves the problem of our awkward second stratum in contemporary society. The vicarious principle here embodied does in fact

push St Paul's "divers gifts within the unity of the Body" far
beyond χαρισμάτα—*spiritual* gifts, for not only is the choir-
office the vicarious worship of the organic community, but
the labour of the *conversi* is equally vicarious and conjoined,
since this supports the bodily needs of the choir. You cannot
worship without a *body*, much though the Puritans would
like to. Without Pelagianism, therefore, we have Cistercian
support for our hypothesis that the vicarious representation of
the Remnant is consistent not only with the service of the
Remnant by the ladies who launder the linen and arrange the
flowers, but also by the man who milks the cows and drives
the lorry. The process is complete when the cowman and lorry
driver give some time to the practice of prayer according to
their capacity; and when the Remnant—including the priest
—gives some time to an ascetical union with the parochial
organism through "secular" work. (The quotation marks are
necessary, since in any Remnant organism the rigid distinction
between "sacred" and "secular" ceases to be.)

The third point of interest is the statutory decree that all
conversi were to remain illiterate. Obstructive obscurantism
if you like—even perhaps in the thirteenth century—but
these *conversi* were monks; their aim was the glory of God in
adoration, and some of them achieved extraordinary heights of
holiness. The emphasis is obviously not on teaching but on
religion: "In the early twelfth century the appeal made by
this vocation [Cistercian *conversi*] to the illiterate, who had for
centuries been neglected by monasticism, was immediate and
widespread."[1]

(*d*) The grange system is the practical step of establishing
little groups of choir-monks and *conversi* in outlying granges
for convenience in farm management. This is interesting
because it gives us a parallel in ecclesiastical organization
similar to that between the medieval abbey and grange, and
the diocese and parish in modern days. A Cistercian grange
would consist of a couple of choir-monks—perhaps only one—
a dozen *conversi*, and the normal secular population of a village
community. Without any exaggeration, such a grange was a
Christian organism in a sense that most modern villages are

[1] Knowles, *Monastic Order*, p. 215.

not. And yet what we may call its spiritual personnel is precisely the sort of thing we would find in the modern parish; and that is more pessimistic than otherwise. A choir monk is equated with the parish priest, who may have a Remnant of one or two living fully to the Rule of the Church. The dozen *conversi* are paralleled by a dozen churchpeople who accept a rule far lower than the Anglican minimum prescribed by the Book of Common Prayer. Such a Rule would be on a par with the *conversi* Rule, for these communicated but seven times a year, said their offices at work—offices as simple as a single paternoster or miserere; that is "saying one's prayers" at the barest minimum. All the difference between the spiritual creativity, the converting power of the Cistercians, and the sterility of to-day is seen in the presence or absence of parochial *pattern*. The difference, in other words, is between a congregation of rather good people and the Body of Christ in place. Contrary to popular notions the *numbers* are much the same, but in one case we have order and in the other chaos. We will then be bold enough to pronounce that our single modern need is not so much recruiting campaigns, but pastoral *shape*.

(4) *St Gilbert of Sempringham*. The normal religious life is one of gradual progress, but events sometimes demand of Christians not only spiritual stamina—long years of plodding endurance—but response to sudden calls to heroic renunciation: hence, whatever the ultimate ideals in view, the initial flight and rigour of monastic reform, followed by modification and compromise aimed at the cloister-world synthesis. The Remnant Concept, as we understand it, seems to be flying in the face of tradition by reversing the process. From the flight to the desert, Benedictinism drew back to the world; it virtually eliminated the double standard by drawing closer and closer to secular life. Remnant parochialism would accentuate the double (or triple or multiple) standard by introducing common Rule to the faithful within the world. The one flees from the secular and then moves back to it, the other begins from the secular and then moves away from it. One would modify extreme rigour, the other would discipline extreme laxity. But no monastic movement has continued

for long in the state of ideal synthesis; to climb down from the heroic heights to meet and sanctify the world, and yet stop short of pure secularism, has ever proved impossible. Cannot the process be reversed? Can we not establish the parochial Remnant on the most modest level consistent with real religion and climb *up* to wherever God chooses to lead? Is some modern flight to the desert the only alternative to the placid mediocrity of the average congregation? The vital significance of the Gilbertine Order is that it is the medieval exception to both general rules; it began parochially and it maintained a purity which never demanded reform.

St Gilbert began—and died—Rector of Sempringham; "the foundation of an Order", writes his biographer, "appears never to have entered his head". His initial step is the direction of seven girls within his parish. He soon builds them a dwelling alongside the parish church, and henceforth writers are apt to speak of a "nunnery", which is moving much too fast and rather too far. Both Rule and organization evolved; the latter comprising a local and domestic arrangement of lay-sisters, *conversi*, and finally canons regular. The early history of Sempringham is a little obscure; doubtless what we would now call "strict enclosure" was an early—and possibly practical—development, and rapid growth would soon make the order extra-parochial. Yet it began not with pre-arranged flight but with growth from the village, and it ever remained intensely local. It began, not with ascetical heroics, but with spiritual direction on the parochial level, and its gradual advance Godwards maintained a purity which the compromising movements with their increasingly worldly bias never managed to consolidate. As we might expect, the Order grew into something not unlike the common monastic pattern. The point at issue here is that the Order evolved rather than devolved. It began parochially, which is the Remnant concept; and led to wherever God thought fit for its age: which is also the Remnant concept.

10

TRANSITION

THE MODERN Remnant evolves out of monasticism because the ascetic upon which it is based grows out of the systematization of the prayer-experience of monastic Order. The pastoral significance of the Reformation, which is sometimes overlooked, is that this transitional process was not allowed to follow its normal course. In England especially, the swift and sudden policy of dissolution cut off the older—and possibly outworn—monastic limb before its Remnant successor had matured. It may well be asked whether the policy of dissolution was an unqualified tragedy or whether it merely speeded a necessary evolutionary process. King Henry VIII can hardly be accused of murdering a pure and vigorous spiritual youth. Did he, in fact, commit little more than a kind of ecclesiastical euthanasia? The real tragedy is that the dissolution in England left the country without the Remnant in any shape at all.

If we accept monasticism at its best as the ideal spiritual partner to medieval secular life, and if we further admit that such a synthesis is hardly compatible with the social structure of our own age, we face the question; into what form would medieval monachism have now evolved had it been allowed to develop, and reform, unimpaired? We are forced to believe that the idea of the parochial Remnant supplies an answer more apposite than Nashdom, Mirfield, and Kelham. Only by the Grace of God has the traditional religious life been reborn within our communion; it is of incalculable value to us, and it is earnestly seeking to serve the world. But it was initiated with an other-worldly intensity as great as any. Despite true missionary zeal there seems no possibility of a link comparable to that between the Cistercian Fathers and Cistercian farming, and between the Cowley Fathers and the Cowley motor works; the mediation of the Remnant is indispensable to both.

But as early as the twelfth century, secular movements had appeared in opposition to established monachism. In Italy, France, and Lombardy there appeared those curious sects known as Cathari, Waldenses, and Humiliati, which paved the way for the flowering of the two great mendicant Orders a century later. These obscure lay movements finally vanished, while the Franciscan and Dominican movements, under the full authority of the Church, became a supreme example of what we have called a divinely sanctioned deviation from the norm. But both are parts of one movement and that movement was anti-monastic. As Pourrat has pointed out, the return of the "invalid" double standard meant much the same as excluding the "secular" standard altogether: "There were not two 'spiritual lives', one for the ascetic, the other for ordinary Christians. There was only one; and that was monastic."[1] Under such circumstances we can hardly speak of a monastic-secular gulf or of the friars' attempt to bridge it. Such a view has been put forward, but as soon as we see the gulf to be non-existent we must conclude that the professed aim of the friars had nothing to do with bridges but that it was concerned with a lay *substitute* for the old monastic Order. The principles involved are so opposed that we might go so far as to believe that eventual monastic dissolution was a foreseen conclusion; even an accepted aim of the Assisi penitents. Despite the heroic renunciation of a St Francis, the very idea of itinerant mendicancy aims at the heart of Monte Cassino and Clairvaux.

St Francis is the outstanding example of the true missionary; a chosen vessel of God called through exceptional spiritual experience to deviate from the norm of Church life because of critical historic circumstances. His life is one of constant adoration in the heart of secular life, and the greatest honour the Church has ever paid him is in calling one of her main divisions of spirituality not "Marthan" or even "Pauline" but "Franciscan". But whatever his obedience to his Lord,

[1] *La Spiritualité chrétienne*, Vol. 1, p. 9.

whatever his example, heroism, and sanctity, he is—and by the nature of things must be—a revolutionary of almost arrogant individualism. As in the case of St Paul the Church showed her wisdom in accepting him as the divinely sanctioned solution to present problems. But he is the last man in the world to start a movement and surround himself by "Franciscan" followers; and that he did so shows him a lesser man than St Paul. The blunt ambition of the early friars is evangelism—even recruitment—with a Dominican emphasis on teaching and the Franciscan on the contagious *attrait* of heroic poverty. Both flock to university centres, one to teach and the other blatantly to attract susceptible young men into the Order. Within the historical context such a direct appeal to a neglected laity is a worthy—indeed a divinely sanctioned— ideal, but its only legitimate outcome is reversion to type; either a reformed monasticism or a revivified parochialism. This latter is Remnant parochialism, which, in view of the movement's anti-monastic beginings, seems its obvious goal. But, at first sight rather ironically, the friars eventually became stabilized after the older monastic pattern. On looking more closely into the situation, however, we see that no other result was possible: the parochial Remnant demands ascetical system as against monastic Order, and in the thirteenth century the former did not exist. The Franciscans won a new, non-monastic type of convert, but with no lay ascetic by which to be guided they either dwindled away or reverted to the older Order.

But the search continued. The Dominicans gave us the canons regular, the Franciscans the idea of the tertiary: significant stepping-stones in the general transition which was going on throughout the whole period. And this ascetical transition, though much less noticed, is every whit as significant to living religion as the parallel movements in dogma, philosophy, and science.

Up to the twelfth century, ascetic, as a practical guide to progressive religion, meant monastic Rule. "As the Church looked to the theologian for the formulation of her doctrine, so she looked to the monk, who had ordered his life in such a way as to find the greatest room for prayer, for expert guidance in the ways of devotion. But here the difficulty began. Monastic piety was bound up with the recitation of 'prayers', the psalter, and the choir offices; and the time available for these occupations in a secular life was all too restricted. Thus for a period Christian piety, in anything like the full sense of the word, was not merely monastic in character; it was also the prerogative of the monks, who alone had leisure for it. . . . It is no small testimony, therefore, to the genius of Christianity that the Middle Ages witnessed a persistent and not entirely unsuccessful demand upon the part of the laity for admission —or re-admission—to the full privileges of religion."[1]

Thus the medieval way to sanctity was to fling oneself into the maelstrom of monastic life and hope for the best. It is empirical experiment, trial and error, but within an ideal environment. Constant corporate prayer, the Gospel story, sermons by saintly superiors and, above all, the genius of St Benedict's Rule created this environment and made the experiment well worth while. Once we accept the priority of religion over theology, of the fundamental cycle of *communis consensus fidelium* leading, on reflection, to formulated tenets, then this initial monastic empiricism is just what we would expect. But we would equally expect monastic Order, in time, to become crystallized into a systematic ascetical theology. Once such a corporate experiment is seen to work it is but human nature to reflect upon the phenomena and consider why it works.

The Cistercians at least seemed aware of the immediate problem, which they tried to solve by widening monastic Order to include *conversi*. This was an invaluable contribution, which nevertheless ended in the same sorry story of secularized monachism. St Francis's error was to throw over too much of monastic Order before he had any developed ascetic with which to replace it.

The weakness of this period was its failure to bring any real order into private prayer; a need to be supplied by the Victorines. St Bernard most certainly saw the value of meditative prayer as an approach to the divine *Man*—he certainly uses his imagination! But if his direction was anything like

[1] *The Vision of God*, p. 360.

some of his allegorical sermons it would have been chaotic in
the hands of a lesser man. To anticipate a distinction which
will be made clear in Part Two of this book, St Bernard may
have been an ascetical artist of unsurpassed genius but he was
most likely a very bad ascetical scientist. The school of St
Victor introduces meditation to theology, and with remarkable
insight to a very modern-sounding psychology as well. They are
making private devotion as orderly as the corporate Office. It
is with them that the word "meditation" takes on its modern
"systematic" meaning. Doubtless this led to over-individual-
ism at the expense of corporate spirituality, since Richard of
St Victor certainly overvalues the contemplative vision as a
personal ideal, and ecstatic experience replaces moral theology
as the test of progress. The point here, however, is that creative
Prayer discipline is beginning to creep from the cloister.

It is sometimes suggested that St François de Sales simply
lifted Prayer out of the monasteries and planted it in the
market place; in fact he only completed a long drawn out
process, and if any single man gave greater impetus to that
process than another, the honour must go to St Thomas
Aquinas. Once the whole of reality is seen as an ordered
hierarchy of existence beginning with God as spirit and
descending to matter, then the ascetical and pastoral implications are revolutionary. In all things we are to "Live like men,
that is like embodied souls; and remember that souls embodied
cannot behave as though they were disembodied." This is the
overall sacramentalism which Dr Kirk calls an "other worldly
naturalism", and if the Victorine's tentative interest in nature
and order inspired Prayer to venture a little way from the
cloister, now it positively overflows into the world. Not only
is prayer an orderly, progressive part of reality, but it lies
between the same two poles: it extends from natural phenomena to God. It begins very much in the world with sense-
experience, we are to "seek God in his creatures"—a process
called the "first form of contemplation"[1]—and this is the

[1] Here we confront a terminological ambiguity notorious in tradi-
tional ascetical writing. Briefly, a "Contemplative" experience to
St Thomas is an immediate flash-photograph glimpse of the Divine
Presence as distinguished from discursive prayer or meditation: what

very infancy of religion. St Thomas's ascetical common sense saw a gradual climb from here to the Vision of God, but moral theology returns as the one guide, and a moral theology which cannot dispense with the corporate; he "brought back the heroics of ascetic religion—always aspiring, often unregulated, sometimes tragically wasteful—to the test of reason, and subordinated them to the supreme rule of the beatific vision as commensurate to human nature."[1] And this is the real meaning of ascetic. But if the ascetical theory of St Thomas comprises several volumes of the *Summa*, it cannot worthily be examined in less. All we wish to insist upon is that in this ascetical stream of development, his place is no less than in dogmatics and philosophy. And this stream flows from monastic Order towards *pastoral* ascetic; it is concerned with religion in the world, the religion of embodied souls in social environment.

The stream flows into practical expression with the *devotio moderna* of the fifteenth century, in which order, discipline, method, and reason create a brotherhood corporate but secular. With meditation at the heart of a corporate spirituality, monasticism gives ground to the Remnant and monastic Order is superseded by ascetical discipline. Between the *devotio moderna* and St Thomas, the work of lay-direction

Tennant would call psychic (ψ) as distinguished from psychological (ps) experience. Our difficulty is that the very earliest, most naïve, and elementary sense of an awareness of God, the very *first* stirrings of religion in the soul, can only be classified as "contemplative". Yet this is obviously very different from the "Contemplative prayer" of a St John of the Cross or a St Teresa. Both are non-intellectual, but the one because it is not yet intellectually formulated, the other because it has transcended all discursive theology: the one is an instinctive or conative glimpse of God, the other is an acquired state of perpetual adoration. In an attempt at clarity the initial stage of religious awareness is referred to as "the first form of" or "natural" contemplation, with a small initial letter, while the *highest* individual achievement in Prayer is "Contemplation" with an initial capital.

Thus the very first stage of "conversion" is contemplative, and all religious people have such contemplative experience: but very few Contemplatives have ever lived. Personal religion therefore always begins with contemplative awareness, and it *might* end in Contemplation, with meditation, affective, etc., prayer form in between.

[1] A. E. Taylor, *St Thomas Aquinas as a Philosopher*, pp. 27–8.

is continued by Walter Hilton—whom we might perhaps see as the pastoral heir of St Gilbert. Between the *Summa Theologica* and the *Imitatio Christi* comes the *Scale of Perfection*, less theological than the one, less emotionally inspiring than the other—and possibly more truly pastoral than either. Ascetical theology, with all its essentially modern and pastoral implications, is consummated with St Ignatius Loyola of *devotio moderna* parentage. It is confirmed and practised by St François de Sales, whose *Devout Life* is in such close kinship with the *Imitatio Christi*; and it tends perhaps to an over-complex schematization in the Spanish Carmelites. Thence it is simplified, purified, and "pastoralized" by the seventeenth-century French Oratorians.

The friars threw over monastic Order and had no pastoral substitute, the later Cistercians tried to extend it further than it could possibly go. Meanwhile, monastic Order was developing into ascetical theology; the medieval Order was undergoing a metamorphosis and its *imago*—or, less ambitiously, its *pupa*—we believe to be the parochial Remnant. It seems therefore established that modern ascetic is not part of monastic Order but its substitute. The Remnant is neither opposed to monastic Order, nor just a mild form of it—but its true and rightful successor.

By analogy, the only way to learn to swim in the Middle Ages was to jump into the river and hope for the best; but wisdom suggested a river full of friends who had already made some progress in the art of swimming. If the worst happened, they could, as a large corporate body, save you from drowning. But in these days of scientifically developed technique and contrivances, all you need is a competent and qualified instructor and you can learn both *gradually* and more or less alone. The riverful of friends who can swim well enough without quite knowing how is no longer necessary. Again, if the worst happens the modern instructor can cope well enough by himself because he has learned life-saving methods. We do not need the safety of numbers in swimming, ascetics, or morals when we have formulated technique.

Fr Poulain is enlightening on this question. He speaks specifically of mental prayer, but as this is normally central to ascetical Rule and indissociable from its other aspects, his basic teaching may be regarded as fundamental to ascetic as such. This is plain enough in his own words: "Before the fifteenth century, or even the sixteenth", he writes, "the usage of methodical mental prayer—prayer, that is to say, where the *subject, method,* and *duration* are determined—is not traceable in the Church.

"In order to avoid all misunderstandings I insist upon this point: that it is solely a question here of methodical mental prayer, and not of that without fixed rules; made when you choose, for as long as you feel the attraction, or on a subject chosen according to the inspiration of the moment. It is clear that from all times persons have reflected with this freedom on the truths of salvation, and have sought to recollect themselves in God without the recitation of formulas. This, I admit, is mental prayer, but of a different kind. . . . It seems that the prayer of the *old Orders* consisted in penetrating the mind with ideas inspired by the Divine Office and Holy Scripture; then in free moments it reverted peacefully to these thoughts without any preconceived plan."[1]

If we accept the basic principle of Rule in religion, as but the spiritual equivalent to the discipline and system needed to learn music, games, mathematics, or anything else, the italicized words are of singular significance. Set chosen *subjects* imply both specific needs of particular souls in their own circumstances, and the acquisition of theological knowledge by a systematic choice of subject matter. *Duration* is of prime importance only amid the distractions of the world and its work, while *method* implies both of the foregoing plus an economy of time when worldly pursuits make it the valuable commodity it is to-day. It is plain that monastic Order eliminates the need for all these things. Here duration of prayer-time is dictated by the minutiae of monastic Order itself, and method matters little when the economy of time means nothing. Monastic Order itself safeguarded the freedom of "feeling" spoken of in this passage, but in secular life prayer made "when you choose, for as long as you feel the

---

[1] A. Poulain, *The Graces of Interior Prayer,* p. 37. Cf. A. Baker, *Holy Wisdom,* pp. 344–5.

attraction, or on a subject chosen according to the inspiration of the moment" must end in the chaos of spiritual eudaemonism —with all the sterility that goes with the primacy of feeling. Ascetical Rule and discipline thus *replaces* monastic Order and discipline.

Poulain now quotes from Dom Martène's Commentary on the Rule of St Benedict: "In the old monastic rules we find no definite hour assigned to mental prayer, because in all places and at all times they were thinking upon Heavenly things. . . . In a word, there was an atmosphere, a continuous *life* of prayer, which was less the result of one particular exercise than of everything taken as a whole. But for those, on the contrary, who mix much with the world, it is generally necessary to give a more definite form to certain religious exercises or to certain of their elements, such as the preparation and the resolution, in order to bring the mind back to the recollection of divine things. In fact we find these forms playing an important part in the more modern Congregations of men or women who have suppressed or curtailed the recitation of the Office in common."[1]

Two comments are pertinent here: first, we note the idea of technical recollection as an essentially "worldly" need and a monastic superfluity—for it is this aspect of Rule by which an integrated life of prayer becomes as possible in the world as in the cloister. Secondly, in "suppressing" the common office, these "modern Congregations"—presumably semi-monastic— have gone much further than a parochial Remnant towards secularization.

To return to Fr Poulain: "Finally, the mode of prayer of the ancients is explained by the intellectual life of their time. Possessing very few books, they did not vary their readings as we do. They accustomed themselves to live with very few ideas, just as is the case now in the changeless East and the convents of the Greek rite. In old days the soul was less complicated, slower than our own, and their prayer felt the effects of this condition.

"Great changes took place in the West after the Renaissance, when human thought became, I will not say deeper, but more

[1] Ibid., p. 39.

restless, a movement that has always gone on becoming more accentuated."

The conclusion, strange as it may seem to modern ears, is that "Because there was a long period when methodical mental prayer was not in use in the Church, we must not conclude that it is useless, or wish to suppress it under pretext of restoring the former spirituality. The methods have been an *advance*, and this advance has been brought about, naturally and necessarily, by changes in the temper of the human mind, as I have showed above."[1] Poulain then goes on to warn against the double exaggeration of either slavery to method or the attempt to advance without method at all; which is simply a restatement of St Benedict's "Rule as means and not end."—and the establishment of this correct proportion as part of modern ascetical knowledge.

Stranger still to modern ears is the fact that religious Rule, corporate discipline, meditative method—the whole ascetical doctrine—is of specifically modern and specifically secular concern. In modern parishes one has only to mention mental prayer, the regular recitation of Offices, or any aspect of ascetical Rule, to be told that all that sort of thing is the business of monks. Even those who ought to know better suggest that these things are not wholly the prerogative of monks and nuns, but "may be useful" to the laity as well. The truth of the matter is that modern ascetic has nothing whatever to do with monks, who are amply served by Order; it is the fruit of a wholly *non*-monastic movement. Ascetical theology is the secular counterpart of monastic Order, and consequently of special import to modern laity; in fact, it is the only possible hope for the layman who professes any religion at all and wishes to remain a layman.[2]

Is this really so strange as may at first appear? One of the fundamental factors in the medieval–modern transition is the change from the intuitive to the reasoned approach to life in general. If the sublime composition of many an English village is the gloriously haphazard fruit of some lost intuitive sense,

[1] A. Poulain, *The Graces of Interior Prayer*, p. 37. Cf. A. Baker, *Holy Wisdom*, pp. 39–41.

[2] See Guibert, *The Theology of the Spiritual Life*, p. 212.

then its modern counterpart—for good or ill—is the planned and blue-printed garden-city. And, forgoing sentiment, we must realize that if a group of modern individuals erected a hundred houses in the same place the result would be very different from Dunster, Kersey, or Finchingfield. But neither could the medievals produce the form, function and amenity of to-day's planning. Whatever the arguments for and against, or the all too obvious dangers of an industrial materialism, the hard fact remains that in all aspects of life, from aesthetics to industry, from cricket to gardening, the scientific, reasoned, synthetic plan is the modern approach. Such is our inheritance which cannot be denied, and all ascetic is doing is to carry over so fundamental a principle into religion.

From this inquiry we may conclude that the policy of dissolution was but the violent end of a long drawn out pastoral process. And parallel with this process, or rather a part of it, is the less dramatic transition from monastic Order to ascetical theory. Our particular interest now becomes an historical one; of vital import to English Christianity is the fact that the Reformation period—in its popular sense of a decade or so in the sixteenth century—came in between the *devotio moderna* and St Ignatius Loyola. If, by King Henry's policy, monastic decline was cut short, the ascetical advance was also checked. By this accident of history the Church in England was left with the corpse of an ancient Remnant and the unborn embryo of another. The monasteries were destroyed a hundred years before the alternative Remnant pattern was complete. The English Church found herself in the throes of this vast domestic crisis in the middle of a pastoral transition, which, when completed by the Ignatian and Salesian formulae, was suspect and "on the other side". It seems rather curious that even to-day, when the Anglican delights to trace his theology and liturgy to the primitive Church, he remains reluctant to look beyond the nineteenth century for pastoral and ascetical practice. It seems a pity that whereas St Thomas Aquinas is a revered doctor of the Church universal, St François de Sales and the Carmelites are "Roman Catholic" and St Ignatius a "Jesuit".

8

The English Church of the mid-sixteenth century thus found herself balanced on a knife-edge. To one side lay the shallow attraction of mass movement, the "National" Church of the Pharisees. On the other was a continual growth toward a new secular Remnant of devotion, creativity, and power. Those responsible for the reform had no easy task; history could not have given them a very clear picture of the real issue at stake. The question is, to which side did the English reform instinctively veer?

The use of the vernacular is obviously essential to meditative prayer and such studies as lead to a properly balanced Prayer-life. On the other side, any English Bible opens the flood-gates to all the perils of private interpretation. But which was intended? Assuredly not the latter, since the Prayer Book points clearly to a creative lay Rule. The Eucharist is not only provided daily but ordered on some seventy-five or eighty days a year—which is considerably more than the medieval Church expected of her laity. The sevenfold Office is concentrated into two longer Offices ("daily throughout the year")—for what other reason than that the secular world should share in the full stream of Christian devotion? And out of all this developed a line of pure and specifically English ascetic: through Lancelot Andrewes, William Law, Jeremy Taylor, George Herbert, thence to the Oxford reform, we can trace a direct line back to Julian of Norwich, Richard Rolle, Walter Hilton, and St Gilbert of Sempringham.

But alas, a knife-edge is a precarious seat; and the gap between Herbert and the Oxford Movement shows a picture of English religion at its worst. Even so dismal a spectacle, however, is not without its interest. These are the *only* two centuries in which the Remnant concept, as pastoral theology, is completely disregarded; significantly the Book of Common Prayer is also disregarded. Seventy-odd holy days "to be observed", seven sacraments, and a daily Office is quite incompatible with "sacrament Sunday" and family prayers. Again it is relevant to ask for whom precisely these Prayer Book directions are intended? Certainly not for the clergy alone. Yet if the whole multitude of the laity are in mind, the compilers were optimistic idealists of a very naïve kind. The alternative is a vague unformulated groping for the reborn Remnant Church.

By general admission, the real strength of the Church Catholic is proved not only by its golden ages but by its powers of recovery from disaster and stagnation. Throughout this unfortunate era the seeds of the Remnant remain buried but still fertile. The groping continues, and the trend of secular philosophy is no small factor in both its latency and eventual germination.

11

THE MODERN AGE

MODERN philosophy begins with Descartes, whose notorious body-mind dualism has issued in a whole series of corollary dichotomies. Although it is a somewhat glib over-simplification, we might say that if Descartes split body and mind, matter and spirit, individual and society, pluralism and theism, particular and universal; then philosophy ever since has been trying to put them together again. The one thing upon which philosophers agree is that they must be put together again: an outlook which may be called sacramentalism.[1] It is known well enough how from Cartesian dualism sprang the two streams ending in subjective idealism on the one hand and dialectical materialism on the other. The influence of philosophy on popular feeling is very subtle and very real, and pastorally these two streams of thought issue either in Puritanism or the "this-worldly" religion of philanthropy, naturalism, and the social gospel. Whenever dualism displaces the sacramental we have multitudinism of one kind or another; either an ethical Puritanism which discounts worship, or a quasi-Pelagianism which we do not hesitate to call materialistic. Once sacramentalism is discounted the vicarious Remnant within organism is plainly impossible.

The *cogito ergo sum* premise stresses man as thinker and man as individual. From the first of these springs the later rational-

---

[1] In spite of its usefulness and, I think, appositeness, I am aware of the danger of using the word "sacramental" in this wide general sense. It has other specialized meanings, and I certainly do not mean to imply naturalistic interpretation of, for example, Eucharistic doctrine. In fact I would argue as strongly as possible against any such view. I think this point follows from my regarding the Incarnation (and all that flows from it) as God's "unique second order activity" in Chapter 12 below.

ism pastorally expressed in teaching as a substitute for direction. Here is the seed of the eighteenth-century emphasis on preaching as means of instilling belief—now hopelessly confused with faith. We are back to the Church as an educative society, a concept which had appeared in the fourth century. We have a new Gnosticism no less dangerous than its predecessor. In the setting of the early seventeenth century, the *individual* emphasis was not unhealthy, but a one-sided individualism is pastorally barren. This trend of thought is continued by Leibniz, attacked by Spinoza, and reinstated by Kant. Then comes Hegel's emphasis on the universal against the individual, with results which are still unpleasantly familiar. Meanwhile modern political theory continues to grope for a synthesis which still seems best expressed as "diversity of gifts within the unity of the body".

In theological terms these dualities add up to Deism, from which most of the evils of multitudinism spring: rationalist teaching, utilitarian ethics, Whig political philosophy, and thence religion-as-philanthropy, Locke's attack on "enthusiasm", and Hume's negative scepticism. We have only to mention such words as vicarious sacrifice, discipline, corporate order, Rule, faith-venture, and ascetic, to see where the pastoral dichotomy lies.

It is plain that rationalism and dogmatic faith cannot live happily together. When the former is ascendant the latter dies, and with it the whole concept of the Church. The process is accentuated by the growing nationalism of the age— multitudinism is obviously latent in the very idea of establishment—but these factors could suggest locality, and so the possibility of a corporate Church in place. If the Church of England had been construed as *The* Church within the sacramental ethos which is England all would have been well, and we might have seen a *devotio moderna* as counterpart to the old monastic Remnant. But history and philosophy were against such a view—with Christian dogma the "Church" had gone—and the Church of England degenerated into an ethical society to which all Englishmen belong: an English Judaism. Church-going by force and under legal penalty is the last straw in the whole farce. Erastianism swung this

Church from one political party to another, first Whig liberalism then Tory convention, while the multitudinist implications of the rising democracy are all too obvious; to the democrat any kind of devolved authority is repellent and sacerdotal authority more repellent than most. Here is the political impetus of Puritanism joining forces with idealist philosophy. But the pastoral significance of this religious monstrosity is that it not only eradicates dogma but replaces applied dogma or ascetical discipline with a moral discipline which is Pelagian and Pharisaic before it begins. This is a more subtle handmaid of multitudinism, since whether or not creative religion is the direct concern of all people equally, morality of some kind undoubtedly is. This story is told often enough; any historian will give a vivid enough picture of these periods, and whatever the historian's viewpoint, its dominant colour is black. These centuries in which religious depravity is seen at its most depressing are governed by the pastoral outlook which we call multitudinist; it would be remarkable if there was no connection between them.

In the introductory section of this book an attempt was made to trace the fundamental cycle of faith issuing in belief, and corporate religion-as-activity crystallizing into theology, which in turn gives expression to the Church as a creative religious organism: a cycle in which theology is applied and becomes ascetical. Now it is important to notice the value and authority which the Church gives to custom as the empirical mediator between religion and theology. Custom is the infant child and theology the full-grown son of *consensus communis fidelium*. But in an age which has thrown over dogmatic theology there can be no *consensus*, arrogant individualism supersedes *communis*, and rationalism has dispensed with *fidelium*. From what source then does our *pastoral* custom spring? Some at least must arise out of the philosophical, political, and social trends of an age which has forgotten dogmatic theology and knows nothing of corporate worship in the Body of Christ. The irony of certain of our practices is that we are calling upon Catholic tradition to maintain the value of custom which arises out of an ethos that denies Catholic tradition. We are using the very idea of pure tradition to justify pastoral customs whose pedigree does not bear looking at.

The lethargy of the English clergy up to the Reform Bill of 1832 is notorious enough. Towards the close of the nineteenth century pressure of social conditions, the cumulative effects of the industrial revolution, the growing unpopularity of the idle clergy and the remedial Christian Socialism of Kingsley and F. D. Maurice combined to wake the "parson" out of his slumbers—slumbers which were not even dogmatic. In an age of social reform and utilitarian ethics it was a little embarrassing to be out of work, and after a two-century lapse from priestly tradition the "parson" could hardly be anything else. If social and political circumstances demanded that he should do something, either they thrust a job upon him or he had to invent one. Whatever the value of this sociological Church work, it is not Catholic custom.

But throughout this era we see glimpses of a return to the Remnant concept, albeit hidden, unformulated, and in opposition to the tenor of the times—a kind of religious-philosophical underground movement. From Leibniz to Lotze we may trace an advance from pure individualism to something like microcosmic representation. The universalism even of Hegel demands "internal relations", which is not so far from the "solidarity of the race with environment" and so from vicariousness. In political theory universalism is personalized in Rousseau's "group-mind", in ethics Kant's objective moral law is to become localized by Bradley into "my station and its duties". Berkeley's idealism seems to be striving towards something like the "first form of contemplation", which is at least religion even if it has little to do with Christianity. Out of all this has arisen the philosophy and epistemology of our own age which (as I will try to show in Part Two of this study) are among our firmest allies. James Ward teaches "plurality-in-unity", which could be the philosophy of the Pauline Church; and he treats of experience as "duality-in-unity", which is as pertinent to Prayer as it is to psychology. And Whitehead has already given us subtitles for the two main divisions of this book: ascetical *process* in parochial *organism*.

But before we reach this stage we must note the anti-rational revolt of Schleiermacher and the Cambridge Platonists; the new-found quest for feeling in religion, for an experiential encounter between God and the soul. Here feeling is undoubtedly over-stressed, but it is a real advance, a step towards religion-as-activity, though as yet, religion in a most muddled transition from rational to ascetical terms: hence Schleiermacher the preacher would teach men how to feel! Similarly, the work of the Cambridge Platonists reads like some extraordinary cross between an eighteenth-century hortatory sermon and the lesser mystics of the Middle Ages. "The truest knowledge of God", writes John Smith, "is not brought out by the labour and sweat of the brain, but that which is kindled within us by a heavenly warmth in our hearts", and "If we would indeed have our knowledge thrive and flourish, we must water the tender plants of it with holiness", and so on. All this concerns both "knowledge" and "heavenly warmth", if it is to "thrive and flourish", we are to "water". This is all a much needed reaction against rationalism; but we can only keep on asking *how?* This train of thought, developed in this century by Dr Otto, is important because in most uncongenial company it gropes for an ascetic which it never quite finds. Here the seeds of real religion remain, ungerminated but alive. Perhaps we can sum up the process by pointing to Schleiermacher's "absolute dependence" as a fact of philosophy and Bossuet's "abandonment to divine providence" as a method of Prayer.

Midway between the Cambridge Platonists and Schleiermacher, and absorbing influences from all sides, comes the evangelical revival of the eighteenth century. The very spirit of this movement suggests an offshoot from the so-called romantic strain, the quest for religion against rationalism which seems to grope after a constructive ascetic. But the influence of idealist philosophy and Puritanism is too strong; the revival finds itself linked not with ascetical but with directly ethical discipline. The Wesleys looked upon a secular position similar to that seen by St Francis, one of clerical laxity, lay lethargy, and general parochial stagnation. In both cases the aim is admittedly evangelism, but can the

Wesleys claim missionary endeavour as "divinely sanctioned deviation from the norm"? The significance of this question is that it is impossible to anwer, the case ever remains unproven; because if the friars were accepted by the Church and backed —whatever their antipathies—by monasticism and rigid dogma, the Wesleys were backed by nothing at all. Can we speak of a deviation from the norm when the norm itself had ceased to exist? Can we fairly blame the evangelicals in their failure to revert to type when there was no type to revert to? Without any accepted dogmatic, without any stabilized Remnant, who can blame the evangelicals when their missionary successes were left high and dry; to be carried hither and thither by every wind of vain doctrine? The regrettable fact is that the prevailing winds were Puritan and their pastoral vanities are still with us. Without the fruits of the Remnant or the sheet-anchor of dogmatic theology, pastoral custom is invented by all and sundry on the whim of the moment. From here we trace the rise of such theological absurdities as total abstinence and Sabbatarianism, which still hold sway in an otherwise enlightened age. The laity of to-day are quite sensible enough to see that any real religion demands discipline, but ambiguity persists as between direct ethical discipline of the Puritan, Pelagian, and Pharisee and the morally creative ascetical discipline of orthodoxy. Even if the Puritan moral code bore any resemblance to Christian moral theology, we are still confusing the map of the spiritual country with the process of travelling. We are still inclined to be muddled over the distinction between the ethics of Sunday dances and the ascetical implications of Ascension Day, between the empty piety of family prayers and the objective Office which the Church shares with the Saints.

Into this peculiar pastoral ethos, the Oxford Movement is born. It begins and virtually ends with the rediscovery of dogmatics, and especially with the doctrine of the Church as the Body of Christ. This is the turn of the tide, and we need not elaborate, except to place the movement in its pastoral environment; a process of special interest to our story. The reform then was doctrinal, but it could not escape from its chaotic pastoral surroundings. It grew up in an age of multitudinist convention, it fell upon a population who, for a variety of reasons, went to church. The only way in which the new-found doctrine of the Church could be expressed to the age's congregation was liturgically, the only way to express the new-found primacy of worship was sacramentally, by ceremonial and ritual. If only the nineteenth-century churches had been as under-crowded as they are to-day, the Oxford reform might have made far greater progress and we would be correspondingly better off. It is true that some bold spirits tried to get rid of the hordes, it is true that Bishop Gore told a bewildered diocese that he did not want any *more* Christians but a few better ones; but the custom of the age was too strong. Thus by a regrettable historical contingency, this doctrinal reform led directly to a revival of liturgical and ritualistic interests. This is, in some ways, tragic, not because ceremonial is unimportant—far from it—but because it came out of its true turn. The obvious child of this doctrinal reform is a rediscovery of ascetical practice in its fullness; for which, with Schleiermacher, the movement continued to grope. It is true that popular Catholic devotion found a new place, the sacrament of penance was rediscovered, and the liturgical movement itself meant an added emphasis on the objective worship of God. Had ascetic been reborn at the end of the nineteenth century, the liturgical problem would have solved itself without all the bitterness, and silliness, of the High Church–Low Church controversy that is still with us. Had the new-found Remnants of zeal been directed rather than taught, the Anglo-Catholic liturgy would have evolved simply and naturally. Had the Eucharist become the centre of ascetical Rule instead of the pivot of theological-political debate, then a chasuble would be a natural part of worship and not a party badge.

However, if things are out of order, we pray that all will come right in the end. We cannot put back the historical clock, so our hope remains in ascetic antedated; by a little careful tunnelling we might succeed in planting a firm creative foundation of ascetic beneath a liturgical movement which, in itself orthodox and good, has nevertheless grown too fast, too superficially, and a little out of season.

The Oxford Reformers remain the champions of religion against nineteenth-century convention; of Prayer and worship against "conscience" and social ethics, and by far their greatest fruit—in itself sufficient to give the movement an honoured place in English religion—is the rebirth of the religious life within our communion. But is not this also, pastorally and historically, a little out of due order? Compared with their medieval counterparts, our modern Orders barely impinge upon the secular parish. Their missions, retreats, literature, and above all their adoration, are of incalculable benefit, but they do not solve the main problem. On the other hand, it must be clearly seen that our present Orders are probably of greater purity than ever before; and we are reluctant to contemplate the beginning of a traditional "climb down" to meet the world. The mediation of the parochial Remnant again suggests itself, backed moreover by certain present-day movements which may well prove of far greater importance than is yet recognized.

Let us first notice the very occasional examples—such as St Philip's, Plaistow, and St Benet's, Cambridge—where our religious Orders have become parochial incumbents. This situation is as ideal as any, but it cannot be very extensive; and extension on any great scale can only risk the integrity of the communities themselves, which God forbid.

But there is a gradually developing interest in the religious life, and a consequent expansion of oblates and tertiaries, obviously capable of practical and parochial experiment. Any parish boasting just two oblates or companions of a religious society could well link its Remnant with that Society; and we should not be so very far from Citeaux. Such secular societies as the Oratory of the Good Shepherd form perhaps the most constructive of all modern attempts to bridge the enclosed order-parochial religion gulf, for here are groups of priests, laymen, and companions, under a common Rule and discipline which is nevertheless readily amenable to almost any parochial circumstances. It is not without relevance to this inquiry that the Oratory of the Good Shepherd should choose Nicholas Ferrar for its patron. If ever there was an attempt to combine medieval and modern, monastic and secular, enclosure and activity, prayer and works, military rigour and domestic humanism, it is in the sublime community at Little Gidding. If we take the developed ascetic of Loyola and the Carmelites, the cell seclusion of the Carthusians, *conversi* from Citeaux, the Benedictine Rule, *devotio moderna*, and Little Gidding, and take them all to Sempringham, the Remnant pedigree is complete: a strange mixture, but the blood is blue.

Not only is the Remnant theologically respectable and worthy of a venture of faith, but the signs suggest God's good time to re-think and practise along the lines it indicates. And this means, in the main, a return to ascetical theology. The next chapter completes the apologetic necessary to the scheme of this book, but it also serves as a link with the main section of the work. The reason for this is that any *pastoral* ascetic must begin on the most elementary level, with sub-Christian or natural prayer. In other words we must start with an ascetic of natural theology.

12

NATURAL THEOLOGY

As soon as an embodied soul acquires self-consciousness a
general sacramentalism presents itself to him. Within or
behind or below or beyond his body and the world of nature, a
realm of spirit lies veiled. Beneath sensible experiences lies
something else—Plato's ideas, Kant's noumenal, Otto's
numinous; the supernatural, the spirit of God. In the eighteenth century the deists and rationalists divorced nature
from God, and the pantheists equated nature with God.
Natural religion inherited a bad name from which it has never
really recovered. But we are slowly returning to the position
from which natural and revealed religion are to be seen as two
parts of a continuous line rather than as parallel and opposing
lines. Between natural and revealed religion there is indeed a
gap; between faith in the God of nature and faith in his
Incarnate Son is a gap which can only be bridged by conversion, which is an act of God himself. But Jesus Christ *is* the
Son of the Father-creator. Similarly between the general
sacramentalism of the world and the unique Sacraments of
the Church there is a gap, but there is still an organic relation
between the order of nature and the order of grace.[1] So
pastoral practice must seek a relation between all these things
—ultimately between the Remnant and those many modern
souls of natural, but not Christian, religion. If God alone can
eliminate the gaps, pastoral prayer may help at least to narrow
them; and the Remnant remains Christ's living agent in
this work.

The present task is to give some account of the relationships
involved between a general theism and Christian theism,

[1] See note on p. 106 above.

between natural and revealed religion, and, more specifically, between the general sacramentalism involved in such prayer experience as the "first form of contemplation" and the spiritual experience and grace conveyed through the Sacraments of the Church. Such a study thus serves as a convenient stepping-stone to the next portion of this work, since it offers a link between ascetical doctrine and sub-Christian or natural ascetic. It also gives added confirmation to the Remnant concept as parochial theology.

Theism rejects Deism on the one hand and pantheism on the other. God and the world are neither separated nor equated. The position may be expressed as a God *of* the world (Theism) against God *and* the world (Deism) or God *is* the world (Pantheism). Our universe is not only made by God but is continuously sustained, or acted upon, by him. There is between God and the world a relation wherein modern Theism is foreshadowed by the Lady Julian's microcosmic universe: "Also in this he showed me a little thing, the quantity of an hazel-nut, in the palm of my hand; and it was as round as a ball. I looked thereupon with eye of my understanding, and thought: *What may this be?* And it was answered generally thus: *It is all that is made.* I marvelled how it might last, for methought it might suddenly have fallen to naught for little[ness]. And I was answered in my understanding: *It lasteth and ever shall [last] for that God loveth it.* And so all-thing hath the being by the love of God.

"In this little thing I saw three properties. The first is that God made it, the second is that God loveth it, the third, that God keepeth it."[1]

That is the contemplative's way of saying that God is the world's creator and that his creative spirit is the abiding spirit of love. Creation is a continuous process. God's love acts upon the world of nature, sustains it, fertilizes it, and tends it; and this is what philosophers are wont to call "divine first order activity". But in a unique position in this God-world relation stands man with his spirituality seeking God in worship and his body "organic to nature". And the religious history of the world is the story of God's special dealings with

[1] Julian of Norwich, *Revelations of Divine Love*, 1st Rev., Cap. v.

his unique sacramental creation, Man. God "spake through
the prophets" and he speaks through and in creation to all
human souls who, like that other "little thing" exist only by
his divine love for his unique creation. God sustains nature,
and inspires man—spectacularly in the case of prophets,
artists, and all kinds of genius, less obviously in other souls.
We may speak both of God's general activity in nature and
his providential actions in human history; and this latter is
called "divine second order activity". The Incarnation of God
of Blessed Mary his Mother is a unique occasion within this
second order activity which deals with human history, and
this Incarnation is extended throughout the same history in
the Church which is his body and the Sacraments which
sustain and vitalize that body.

We have, therefore, God generally active upon his creation,
with man as unique to that creation; a fundamental, general,
and continuous flow of love from the father of all to all at
large. But within such a theistic scheme—and, we may believe,
as part of it—there is the unique channel of grace which
is the Church, a channel through which God acts upon his
world, through which his Blood flows and overflows onto his
world; as it were supplementing his first order providence,
and sanctifying that which sin has broken off. It is within this
Incarnational second order stream, within this Church—and
only within it—that we can speak of man "co-operating"
with God in nature. There is no opposition but a clear distinction between a communicant ploughman and a merely
religious ploughman. The first is truly freed by ascetical
discipline: by free will he "co-operates" with the God of
Creation and the God of the Cross, by adoration he synthesizes
the first and second order activities of God. The second
ploughman is but the enlightened receiver of God's providential blessing. The first gives God glory and man blessing
by faith, the second has at most an individual belief, an
intellectual humility, a feeling perhaps of "absolute dependence". In Christ's own words, the one is a son and the other
a servant.[1] But there seems no special reason for supposing
any opposition between the various ways, means, methods,

[1] Cf. the theological distinction between *gratia Dei* and *gratia Christi*.

and activities of God, or for imagining that the Church is to replace the initial plan of God's love in creation and nature and all human spirituality of whatever kind. There seems no reason for supposing that this uniquely created Church exhausts God and deposes his original creative love. On the other hand, it does seem reasonable to suppose that the Church is part of a much larger plan—a unique and glorious part, but a part in so far as it sanctifies and exudes creative love to all other parts. And this is simply the Remnant hypothesis in philosophical language.

By analogy we can see the world as a garden, and rain as the direct first order activity of God upon it. This creative substance, this gracious purity, rain, descends from heaven fertilizing and beautifying the garden. But because of sin, mankind somehow upsets the divine operation and we experience floods and droughts and other disasters of the kind. Something goes wrong with the whole scheme of things and the human world ceases to be wholly at one with God. By the Incarnation a unique pipeline is established between heaven and earth: the two are linked and at one. And this pipeline extends through the ages as the Church—a pipe through which the crystal purity of God's grace may flow by the unique means of sacraments and worship. Now there is obviously no dualism or antagonism between the first and unique second order activities here pictured—there is no enmity between the rain and the garden hose, nor is there essential difference between the creative power of them; in fact it is identical, water or love or grace, and it springs from the same God. But by the divine economy the water from the pipeline is always available, it can be manipulated by men, it rushes out of the nozzle with a force which can be directed—and misdirected. Faced by drought the merely religious gardeners can do nothing very much but stimulate a subjective sense of attrition and naïvely pray for rain. Within the second order, the Church, we have a synthesis of three things at least: contrition, vicarious prayer, to God and on behalf of the suffering world, *and* a pipeline. But the efficient working of these latter demands training, discipline, and technique—ascetical Rule.

The purpose of the garden is to give glory to God, and the purpose of the pipeline equipment is to help it so to do. It is to be efficient, pure, clean, and controlled; it need not be over-large or over-long. Let us suppose that this water is played onto a patch of leguminous flowers in the garden. The more they are watered and fertilized and tended, the more they give glory to God—and that is their prime purpose. But in so doing they fix nitrates in their immediate environment, which becomes more fertile and more productive of other plants and flowers, which also give glory to God. And the watered flowers bear fruit and seeds which spread to other parts of the garden. So it might be well to extend the pipeline by missionary activity. But that is a work subsidiary to the further tending of flowers, for the one and only reason that they lift up their heads and sing *benedicite*. Christian flowers are leguminous. The more they grow to God's glory, the more colour and blossom they display, and the more heavenward they reach; then the more fertility there is in the soil of their environment, the more nourishment is fixed for their offspring and their friends. Christian flowers, by concentrating heavenwards, fertilize the world.

Let us look again at the natural world around us, and, assuming that there is some such thing as spirit, or noumenon, or supernature, see what this analogy suggests. The Remnant concept, accepting the primacy of prayer, assumes some such thing as spiritual power sacramentally purveyed. It assumes that a life of adoration is somehow contagious, that the only converting power which is of the Holy Spirit flows through the Body of Christ in place, and out onto the world. This essential pre-supposition of Remnant theology is contained in St Teresa's concept of "the apostolate by contemplation" and again in St Thomas's definition of prayer: "Loving God in act, so that the divine life may communicate itself to us and through us to the world."[1]

What then can we know of the ways and workings of this spiritual world? In terms of logical belief we can know nothing at all, and if we accept St Thomas's "analogical discontinuity" we can still prove nothing. This is the fundamental truth

[1] See D. Fahey, *Mental Prayer according to St Thomas Aquinas.*

9

behind the distrust shown by Dr Tennant and others of the mystical, and of religious experience in general.[1] This spiritual realm behind our phenomenal world is "scientifically intractable",[2] and yet Theism in any form hints, assumes, or guesses at, a link between God and his world; that is, between God who is spirit and the world through which that spirit is expressed. This assumption lies at the heart of the experience of all religious men—it is the initial venture of faith. The idea lies behind the theories of Malebranche and the occasionalists, following from Leibniz's "pre-established harmony". It is assumed by Kant's phenomena–noumena theories and is necessary to his transcendental ethic. The monism of Spinoza sees mind and extension as two attributes of a God of multiform attributes, yet Spinoza formulates three types of "knowledge": rational knowledge of "distinct ideas", "opinion" of "confused ideas", and "intuitive knowledge". If this third derives from a "primary adequate idea of God", then we are in the realms of the spirit, we are talking about Prayer and religious experience, and it might well be suggested that Spinoza is not far from a third known attribute of God—the "attribute of intuition" or even "spirit". Is this the fundamental weakness of the "hideous atheist" who is also "God-intoxicated", of the dualism involved in a rationalist who nevertheless knows by experience what the word "religion" means? What concerns us here is simply this: that if Spinoza had tried to bring his spiritual experience—"intuitive knowledge" or "intellectual love of God"—into his general philosophy, he would have found a complete analogy between the modes of extension and spirit: between, that is, nature and spirit. This he rightly would not allow, and this is what Berkeley did allow when he spoke of "divine visual language"; here the ways of nature are the "thoughts of God" plainly set out to be read off by a kind of one-sided sacramentalism.

[1] *Philosophical Theology*, Vol. I, pp. 311 ff.

[2] I am not here agreeing with Dr Tennant's general teaching against mysticism. I agree with him that mystical knowledge is "philosophically intractable" not because it is false but because it is so difficult to interpret, translate, and put into words. See E. L. Mascall, *Christ, the Christian and the Church*, pp. 61–2.

The problem becomes "reciprocal action" in Lotze, and even Tennant himself is forced to offer a vague relation from the phenomenal to the ontological by repetitive use of the ambiguous term *rapport*. But Tennant nevertheless gives us the key to the solution in his invaluable "faith"-"belief" distinction. All experience begins with the sensible, and the God of the spirit-world is the same God of the world of nature; so we can have not only faith but reasonable faith in assuming the two to have something in common. The general sacramentalism of Theism, which assumes that the whole universe is to God what the body is to the human spirit, suggests that the world of the spirit has common properties with the world of nature. This indeed is confirmed by God's own revealing Incarnation.

But if we are to speculate reasonably about these things we must ask what are the properties of the natural world which faith carries over, creatively, into parochial theology. These may conveniently and briefly be discussed under four heads:

(1) The world we know is a plurality in unity, a plurality of beings involved in an organic relationship. It becomes a whole by virtue of an incomprehensible complex of interrelated cycles, which suggests

(2) that the natural world is one of fundamental order and relative contingency. In other words, it is an orderly system of cycles; of seasons, reproduction, fertility, etc. But it is a living organism controlled by God, and not a machine.

(3) The world is governed by the principles of evolution, or, in the better word of James Ward, epigenesis; it not only moves, but moves to a teleological plan. This in turn suggests

(4) a temporal hierarchy of being; a development from simple organisms to complex organic cycles; but all ultimately forming one organic cycle of infinite complexity.

What are the spiritual analogies of these material things? (1) *Plurality in unity* is St Paul's doctrine of the Church—individual members within the bodily whole. A complex interrelationship is only a Theistic enlarging of the solidarity of the race doctrine, and this is the basis of vicariousness in Prayer. What is usually called "the axiom of internal relations"—associated with modern monism in general and with

Hegel in particular—gives us the clue to an overall inter-dependence in nature which suggests a similar interplay in the realm of the spirit. If such an event in nature has repercussions in everything else, then each prayer, each Eucharist, each act of love reverberates throughout the spiritual world: "For their sakes I sanctify myself."

If we return from monism to a thoroughgoing Pluralism exemplified in the philosophy of Leibniz, we are confronted with the microcosmic principle wherein each "monad" recapitulates the world in itself. By the notion of plurality-in-unity we may thus postulate a spiritual world governed by vicariousness acting through the microcosmic group; the complete Body of Christ in place. Whitehead's "philosophy of organism" is in support of the Remnant concept.

The "Philosophy of Organism" is to Professor Emmet "the notion of process concerned as a complex activity with internal relations between its various factors".[1] Therefore the cosmos is a unity or a "patterned process"; there is a "mutual sensibility" of bodies so that everything in the universe is "sensitive" to the presence of everything else. That in itself is enough to suggest a spirit world, the Godward side of the universal sacrament, working in accord with the phenomenal characteristics of fundamental order and relative contingency, but Whitehead goes much further in bridging the notorious gap with his conception of "eternal objects" which are frequently compared with the platonic "forms" of eternal reality. The "process" which is the world is now a flux of events with spatial-temporal characteristics, the eternal objects comprise the "realm of possibility" and are abstractive until they ingress into the cosmic flux. This concrescence Whitehead calls an "actual occasion", and it is determined by God. The actual world consists of such "actual occasions" or "events", the word "prehension" is used to denote this active taking into relation, and the underlying process of "prehension" is *feeling*.

This philosophy is of value here because, by translation, multitudinism as "individual" prayer and religion is bound to

[1] *Whitehead's Philosophy of Organism*, Chapter IV, and see further, Chapter IX.

a world-view of extreme pluralism of a Leibnizian kind. And if the cosmos is organic, if it is in any sense a whole, and if this one is a synthesis of many—if, that is, the word individuality means anything at all; then any exclusive pastoral view, from insular monachism to a nice little nucleus, finds itself in a philosophical vacuum. If there is any theistic *rapport* between God and the world, any possible or feasible analogy between soul and body, or spiritual and phenomenal environment, then only such conceptions as vicariousness, microcosm, spiritual hierarchies, related processes, organism, and so forth are consistent with it: and these things spell Remnant theology.

(2) *Fundamental order and relative contingency* in cosmic nature suggest the same in the world of the spirit. Order itself suggests ascetical Rule as the norm of creative progress and a certain contingency is only what all the saints, following St Benedict, mean by "Rule and method as means to ends and not ends in themselves". Order in spiritual activity makes human souls into agents of free will, of moral value and capable of sonship with God. Contingency saves the cosmos from mechanism and turns Prayer from formal duty into adventurous search. Order makes possible ascetical direction, contingency places all power in the hands of God the Holy Ghost. Order, moreover, is analogous to what we have described as divine first order activity, and contingency is analogous to divine second order activity. In this light the two conditions live peaceably together as parts of God's world and its ways.

But as we consider internal relations in nature in terms of more and more complex natural cycles, we are bound to speculate upon the existence of corresponding "spiritual cycles"; or upon God's first order activity in the spiritual realm. In nature we know that if we want bread we must begin by ploughing, cultivating, and fertilizing, and then we must drill seed and continue with like cultivations until, by a complex process during a period of nine or ten months, wheat produces wheat. But this cycle in nature is only a part of other cycles; wheat follows legume because of nitrogen fixation properties which are peculiar to these latter, and roots, leys, fallows, green manure, and so forth fit in with the agricultural cycle we call rotation of crops. This process corresponds with other cycles of animal nutrition—wheat-straw-stock-muck— in nature we have indeed wheels within wheels, cycles within cycles, of ever growing complexity. All this theism claims to be the first-order activity of God. In agriculture divine second-order activity is allowed for by "miracle" in a fairly common-sense sort of way—that is, by the inexplicable successes and failures which farmers know. It is not uncommon to meet with examples of strange interconnected cycles in nature, such as liver fluke in sheep traceable to the presence in pasture of certain small snails, or the connection traceable between cats and red-clover through bees and field-mice, quoted by Darwin in *Origin of Species*. The condition of order gives to nature an integrated wholeness by connected cycles of immense complexity, and this complexity increases as we move up the evolutionary scale of nature.

This is in itself sufficient to suggest that God's spiritual world is something of similar order, similar cycles, and an even more intricate complexity; that God's activity in the realms of the spirit concerns an equivalent to first-order as well as second-order activity. Such a possibility is important, because we are prone to doubt the miraculous or direct second-order activity of God in nature and trust wholly in what used to be called natural law, whereas in Prayer the position is reversed—*all* Prayer we are apt to regard either as miraculous or as negative, all Prayer we are apt to see as a direct, isolated, and unique intercourse with God; that is, as second-order activity. The relative contingency of the world certainly allows for such possibility, but its fundamental order equally suggests interconnected streams of spiritual power arising out of an orderly sequence of regular Offices, Sacraments, inter-cessions and praise. And these orderly sequences in individuals fit into more complex and more creative cycles as individuals combine in common corporate harmonies, which in turn form cycles with other groups and other places. By Christian theology all are but lower parts of hierarchical cycles which contain angels, archangels, seraphim, and cherubim, and the whole host of heaven. The threefold Church of orthodoxy is analogous to nutritional and fertility cycles in agriculture and nature.

Professor James Ward[1] sees an analogy between this external correlation of all living things, which he calls "bionomics", and a similar internal relation in each organism which he calls "physionomics". We are merely continuing the process into something that might possibly be called "spiritonomics"—the laws governing the spiritual world according to a first-order activity of God. Speculation of this kind may be exciting but it is open to the objection that it leads to a new Gnosticism as fantastic as the spiritual hierarchies of Cerinthus and Basilides. The difference is that the Gnostics' only aim was *to know*, theirs was a pride which bluntly sought the tree of knowledge in order to eat of its fruit and bask in its comfortable shade. We have no desire at all either to know or to teach, but simply to substantiate a venture of faith by analogical probability. But if nature has any possible analogy to God's ways then one has only to open one's eyes and much of our "simple evangelism" becomes about the most improbable of all methods of such service. We might add that if the Gnostics defied the traditions of the Church it was not on the score of the existence of heavenly hierarchies as such; indeed the doctrine of the threefold Church, of purgatory and paradise, angels and archangels, of half our Lord's parables and St John's apocalypse, are all full of the idea. By contrast, the fundamental points which here arise suggest firstly, that our over-individualized modern prayer is an absurdly naïve concept. At the very least we may expect complexity and correlation in the realms of the spirit which imply ascetical order and corporate creativity. And this alone is sufficient to justify a *faith* in Remnant organism against the simplicity of multitudinist individualism. Nature surely dictates that nothing is creative *by itself*.

(3) *Evolution*, or in Ward's term, *epigenesis*, suggests organic growth, but it also implies conational adaptability to environment. By spiritual analogy it suggests a fundamental pattern of spiritual progress which begins with and evolves from the establishment of a sacramental harmony with a

[1] *The Realm of Ends*, pp. 56 ff.

specific environment, and this is what we call "the first form
of contemplation". As species in the biological world evolve
by the adaptability of their members to environment, and
in man by his civilizing adaptation of nature to himself, so
monasticism, for example, is concerned with Prayer form and
ascetic organization, in place, which adapts natural and
cultural things to spiritual purposes. Again it appears improbable that the Remnant of medieval genius is adaptable to a
twentieth-century world. Such natural process infers the
spiritual importance of Remnant organism, growing, not only
in progressive spirituality, but also in harmony with a specific
parochial environment. We must remain faithful to orthodox
ascetical theology as the basis, but there is always the need of
local development evolving from *communis consensus fidelium*.
We must not fear what may be called "devout experiment" in
prayer technique, and this individuality of a parochial kind,
though rooted and grounded in orthodoxy, is recognized by
the living Church, which gives a measure of authority to
custom and local cult. Thus is explained the Christian
paradox whereby true individuality in Prayer and liturgy
springs only from a sinking of individuality in corporate
Rule.

(4) But there is, in nature, a *hierarchy* of development,
which again suggests religion as progressive activity, but
which also infers an increasing complexity as we climb from
lower to higher strata. This is important because natural
reproduction becomes analogous to spiritual reproduction or
what is usually called conversion, and as reproduction grows
in complexity from amoeba to man, so we must assume the
process of religious reproduction to be very complex indeed.
A unicellular hydra is reproduced by the simplest possible
process of dividing itself in two, and this is analogous to the
naïve sort of religion which would *preach* and *teach* conversion.
The reproduction of higher organisms such as mammalia
becomes a complex of cycles, and we can only assume that
the even higher reproduction of spiritualities is more complex
still. To reproduce wheat, as we have seen, demands not a
simple hydra-like division of wheat grains but ploughing,
cultivating, draining, and fertilizing operations all within

correlated cycles of rotation and animal nutrition. The analogous inference is that religious conversions begin, not with simple division or sharing of belief, but with a complex of corporate and environmental Prayer. Faith begets faith just as cow begets cow, but in neither case is the process simple, and sacramentalism suggests a spiritual cycle beginning with faith-prayer-works-faith. This is apparent in the whole world of Christian culture, since the converting religious influence of, say, a Michelangelo is expressed through the cycle of faith-meditation-painting-faith, and this influence is a thousand times more fruitful than anything Michelangelo would have achieved by renouncing painting for more direct methods. All Christian achievement derives from the fundamental primacy of adoring worship expressed by any means with which we are gifted, and the spiritual power of any work, ἐν χριστῷ, is as real as the Sistine chapel, if less obvious.

If the yield of a crop of red clover depends on the cat population in the neighbourhood, if the cure for liver fluke is achieved by killing snails, then it is reasonable to suppose that the Remnant's Office has something to do with the sudden or gradual conversion of the postman's daughter—especially if the Remnant are in contagious harmony with an all-embracing environment.

It is well humbly to realize our inability to comprehend even the observable intricacies of natural order. Higher still is the largely unknown realm of mind, with its greater complexity, which hints at such phenomena as mental telepathy in such a way that we might reasonably postulate a "spiritual telepathy". We know for example that football teams win more matches on their home ground than on others. Logically it can make no difference where a game is played. Logically the home crowd cheering on their team by a sort of "volitional telepathy"—a corporate willing which *seems* to be actively transferable—should have no real effect on the game at all: yet league tables suggest that it does. If footballers really play better under such circumstances, then we are getting very near indeed to the "contemplative harmony in place" of natural ascetic.

My only point here is that in view of such comparatively

commonplace examples, and in view of the immense complexity of spiritual things like conversion, faith, and *attrait* for prayer, many of our evangelistic stunts appear extremely puerile. The consistent worship of the Remnant in place seems a much more reasonable method.

PART TWO

TOWARDS A PASTORAL ASCETIC

13

INTRODUCTION:
THE ELEMENTS OF DIRECTION

I HAVE defined ascetical theology as applied dogmatics, so that any pretence at an ascetical *summa* would need to occupy many volumes. Meanwhile, I accept both the general consensus of the ascetical writings of the Church's saints and doctors, and also the Anglican right freely to criticize any specific portions of it. If pastoral priesthood is to take the guidance of souls seriously we can only presuppose that it is acquainted with the ascetical ethos of the Church and that this acquaintance has been, or rather is being, gained by use as well as study. Having reserved the right to criticize, I would point out, for example, that much rather shallow criticism of St Ignatius Loyola would be avoided if only the spiritual exercises were *used* rather than studied. On the other hand, I may applaud Frederick William Faber's well-known conclusion: "This, then, my dear brethren, is St Ignatius's way to heaven; and, thank God, it is not the only way!"

The general position is summed up very well by Fr Patrick Thompson,[1] who distinguishes between prayer as an art and a science:

"Teaching of art can only be based on what the consecutive achievement of the ages has built up—technique in fact.

"Dancing is an art. So is prayer. Dancing is not to be learned in isolation from tradition. Neither is prayer. Dancing is not a science. Neither is prayer. But there is a science of the dance. It is anatomy which governs the possibilities, in movement and repose, of the human frame. And there is a science of prayer. It is the theology of grace, of the supernatural life, the

---

[1] *Priesthood*, ed. H. S. Box, pp. 267 ff.

anatomy of the mystical body, and the biochemistry of its cells.

"Dancing can be learned without learning anatomy. And the art of prayer can be learned without learning the relevant science. But neither prayer nor dancing can be efficiently or safely taught save by those who are themselves acquainted with the relevant sciences. That is why I say there is a science and an art of prayer, and that the priest must know the one and can impart the other."

This passage is both illustrative of the position maintained in the preceding section of this work and a guide to the formulation of the present section. Despite a somewhat ambiguous use of the words "teach" and "learn", Fr Thompson is quite clear in the distinction between science and art, which seem to be exactly equivalent to dogma pure and applied—by dogma "the priest must know", by ascetic he "can impart"; and dancing and prayer can be "learned" (I would prefer "developed" or "acquired") without anatomy or dogma— that is without teaching but by direction. Now this direction ("teaching of art") implies in Prayer the science of ascetic— "technique, in fact"—which is the living experience of the Church; in other words, tradition in its living and essentially present sense. This preliminary point explains my attitude to the bulk of Christian ascetical theology embodied in the writings of the Saints—it is to be accepted because our art and science cannot, as well as dare not, base itself on anything but traditional achievement or orthodoxy. And to all this great bulk of writing and experience I give what Anglican genius for both dogma and freedom calls a general assent. But if anything really lives then it must develop, change, and be reinterpreted; and so we may reasonably claim to doubt any detail of ascetical practice and fairly to face any conflict which may arise between the medieval ascetics and the modern relevant sciences—a conflict, it may be added, which proves to be remarkably rare.

But traditional ascetic must also be brought into line with the modern intellectual temper; we have to bear in mind throughout that our age is far more interested in the reason why, the science of things, than was the Middle Ages, and therefore a synthesis of the modern sciences with the older practices—invariably accepted on faith or authority or experience—is of the first importance. The very principle of *consensus communis fidelium* infers that the science of ascetical theology necessarily succeeds the art of ascetical practice; men danced long before they knew anatomy. But in an age of healthy questioning, ascetical science is apt to be asked for before conative-faith-venture will practise prayer. To-day mental prayer would be much more acceptable—according to any method you like—were we to succeed in rendering it reputable in the light of epistemology, pure psychology, and a philosophy of history.[1] Similarly, the fundamental Rule of the Church[2]—Mass, Office, private prayer—is dull and uninspiring to so many modern Christians because it is presented as convention rather than ascetic. It is demanded only as duty and on authority; two very important motives, but by no means the only ones. In the past this basic scheme has been proved by experience to be creative and progressive —it is no sin if the moderns ask how and why it is so, and more pertinently how is it to be *used* creatively rather than conventionally. As I hope to show a little later, the modern sciences can help to explain this without altering the traditional scheme in any way—what must be prevented is the misuse which illicit custom is apt to make of this tradition.

Contemporary work on ascetical theology is inclined to be individualistic. As we have seen, we tend to examine the "biochemistry of its cells" without relation to the "anatomy of the mystical body". But there is a further tendency even to departmentalize the unisolable reactions of the individual cell. Thus we hear and read much about the Mass, and the Office, and mental prayer, and liturgical prayer and vocal prayer and so on—occasionally these things are treated ascetically rather than dogmatically—but very seldom do we hear of any necessary interrelation between them all. In ascetic, even from the individual aspect, we are confronted with precisely the same departmental error that is found in parochial theology—we find hosts of good things—valuable materials—but very little constructive pattern. Our modern

[1] See below, Chapter 20.   [2] See below, Chapters 18, 19, 20.

ascetical direction, like our modern pastoral practice, lacks form and shape. It is this fundamental form, shape, and pattern inherent in Christian spirituality with which we are concerned, rather than with original methods or detailed commentaries on ancient methods of prayer in its manifold branches. This must be so because all souls are unique: it can never be repeated too often that the first quality needed in direction is self-effacement. The one approach of the director to the soul is by means of objective empathy, and thence perhaps a loving sympathy. We are to develop unique spirituality, and growth comes only from the gracious work of the Holy Spirit. We are not to mould souls into a set pattern, there can be no fundamental method—and yet if Christ is One Mystical Body then the cells, however unique their bio-chemistry, must conform to a fundamental pattern; there can be only one "anatomy of the mystical body" because it is only One Body.

As each oak tree and each leaf is unique, so is each Christian soul. But it is nevertheless true to say that the shape of an oak tree or its leaf conforms to a single fundamental pattern. With the Rule of the Church in mind—Mass-Office-private prayer—we might describe Christian ascetic at its most fundamental as three-sided, however many variations there may be on this pattern. It is with the pattern that we are concerned; individual details, sins, usable and unusable methods, times, periods, and proportions are all a matter for direction, in the right sense individual. And this uniqueness of the human soul is the obvious reason why anything like an ascetical *summa* means a library rather than a book. Direction remains a particular art based on a universal science. If the diversity of the Saints baffles analysis, their writings are nevertheless reducible to Christian form.

So, returning to Fr Thompson, "neither prayer nor dancing can be efficiently or *safely* taught save by those who are them-selves acquainted with the relevant *sciences*." (Italics mine.)

I summarize my aim by making another distinction within the ascetical corpus which is possibly the most vital, and most neglected, of all. To-day, whenever religion is taken seriously, there is apt to be so much stress on progress that we completely disregard spiritual health. As a practical distinction we would say that a pastoral ascetic is concerned entirely with the latter; the director is to maintain health, while progress can safely be left to the Holy Ghost. And this preoccupation with health means an initial preoccupation with ascetical science. If priests are to seek to guide souls in Prayer—and that is their true pastoral function—they must do so with safety; they are to apply the fundamental patterns of ascetical knowledge which tend to keep the soul healthy—they must be ascetical scientists before they dare to be ascetical artists. Like the newly qualified surgeon, the priest must perform his operations efficiently before he can do them brilliantly. It is, in practice, such vague advice as "Fr Brown's latest little book is very helpful", which causes so much spiritual ill-health.[1] It is not only useless but dangerous to suggest that brown bread or aspirin or beefsteak pie is very good for someone who wants a balanced diet. Two glasses of port after dinner are very good indeed, but an unwise prescription for the gout. I am not interested in psychological stunts, oddities, or even true brilliance. I only hope to aid in the creation of Remnants whose members are spiritually healthy and quietly efficient. Pastoral ascetic has not the least concern with visionaries, mystics, and contemplatives: if such do arise from time to time in our parishes we can give thanks to God and legitimately seek for specialists to look after them.

By the divine dispensation, health and growth are closely connected. This distinction and correlation is so important that two explanatory analogies are worth considering, and the physical analogy is the obvious one to make first.

The mother of a child is concerned with both his health and growth. These are closely related, and all the mother can do, in practice, about insuring growth is to concentrate entirely upon maintaining health. Both are the gifts of

[1] Is it always wise to publish personal "letters of direction"? The popular letters of the Abbé de Tourville for example? Written to devout souls under the Papal discipline of nineteenth-century France, these letters are invigorating for their inspired humanism, their anti-formalism and their spiritual boldness. But is this a safe book to leave in the tract case of an English parish church in 1956? I have no wish for an Anglican "Index"—personal direction is the real need.

God, and yet he deigns to give the human mother a great measure of control over health and, directly, none at all over growth. And the one essential guide to the mother in her duty of maintaining health is a scientific technique which is part of a living tradition. She knows all about balanced and progressive diet, sleep, exercise, fresh air, hygiene, and so on, and she is quite confident that if this fundamental pattern is followed health will be maintained and growth can safely be left to God. She is concerned with slow, normal development, and nothing akin to brilliance; she knows and fears the disastrous. repercussions of too rapid growth. Progress is always presupposed rather than contrived. I suggest that it is the same in ascetic.

For the second analogy, let us assume that a farmer keeps rigidly to a Norfolk-four-course system. According to both science and tradition he is safe, because he is ensuring fertility or soil health—which is almost as onerous a responsibility of divine stewardship as cure of souls. Now if the farmer follows this basic pattern he may justifiably experiment in details. A proportion of his land will come in for a straw crop, and he may choose between wheat, oats, barley, rye, maize, millet or any other cereal; and by trial and error he may improve as a farmer by finding out which crops are suited to particular fields. He may discover a need for draining or liming, or some other tillage operation. He may have two or three failures by trying barley, oats, and rye on land which is better suited to wheat. Such failures will not be disastrous, however, because the general health of his farm will be assured by his rigid pattern of time-honoured tradition and scientific standing—the Norfolk-four-course. What the farmer dare not do is eliminate his white straw crop altogether, or alter his proportion of acreage, or leave out the muck before roots, and so upset the fundamental balance of his system —that would be dangerous. The point of this analogy is that if the farmer keeps to such a safe system, he can be comparatively young and inexperienced without coming to much harm; he is free to farm empirically, he can gain knowledge day by day. He can, in James Ward's definition of experience, "become expert by experiment". He may finish as an artist, an expert, or a specialist, but he is from the very beginning orthodox and efficient.

Direction of souls is empirical in two senses: as distinct from the dogmatic direction of medieval authoritarianism, and in the sense of a certain necessary trial and error. It is assumed that the priest with cure of souls knows, by experience and experiment, various methods of meditation; it is assumed that the writings of the Saints have ceased to be, for him, a homogeneous collection of holy books and are seen to have clearly defined characteristics; that the Saints, in fact, have ceased to be a standard collection of holy men and have become mentally classified into schools and groups of distinct but overlapping emphases. This is only to suppose that he can understand and recognize the difference between a passage from Avila and a passage from Lisieux, as a musician can distinguish between a symphony by Brahms and a symphony by Mozart. One of the essentials in direction is finding the right method, the right saintly writer, the right school of ascetical thought for the particular soul in question: the right white straw crop for the particular field. Normally, therefore, one might consider St Thérèse of Lisieux more suitable for what William James calls a "once born" schoolgirl than St Augustine's Confessions. The Ignatian fifth method would not be given to a spiritually virile but illiterate ploughboy—it would be like drilling wheat on poor light land. So much is obvious; choosing exactly the right methods and readings and prayer-forms for individual souls is not: it is a very complex and difficult business. But if it is set within a traditional, scientific time-honoured pattern; not "Norfolk-four-course" but perhaps the "three-course" Rule of the Church—properly applied—then we too can faith-venture empirically, we can experiment and even make a mistake or two: the soul is safe. We may have spiritual mishaps but we will not be responsible for disaster. And if we set individual souls within the wider framework of the corporate Remnant, then spiritual health is doubly secure; growth can be left to the Holy Ghost with as much confidence as the farmer shows in leaving his wheat, or the mother her child. But such faith in him does not excuse farmer and mother from their stewardship and its responsibility. The lambs of the Good Shepherd were not entrusted to St Peter to be taught, regimented, forced, or neglected, but to be fed.

It will make for clarity if I state here and now the conclusions we are to reach and our method of reaching them. If ascetic really is applied dogmatic then we will expect our ascetical patterns to grow out of the application of the fundamental Christian doctrines of Incarnation, Atonement, and the Holy Trinity; and this pattern will be seen to be embodied in the traditional threefold Rule of the Church when ascetically applied. This is in fundamental agreement with both Christian ascetic culminating in St Ignatius Loyola and the modern psychological philosophy of such writers as Professor James Ward and Dr F. R. Tennant.

But before proceeding to this inquiry we must tackle the problem of the "hierarchy" muddle. Our purpose, we have explained, is to maintain the health which promotes growth; but there is much ambiguity as to what spiritual progress really means. The right and wrong conceptions of spiritual progress will be found to be closely linked with spiritual health and spiritual ill-health.

The crux of the ambiguity is seen in two different conceptions of progression, which need to be carefully distinguished. There is firstly a progressive hierarchy or *scale*, and secondly a progression in *value*. The first is applicable to the general historical progress of religious consciousness in the spiritual evolution of the race; the progress, for example, from Moses' utilitarian polytheism to the transcendentalism of Deutero-Isaiah, thence to Christianity. This is basically the progress from natural religion to the fullness of life in Christ and it is recapitulated in every human life. Thus the spiritual consciousness of a child usually goes through the stages of Mosaic polytheism—a mere awareness of supernatural forces, whether "gods" or "fairies"—to Christian prayer. St Thomas Aquinas's sacramentalism, and his tenet that we are to pray as *men* and not disembodied spirits, present us with a natural hierarchy of development which issues in the classical "three ways". Religion, like everything else, begins with (1) sense-life, followed by (2) "natural life", ruled by intellect and will.

This is the stage of the purgative way. Next (3) comes the "supernatural life" of grace, the life of "infused" moral virtue—the "theological" virtues and the gifts of the spirit, and this leads to (4) life within the mystical Body of our Lord Jesus Christ, which is the illuminative way. The last stage is union with "God as he is in himself" or pure Contemplation or the unitive way. Clearly this is but an ascetical scheme of general classification, an outline map of the spiritual country, not to be used too rigidly. Natural and Christian Prayer obviously overlap, and so do the "three ways", since all the Saints remain to some extent in a life of purgation and the vast body of Christian people are occasionally illuminated by grace. But the vitally important thing is that this is, pastorally speaking, a progressive scale quite distinct from value. In other words, souls are to pray as they can and not as they cannot—their spiritual progress is dependent upon vocation, election, and diversities of gifts, and as members of the Body of Christ they are "comely" and "less comely", "babes in Christ", "weak brethren" and "strong men". They have different but interdependent functions, and so they are basically of equal value because value intrinsically belongs to the organic Body rather than to its members individually.[1] Thus an individual's progress in scale or function is when his Prayer life becomes largely illuminative rather than largely purgative, or possibly when his prayer is more generally contemplative than meditative. But this is entirely a matter of scientific, ascetical fact, and is dependent upon vocation or election by God rather than ascetical struggle; it is progress by infusion rather than acquisition.

An individual's progress in value, on the other hand, is simply when he prays better, when his faith deepens and his worship expands, when his adoration becomes more real, and —be it never forgotten—such progress is to be tested by the one valid yardstick, moral theology. Suppose, for example, that after struggle and practice a ploughman manages at last to say the two words "Our Father" adoringly, and that in similar circumstances a religious achieves mystical union: by

[1] See E. L. Mascall, *Christ, The Christian and The Church*, p. 219.

the useful classification of ascetical science we may truly regard the latter as higher in scale, further up the spiritual hierarchy; but within the Body of Christ both these prayers are of equal value. The essential value is the adoration of God, the method and form of such adoration is a question of function and vocation.

This links up with the fundamental health-growth distinction in pastoral practice in that our aim is to maintain health, and so direction seeks only to promote progress in value; it is not concerned with progress in scale, which is the prerogative of God alone. If a soul's private prayer is generally centred around meditation, direction seeks to keep this soul spiritually healthy, so that it may meditate better; pastoral direction has no immediate interest in substituting this form of prayer by something "higher up the scale".

Assuming that the game of cricket comprises an organic athletic ethos wherein both international and keen village rabbit have true places, we can discern three distinct classes, grades or, analogously, "ways": club cricket, county cricket, and test matches. All cricketers can be placed, for convenience, in one or other of these three grades, which nevertheless overlap. And the grades depend upon temperament, circumstances, choice of career, health, etc., as well as upon innate gifts and propensities. Thus a man may play club cricket on Saturdays and work as a solicitor during the week, yet be a better player than the last professional in the county side; but this professional is, as plain fact, in a higher grade. In other words, Saints can remain in the illuminative way where their prayer and worship are of higher value but in a lower grade than a less holy Contemplative. The adoring "Our Father" of the ploughman and the mystical experience of the religious are comparable to an innings of a 100 runs in a village match and 100 runs in a test match. In the hierarchy sense we may call the latter of a higher order, within the ethos of "organic cricket"; but both innings are of equal value. And under adverse environmental and psychological circumstances 50 runs out of a total of 75 for one's county may well be an intrinsically better innings than 80 runs out of a total of 650 for 5 wickets in an international encounter. The ramifications are infinite, which explains the ambiguity of the general hierarchy confusion in ascetical thinking. But most of this difficulty disappears as soon as we distinguish between two distinct patterns of language—a calculable hierarchy of grades, and a more continuous stream of progress in terms of value.

The pastoral importance of this particular analogy is seen when we return to our former equation of director with coach. A club player can advance either by becoming a county player—that is, by grade; or by playing better and better for his same club—that is, by value: and it is with this latter progress only that the club coach or director is concerned. The coach's job is to correct faults, perfect technique, and generally improve the player's ability—such a player might possibly be selected for the county eleven, but that is contingent to the coach's immediate work. Any member of the parochial Remnant might be selected, or elected, or called by God to the complete Contemplative life—within or without community walls; but such a contingency is God's business and not the aim of direction. And if a soul—or a batsman—is selected for a higher grade, then it gives him a different function or calling within the whole organic ethos of the mystical Body, but it makes no difference at all to his fundamental value as a growing soul. We might suggest as a tentative hypothesis some such concept as "my station and its duties" in ascetic as well as ethical theory.

So far so good. But an added complication arises when we face the whole significance of a *pastoral* ascetic, for here we find one vital period in the soul's life when progress in grade and value do coincide; that is the period of growth from natural spiritual experience through initial conversion to the fullness of Christian Prayer. The method of achieving this growth in different souls is always, it should be remembered, the direction of the corporate Remnant; both parochially and individually. We can only plant and water with Apollos and Paul, and leave the increase to God. But we will be confronted with the parochial second stratum, either on the level of specific natural religion or in the persons of those whose experience of Christian conversion is true enough but who would live to the Rule of the Church only as a formal duty at best. These are the true "babes in Christ", truly in Christ yet very much babes; and the full threefold Rule of the Church—the Rule of the Remnant—is comparatively solid food. St Paul's Corinthian analogy helps us to understand our problem when the threefold Rule is likened to a balanced diet of say milk, soup, and beefsteak. These three foodstuffs obviously form a "hierarchy" of diet from infancy to maturity, since we are capable of assimilating, using, and digesting them only in this order and gradually over a period of years. But this hierarchy obviously differs from that of the "three ways", since the normal adult is in need of all three for a balanced diet; and progress both of stage and value is implied when soup is added to milk, and finally when beef-steak can be digested by the adult. It is still unnecessary to decide whether milk is "better" or "higher" than beef, as it is equally sterile to argue whether meditation is "better" or "higher" than the corporate liturgical Office. Complete adult health demands *both*—balanced by other foods too—but milk and meditation, we suggest, usually precede beef and the corporate Office as more easily digestible by the babes. Thus newer grades and higher values coincide, and this startling statement hints at a disregard for ascetical dietetics which seems to rule our parishes. We are regularly serving up roast beef and beer in Sunday school and tepid milk for Evensong. The reason, in all fairness, is that this particular period of religious growth is the most neglected in ascetical thinking because the "sub-Christian member of the Church" or "second stratum" is a mainly modern species about which the Middle Ages obviously had little to say. The Cistercian *conversi* is the nearest counterpart to the curious modern type of a "Church-man" who is "fairly regular". But nowadays the latter forms the varied majority rather than a distinct well-defined class within an order, and *conversi* are only found in the pre-ascetic age. The sixteenth- and seventeenth-century ascetics of St Ignatius, St François de Sales, St Teresa and St John of the Cross give us an organized and systematized substitute for monastic Order, but they have nothing much to say about sub-standard, or sub-Rule Christian souls. The monasteries had been as spiritual clinics, with complete meals laid on by expert administrators; the later ascetic developed a scheme of balanced dietetics which could be applied by individuals in their home environment. But these provisions are strictly for adults; in the Middle Ages there was no need for the progressive baby-feedings which would be a large part of modern pastoral practice.

In short, a Prayer-life lived on the basis of the Rule of the Church is radically different from an individually constructed jumble of fairly regular worship and undirected attempts at private prayer. And life by Rule is, in practice, the result of sub-Christian spiritual growth as well as a mere will-to-duty. The conception of duty and volitional discipline must obviously play no mean part in the acceptance of direction and Rule—it is right, proper, and creative that the Office and the Mass should sometimes bore us, and that our mental prayer should sometimes be dull and arid. There are times, many times, when our Rule is distasteful; but our motive needs to be more than mere duty; we cannot merely live to Rule by a superlative degree of human will-power. There must be vocation in some degree, there must be zeal, faith-venture, and love, "for their sakes", or we sink into a veiled Pharisaism. Thus this elementary ascetic, this spiritual baby-culture of pastoral direction, has to correlate progress in value with progress by stage. Our aim is not to lift souls through the stages of the "three ways", it is not to turn meditatives into Contemplatives; it is to promote progress in value only. But here, in this one instance, we are bound to aim not only at better prayers, better worship, greater recollection, piecemeal, but at raising the soul onto the different and higher plane of life within the full corporate Rule of the Church: that is life truly, creatively, and vicariously, in Christ.

It is also to be noted that any sort of corporate Prayer constitutes a higher grade than individual prayer, although in Rule these become correlates. This point is to be discussed more fully later, but it is important here because our babe-adult analogy suggests the great skill needed in calculating the exact day on which to introduce the next stage of diet; from milk to soup to beef. Or, by our other analogy, the skill needed to time the exact moment when the promising schoolboy is to be blooded into the county game. Any experienced coach becomes reminiscent over the sad cases of brilliant schoolboys ruined by playing first-class cricket too early, or too late, in their careers. Urging a soul to "go to church" indiscriminately, without direction and without the first flush of the experience of spiritual growth, is like sending a boy straight from prep school to a test match and wondering why he consequently gives up cricket. The babes will not develop by having raw beef rammed down their throats.

Now all these babes we have been considering, the parochial second stratum (and incidentally the vast majority of the contemporary congregation), we assume to have experienced some sort of conversion. They are those souls with some real self-recognized religion, who, because of grace, environment, upbringing, or social tradition look to the Church as a relevant part of religion. They have not reached full Christian maturity, they have little recognizable vocation, and no zealous urge to fling themselves wholeheartedly into the Church's Rule. But they are not unwilling to be gently guided. They cannot simply accept ascetical Rule, but they might one day reach it. These are potential members of the Remnant, but they are not yet of vicarious, or creative corporate power.

This general introduction would be incomplete if we left the matter at this point. We have exhausted the Christianity of our parochial organism, but quite a lot of real *religion* remains. The parochial third stratum—the multitudes—are admittedly sub-Christian, in the sense of "naturally" religious; we cannot convert except by the objective worship of the Remnant which is the agent of the converting Christ. But is there any possibility of a thoroughgoing natural ascetic? If "God alone gives the increase" and if the Remnant performs the major tillage operations, can we nevertheless do any specific, even surreptitious, planting and watering on this level? Once the Remnant concept is accepted in its fullness, the question becomes more interesting than important, and we can postpone our speculations, but if we are seriously concerned with *pastoral* ascetic we must at least examine the ascetical implications of natural religion if only as prologomena to sub-standard direction of the willing second stratum, and so on to the fullness of Christian health promoted and maintained by the Rule of the Church. If we are to understand *progressive* dietetics we must begin with a baby rather than an adult. The medieval thinkers and ascetics are of little direct assistance because they assume spiritual manhood as their starting-point—often quite immature manhood, it is true, but full manhood nevertheless. Thus those inspired with sufficient zeal and vocation to submit wholeheartedly to the dogmatic direction of St Teresa or St Ignatius are bluntly—and accurately—called beginners. Nevertheless in modern pastoral practice we are faced with these two lower grades: tentative Christianity and natural religion. We have no alternative but to turn to religious philosophy and psychology; to an examination of religious experience from the natural to the full Christian plane of prayer and worship in the Holy Trinity.

But if the Remnant concept is really accepted, then nine-tenths of our pastoral practice consists of the direction of the Remnant alone. This is what really matters; and for this the later medieval Saints give us all we require. Why, it may be asked, bother with this sub-Christian and natural religion at all? The need to keep things in perspective and to give the greater proportion of time and effort to the Remnant itself is admittedly great. But the answer to this question is, first, that we must begin at the beginning. Our age demands reason rather than, or at least as well as, authority. A synthesis of modern-medieval thought is therefore important; and if modern sciences can show traditional Christian ascetic to be an harmonious development from natural theism it is all to the good. The medieval community vowed dogmatic obedience —even the modern Remnant have the right to ask "Why?", and it is important that there should be an answer. Secondly, although the individual Christian is to be directed by traditional methods, parochial theology demands both an individual and a corporate pattern, and many aspects of such a pattern depend on the examination of sub-Christian and natural religion. What is called "the first form of contemplation" is basically natural rather than Christian. But it becomes important to the Remnant pattern which depends on "contemplative union with place" for a true vicariousness.

Thirdly, although we agree that a priest accepting the Remnant pattern in practice will begin only with the direction of the Remnant, and that this will always have the prior right to his prayer and time, the second stratum must not wholly be disregarded—at least we have one-tenth of our energy left. Moreover, if the Remnant is taken seriously we can confidently assume that the second and third strata will demand more and more of their priest's time. There will be, in fact, conversions, and it is well to be prepared for ascetical schemes for which the medievals had no use. If the Remnant really plants in prayer and waters in worship, there need be no doubt of God giving the increase—so long as we leave his prerogative to him. And if Part One of this work has any meaning at all it may be claimed that the whole tradition of theology and history supports our hope.

14

"RELIGIOUS EXPERIENCE"

"RELIGIOUS experience", wrote the late Archbishop Temple in *Christus Veritas*, "is the special way in which the whole of life is experienced by the 'religious' man." Conversely, the only fundamental difference between the sense experience of a man and a gorilla is that the one is religious and the other is not. The only thing which makes any experience religious is simply religion.

Religion we have defined as an activity, and modern philosophy and psychology are wont to define reality and experience also as activity. Thus the fundamental experience of man in his environment is the beginning of both experience and religious experience. That is St Thomas's dictum that, like everything else in human experience, religion begins with "sense-life". So, accepting "religiousness", we assume that the activity which the theologian calls Prayer follows a similar pattern to that activity which the psychologist calls simply experience. That is in accord with St Thomas Aquinas, Dr Temple, and what we might call general orthodoxy, and if it seems strangely discordant with, say, *The Dark Night of the Soul*, it is only because St John of the Cross was not concerned with pastoral ascetics and did not—for us—begin nearly low enough.[1]

Thus religious experience has the same ground as simple psychological experience, which a religious psychologist like Professor James Ward describes as an activity between subject and object; between a subject or ego or self—in religious terms, a soul—and its objective environment reducible to sense data. And this experience is a duality-in-unity, that is to say

[1] See von Hügel, *Essays and Addresses*, Vol. 1, i, 8; *Progress in Religion*, esp. pp. 70 ff.

that subject and object are logically, but not actually, separable; or that experiential activity demands a unity of both and neither subjects nor objects can exist apart. This again is a sacramentalism which rejects Cartesian dualism, from which springs materialism and subjective idealism respectively. The basic elements of this duality-in-unity are, on the subjective side, cognition, feeling, and conation, but again within an integral unity of the subject or self. These three elements are again logically distinguishable but not actually separable. On the objective side we have sense-data. Concerning ourselves with practical ascetic rather than psychological intricacy we can describe all experience as an activity between "self" and "things" which is fundamentally a duality-in-unity, and say (as Ward says) that the subjective side of experience is reducible to "I know something, I feel somehow, I do something". We have here, in germ, the generally accepted threefold analysis of religious activity— intellect, feeling, willing (as against, for example, both the old bi-partite scheme which excluded feeling, and the later reaction of Schleiermacher which almost excluded the other two).

Never forgetting the unity of the subject or self, we may ask if any of these are, *ascetically*, fundamental? Does religion generally make itself known by cognition or feeling or conation, or as these develop, by intellect or feeling or willing? The answer is that religious experience must embrace or contain all three, and yet ascetic is obviously more directly concerned with volition. We cannot eliminate feeling, nor have we ever wished to eliminate intellection; for as Dr Matthews insists, reason plays a part in all religious experience. What we do insist upon is that our emphasis on religious teaching creates not religion at all, but a modern gnosticism, and an overstressed feeling spells non-corporate quasi-mysticism. However, "in the present day psychologists are beginning more and more generally to insist that not intellect but will, not cognition but conation, not sensitivity but activity, is the clue to a true understanding of the character and development of experience."[1] If the prefix "religious" is

[1] James Ward, *Psychological Principles* (ed. 1933), p. 20; and cf. St John of the Cross, *Ascent of Mount Carmel*, Book 2, Cap. 4.

added to this last word we may claim support for our own contention—"not intellect but will, not cognition but Prayer, not sensitivity but ascetic. . . ." Religious experience progresses by means of reasoned Rule, and although healthy feeling plays a part in such a process, the prior motive force in following reasoned Rule is conative-faith-venture, thence volition.

The point here is that what we mean by religious experience demands three qualifications. First, it is experience by a self *of* something objective, therefore not a "mere" feeling or emotion—if such be possible. Secondly, this experience is a duality-in-unity. Thirdly, the experiencing self is a unity which is analysable into correlated cognition, feeling, and conation. But two other qualifications of this scheme must be admitted: firstly, despite the necessary duality-in-unity of all experience there may be greater or lesser emphasis upon one side or the other. Thus we may rightly speak of subjective and objective experience and subjective and objective religious activity. The experience of an aesthete looking at a rose or of a glutton savouring a pork-chop may be said to be subjective, since the practical emphasis of the experiential encounter is upon the side of the subject. The experiences of a scientist looking at a microscopic slide, a botanist looking at a rose or a cook looking at a pork-chop may be called objective, since the subjects are generally self-forgetful and the emphasis of their attention is on the object in each case. Similarly, self-examination of conscience in prayer before confession may be called subjective prayer, and the adoration of our Lord at the altar objective prayer.

The second qualification is that although cognition-feeling-conation are all present and inseparable within any actual experience, yet here again we may discern variable emphases. For example, re-reading portions of James Ward's *Psychological Principles* might induce a marked consciousness of the supremacy of cognition; a hot bath following a piece of very cold outdoor work brings a pleasurable feeling to the fore in most people; it is only by conation and volition that a book such as this is written at all. But the important point is that a religious man reading the dullest dogmatic implies religious experience just as much as the Contemplative's feeling of the presence of God. That is to say, whichever constituent of experience, at whatever stage—cognition, feeling, conation; intellection, moral consciousness or feeling, or conscious volition; whichever of these is, so to speak, to the fore, we have religious experience. This is doubly important when we consider how, in mature personality with which ascetic has to deal, these basic factors—developed into the refinements of intellect, aesthetic and moral feeling, and purposeful volition —vary their proportion within a constant personality. The religious theologian delighting in the intricacies of scholastic philosophy does not know what he is saying when he denies his capacity for religious experience. Nor, when he claims it, does the irreligious aesthete swooning before a sunset.

The thousand definitions of religion to be found in theistic literature may be roughly divided into two main types: those whose operative stress is upon the idea of *unity* and *harmony* and those emphasizing the idea of *encounter*. Here are some examples of the first: "Religion is an emotion resting on a conviction of a harmony between ourselves and the universe at large."[1] "The fundamental spring of religious experience is the thirst for unity."[2] "In religion the spirit of man discerns itself to be at home in the universe."[3] "Religion in the broadest and most general terms possible . . . consists of the belief that there is an unseen order, and that our supreme good lies in harmoniously adjusting ourselves thereto."[4] It is this kind of experience which the theologian is wont to call the "first form of contemplation", or, allowing our middle term, "contemplative harmony with environment". Examples of the second are too common and obvious to detain us, since encounter between the soul and God is everywhere accepted as fundamental to all theism. But it is to be noticed in passing that these two types of definition imply a progression. The first is natural religion at its most

[1] J. M. E. McTaggart, *Some Dogmas of Religion*, p. 3.
[2] W. R. Matthews, *God in Christian Thought and Experience*, p. 18 ff.
[3] H. H. Farmer, *The World and God*, p. 42; see also Farmer's discussion of this subject, ibid., pp. 38–43.
[4] W. James, *The Varieties of Religious Experience*, p. 53.

primitive, the second is natural theism, which follows as soon as unity both of self and of the universe suggest the idea "which most men call God". It is also plain that the first emphasis is mainly subjective or, in theological terms, immanental while the second is objective or transcendental— this is simply the progression from Moses, for example, to the Second Isaiah.[1]

The study of primitive religion, glibly so called, may also be passed over, since in pastoral practice of modern times the general idea of God is so fundamental to our whole civilized tradition that we need start no lower than natural theism. In other words, we can couple these two sorts of definitions together and assume that to modern souls, harmony with the universe means harmony with an immediate environment, and so with the whole unifying principle or God. To all men who can be called religious the universe is sacramental: they see a phenomenal universe, and are aware of an unseen spiritual order beyond or behind or in or through it. This is the sphere of the spirit, and of God, and, due mainly to the systematizing of Christian tradition by St Thomas, this spiritual or religious realm may only be reached by way of the sensible world. The key to the sacramental "inward and spiritual" is attention to its "outward and visible sign". We have seen that by a general theistic sacramentalism the visible universe is to God as the body is to the soul in man, and in both cases encounter and union are achieved through sacramental means. The initial religious struggle for harmony with God must therefore begin in a harmony with immediate environment sacramentally interpreted.

Experience we have defined as a duality-in-unity, or an activity between subject and object. Thus religious experience is such activity where the ultimate object is God, or where the objects of sense data are sacramentally perceived. This activity of religious experience is clarified by Dr Tennant's

[1] Perhaps we see an intermediate stage in such progression in another definition from McTaggart: "Religion is the influence which draws men's thoughts away from their personal interests, making them intensely aware of other existences, to which it binds them by strong ties, sometimes of admiration, sometimes of awe, sometimes of duty, sometimes of love." *Natural Religion: Some Dogmas of Religion*, p. 8.

threefold distinction of object (o) which is the objective image over against the individual subject, Object (O) which equals the universal Object common to many individual subjects and object (ω) or the ontological counterpart of phenomena.[1] Thus religious experience may be described as a duality-in-unity between subject, analysable into cognition-feeling-conation and object (o), Object (O), thence object (ω); and experience becomes religious by virtue of a cognition of, a feeling for, and hence a particularly conative activity towards, the universal, unifying object (ω) of which phenomena (O) is the sacramental sign.

Now, pastorally, environment is a sacramental complex of nature, society, traditions, customs, laws, etc., and we can achieve a unified harmony with this in one of three ways: by a forceful subjection of environment to self, such as that adopted by a tyrant ruler of a country, parish, or home; by wholly yielding self to environment, as a fatalist or a slave does; or by a mutual *rapport* of environment and self in an encounter which is best described by the word "love"— despite its general ambiguity. In other words, the unity which is experience can be described, according to emphasis, as subjective, objective, or harmonious, mutual or loving.

Analogically, let us consider an encounter between a specific sacramental self or environment which we will call George and another such which we will call Mary. Such an encounter implies what Professor Farmer calls "value-resistance".[2] Two cognitive, feeling, conative selves meet in an environment—for simplicity consisting simply of two human bodies—and this creates what Farmer calls a polarity or tension of wills: "The other's will presents itself as an inaccessible source of activity, continuously creating as it were, an invisible frontier between his being and ours, a frontier where there is always at least potential resistance, and over which there is no passing save in so far as he invites us so to do."[3] In other words a meeting between two persons, or person and environment (cognition), immediately implies some kind of feeling, which in turn inspires a conative activity.

[1] *Philosophical Theology*, Vol. I, pp. 19–21.
[2] *The World and God*, pp. 19–22.   [3] Ibid., p. 19.

However blasé and sophisticated we pretend to be, the first introduction to another person, or the first sight of an environmental scene, causes a tension within us; some adjustment is necessary before a perfect harmony is reached. Now let us suppose that the feeling in George cognizing Mary is one of great pleasure, and his conative urge is to kiss her—conative activity not wholly reciprocated by Mary. Either he can simply kiss her, tyrant fashion and by force, whether she likes it or not, or by yielding wholly to her will, he can give up all idea of so doing. The encounter can be subjective or objective. But suppose George and Mary take less drastic action, and indulge the slow, disciplined, harmonizing process of courtship, then it may become possible not simply for George to kiss Mary, nor for Mary to kiss George, nor for both to refrain from kissing; but for George and Mary simply to kiss one another: this end-process, allowing ambiguities forementioned, we will call the sacramental sign of love. Recalling the accepted definition of Archbishop Temple, it is obvious enough that this experience of unity and harmony, this harmonious encounter, this experiential activity of duality-in-unity between George and Mary, is a religious experience just in so far as George and Mary are religious people. If we assume that they *are* religious people then this sacramental experience is the simplest possible example of what is called "the first form of contemplation".

If we analyse this analogy we find five points of some consequence to our general inquiry. First, we notice that the realization of this lover's embrace is not attainable by the short direct method of either forceful tyrant or yielding slave; there is no love between two people one of whom submits to every whim of the other, because there is no *rapport* or "value-resistance". The only method of attaining this lover's embrace is by the slow gradual process of courtship; which, by translating our analogy, is the working out of an initial faith-venture by ascetical activity. Secondly, this disciplinary process involves, in ascetical terms, an initial simplification or unification of the subjective self or soul. Looking at it from George's viewpoint, Mary demands *all* his interest; anything which conflicts with love for Mary must go, all other interests, emotions, and activities are to be concentrated into a unity and directed towards Mary until she is the reason for George's work, the inspirer of his noblest aspirations, she is "ever in his thoughts"; and this is what spiritual language calls Recollection.[1] Thirdly, this state is procured by George's self-surrender, which is not a mere passive yielding but a conative disciplinary *activity*. It is the active fight against all other interests which happen to conflict with the absolute demand of Mary's love. If these are normally good, healthy interests, we call it mortification. If they are evil emotions and interests we call it purgation. And the whole disciplinary activity is contained in what Professor Ward calls "attention"[2]—the volitional control of thoughts, feelings, and actions so that George attends solely to Mary and excludes everything else.

Fourthly, there are the results of this achieved encounter, this embrace of subjective-objective balance: a feeling of peace or harmony, and also a feeling of what von Hügel and others call "simultaneity"; time, an experience peculiar to creatures, is suppressed by the uprising of the spiritual in George and Mary. "Time stood still", "the moment charged with eternity", "blissful unawareness of all around them" and suchlike may be clichés, but they are nevertheless fairly accurate descriptions of this kind of experience. And fifthly, these feelings of peace, harmony, simultaneity are acquired by the mutual loving embrace of Mary, but to George it is a peace and harmony not only with Mary but with the universe. Mary *is* the universe in microcosm, she recapitulates within herself all values, all desires, all activities; everything else —houses, work, moon and stars, motor-cars and income-tax

[1] Ambiguity of ascetical terms makes it necessary to distinguish between the Recollection, which is defined by Evelyn Underhill as "emotion disciplined by will"—i.e., the disciplinary process of self-simplification or unification—of integrating the whole self and drawing it Godwards; and the recollection which is simply that part of ascetical Rule whereby we "recollect" the presence of God momentarily at intervals throughout the day. Guibert thus distinguishes between "habitual" and "actual" recollection in these two senses. *The Theology of the Spiritual Life*, p. 216 ff.

[2] *Psychological Principles*, pp. 60–6.

—simply ceases to exist as isolable or "real": everything "looks different", everything is Mary. When this state of feeling is upset, as we believe it sometimes is, it is not only useless but flagrantly untrue to console poor George by suggesting that there are plenty of other nice girls in the world. The whole trouble is that there are not. Mary is not one girl among many, but girlhood. She *is* the world in microcosm, the universe is wholly and completely recapitulated in her.[1]

Now if George and Mary are religious people, this is religious experience in its simplest form, "the first form of contemplation", and it is adequately described by McTaggart, Matthews, von Hügel, and James. If George and Mary are fully and maturely Christian then theirs is Christian religious experience, for they truly see Christ in one another and are mutually in him. And if George is not merely naturally contemplative but a sanctified Contemplative, then we can simply substitute God for Mary in each of our five points above.

The trouble with George and Mary's contemplative embrace, of course, is that it does not last very long: "the moment that seems eternity" remains very much a moment so soon as the rent, rates, creditors, Willy's measles, and Bessie's education all come into it. The initial harmony is upset by quarrels, and without continued ascetical courtship the subjective-objective equilibrium is upset. George sinks to the level of being either domineering or henpecked. As sacramental environments two embodied souls are not wide enough to ensure any constant, long-lived, if less intense, state of Recollection. In other words they are not, in themselves, sacramental enough; the moment may "seem like eternity", but sooner or later they are going to get tired and hungry, their environment has to widen into a home, a street, a village, a society, and if they are Christians then at least a parish. Their acquired Recollection has to extend to this wider environment, which demands more arduous mortification and more thorough purgation; and

[1] Perhaps this analogy helps us to see that Prayer leading to love for God in Christ does not merely *lead* to, but verily involves love for our fellow men; because Christ truly is the recapitulation of all humanity. The point illustrates the inadequacy of a merely ethical exhortation to love our fellows divorced from Prayer. Pastoral and parochial love is the fruit of ascetic rather than morals.

this helps to explain why the lover's embrace is not only an example of the first form of contemplation which is the beginning of religious awareness, but a very elementary form even of that. The pastoral tragedy instilled by the second-rate love-story is that instead of looking back nostalgically upon dear Albert's proposal or trying to recapture the lost moment, married people to-day do not see all this as the most elementary beginning of religion-as-activity, forget it, and press on towards truly "higher" forms of the same thing like mutual Eucharistic worship in the Sanctified Body.

But the first form of contemplation in this wider environment—in its second degree as it were—is common enough to be recognized. It is simply the feeling of "being at home" in a place and among those who inhabit that place. Literally, "feeling at home" is a useful example of which we will make further use presently, but any environmental-self *rapport*, such as is achieved by a farmer on his farm, a music-lover in the concert hall, the cricket enthusiast at Lord's or the sailor on his ship, presupposes the same five basic factors of our ascetical analysis of the lover's embrace, generally in a more stable though less intense form. The subjects here are conscious of (1) a harmonious encounter as the result of a gradual *process*, getting to know the finer points of agriculture, music, cricket, or seamanship—in Ward's phrase a process of "becoming expert by experiment". And there is a subject-object balance. A farmer or musician will talk of what the land or music *gives* to him while he is conscious of a self-giving or going out to it. (2) This state is achieved by a disciplinary, ordered process of attention; you do not "become expert" at farming or music or cricket except by concentrating and excluding other interests, by training and practice which demand sacrifices. And this is (3) a self-surrender to the demands which the acquisition of these skills make. (4) This sense of peace and harmony with an environment implies not complete simultaneity, but at least a certain timelessness. To the music-lover the two-hour concert passes all too quickly—he is absorbed in it; whereas to his poor tone-deaf friend dragged along unwittingly, these two clock hours seem endless. (5) The experience is qualified by a more general though less intense sense of union with something far more fundamental than the immediate environmental object of attention. *Rapport* exists between subjective self and something far bigger and deeper than a particular field or a particular performance of a particular musical phrase; we speak naturally of "knowing" the Land—*all* Land and the unifying principle behind it and the universe at large. We "know" the symphony, or Brahms, or music, which is again the unification of the whole at that mystic moment. And if it is useless to remind poor George of all the other girls he will love in the future, it is just as useless to speak of income-tax or world-economics or the international situation to a man supremely concerned with his team's performance in a cricket match.

The relevance of such an analogy to pastoral ascetic is that these common experiences are achieved by a slow period of sacrifice and discipline. Real contemplative union with land belongs not to the urban aesthete on holiday, swooning in ecstasy before the August cornfield, but to the farm-worker who, possibly oblivious of any aesthetic emotion, rises at 5 on winter mornings to milk cows and cut kale; he, that is, who lives to a disciplined rule. If our critic urges the phenomenon of "love at first sight" or George-Mary harmony in a single conative *rapport*, without the discipline of courtship, then we can only liken it to sudden conversion of a semi-mystical kind wherein the sudden inrush of grace immediately transforms our whole experience. We need not deny such a possibility, but it is the prerogative of God alone, and outside our immediate concern. The normal experience of men entails the necessity of "courtship" or ascetical Rule, experiment, and discipline. What we here describe by the word "love"— for it applies in all these cases—is thus not to be confused with the exaggerated mystical variety which in ascetical language is wholly infused. It must be freely admitted that *any* sort of love is impossible without the infused grace of God; but this love expressed in the first form of contemplation is very largely acquired. The first conative urge, the fundamental activity towards something, be it music, land, cricket, or Mary, may be associated with the initial fertilization by grace: it is God-infused. But all else is acquired by discipline, recollection, purgation, mortification, attention, and the rest. Of course, on what we have formerly called God's first-order level of activity, grace continues to flow in support of our self-discipline; but the absence of such discipline means the elimination of human free will—hence any possibility of *rapport* in love between the soul and God. In a Christian context this discipline is the ascetic formulated by empirical tradition, whereby added support of grace flows to the soul through the Sacraments; that is, according to the unique second-order activity.

The environment with which we can become in contemplative harmony, in which we can be lovingly "at home", can be expanded still further. We can truly be said to love our village or town or county or country—even the universe at large, which by the principle of recapitulation or microcosm becomes much the same thing. "God so loved the *world*"—yet the Son of God so loved by a microcosmic love for a few square miles of Palestine. All that concerns us, in following him, in being his Body in place as his Body was, and remained, in place, is contemplative harmony with, union with, love for, that environmental organism which we have called a parish.[1]

It should be plain enough that we are not talking about any occult mystic state, but the commonest and most elementary manifestation of religious experience. The first form of contemplation depends as much on the grace of God as every other good in human life; on sacramental grace or "first order" grace depending upon whether we are Christian or merely religious. Of the most vital significance is the fact that this contemplative love is the beginning of natural religion which may develop into Christianity, the beginning of Christian religion which is to maintain health and grow, and the beginning of pastoral practice so far as Remnant theology is concerned. Upon a real contemplative harmony with, or love for parochial organism, a loving *rapport* between priest-Remnant and parish, the vicarious principle depends. If vicarious Prayer and worship are to constitute creative ascetical practice and not merely a comfortable bit of theory, then the discipline, sacrifice, order and courtship which leads

[1] See Supplementary Note 2, below.

to it is parochial priesthood's first concern. For only thereby can Prayer and worship, as a whole unified life, be truly vicarious and not merely intercessory. This does not lessen the importance of simple intercession as an essential part of Christian Prayer, but sanctification "for their sakes" makes *all* Prayer and all life intercessory in a much deeper sense. Only by simple direct intercession can we pray *for* foreign missions, the sick, or John Smith whom we once met in Newcastle. But to pray for his beloved wife a man only has to pray— "the twain are one flesh", "the one is sanctified in the other", "for their"—and her—"sake I sanctify myself". The one is for—because of; the other is for—on behalf of; only the latter is wholly and truly vicarious, and the parish demands nothing less than this latter from priest and Remnant. The Church which is the spouse of Christ can be nothing less than the spouse of the parish.

We are now in a position to trace the religious life, stage by stage, from sense-experience to pure Contemplation. From the first form of "natural contemplation" or elementary religious awareness to the fullness of Christianity as set out in the Thomist scheme formulated on pages 138–9 above, and we can best illustrate this analogously from the example of the home as an environmental sacrament.

Let us begin then, with a family—that is, with a society of parents and children, and a house. Neither of these can properly be called a home if sacramentalism means anything at all. (And, incidentally, if those politicians who say so much about the urgent need of homes for the people were in earnest, they would have to begin not with the economics of building but with the first form of contemplation.) We certainly need houses, but we need homes even more. Bringing these two sacramental parts together, the spiritualized family (albeit expressed through living bodies), and the material environment or setting of bricks and mortar, we may now imagine a furniture van drawn up at the door. The first stage in making a home is to adapt the family to this environment and, so far as is possible, to adapt the environment to the family. We allot each room to a particular use and arrange the furniture accordingly. This is the first stage of progress towards an

environmental harmony. It is as the *sense life* of St Thomas
and it is not so very far from biological adaptation in evolutionary theory. If we assume that the giraffe really did grow
a long neck because the only edible vegetation grew on the
tree-tops, then putting the hatstand in the hall rather than in
the bathroom or the draining-board next to the sink rather
than in the attic is a similar concession to need; this arrangement of hatstand or draining-board makes for peace, order,
and harmony.

St Thomas's next stage he calls the *natural life* of man,
which is ordered by the specifically human attributes of
reason and will. So soon as human society comes into the
picture we arrive at a moral element, if only in a utilitarian
sense. Mother, father, son, and daughter may all want the
bathroom at the same time, and harmony can only be restored
by a measure of self-sacrifice. Three of them must give way to
the fourth. One member of the family must do the washing-
up and allow the others to do other duties, which again adds
to the general harmony. And here reason plays its part. If we
know that the furnace takes an hour and a half to heat water
for two baths, or that the stove boils a kettle in ten minutes,
or that the hall fire smokes when the wind is in the east, this
knowledge makes for harmony—we can order things accordingly, and the process of unification begins. Many rooms, different
people, and pieces of furniture are becoming an integrated
whole, and the people are attaining sympathy with this whole
and with one another.

Next comes the *supernatural life of grace,* which we can
divide into first- and second-order activity of God in *rapport*
with the environment. In the former case we have infused
moral virtues whereby our ethical considerations progress from
a mere utilitarianism to an intuitive ethic qualified by loving
service. We let our mother use the bathroom first not only
for convenience but in love, and we accept our father's
decisions not simply because he is stronger or holds the purse
strings, but because we all prefer to do so. We may speak of
being "at home" or of "going home" or of "longing to be
home"; now such phrases really mean something. In the
latter case, the second-order activity of God, we are getting

close to stage four, because we are somewhere near to the religion of the major prophets. There is felt to be a specific, individualized, *rapport* with God; we are becoming "prophetic". We have the idea of asking God to guide our decisions and his response is obeyed on the same level as utilitarian ethic or reason. This "home", practical, ethical, spiritual, and social, is becoming more and more unified in God because more and more controlled by God.

The fourth stage is of "*the fullness of the measure of the stature of Christ*". Our unified, simplified home is integrated in and through its members, not only in *rapport* with a theistic God but with God-in-Christ; they have become the Body of Christ in place united in the adoration of the Father. Ascetically we are now on firm ground and no difficulties and disharmonies are without solution, for we may speak freely of *sin* and redemption, mortification, recollection, humility, love, worship, penance, and sacrifice. Christ unifies and upholds our home in love, and Christian experience suggests channels of grace, motives, power, and technique, whereby all this is to be achieved.

Within such an environment, the fifth stage may, if God so wills, be reached. The family truly may feel and know the very Presence of Christ in and through all things, they may live or die—it matters not which—in the adorable Presence of God—they may see him at a simple glance, which is pure Contemplation. This whole process is epitomized in what is sometimes distinguished as contemplative harmony with the sanctified world of becoming, and thence the ontological world of being, and thence the Contemplation of God. But with stage five we need not concern ourselves, since this is the pure election of God and has nothing to do with pastoral ascetics. There remain three points of interest to us by way of synopsis.

(1) The scheme set out in this analogy contains two essential "gaps"—the gap between sense-life shared with the animals like the giraffe, and religion manifested by infused moral virtues and God-implanted reason; and the gap between natural religion and elementary—even sub-Christianity. These gaps we can narrow but never bridge. If we could, the result would be to rationalize all things and leave no room for

faith. There would be no higher value than mathematics. Like the evolutionists in biology, we have narrowed the gap between amoeba and angel to that between ape and man, but gap—in both cases—there still must be. Rejoicing in the gaps which allow faith-venture, however, we have a hierarchical scheme of things, an ascetical ladder with a couple of rungs missing, which itself inspires faith-venture. For we can see, reasonably if not logically, that the fullness of our integral Christian "home" begins with shifting furniture about. Pastoral practice may well make a venture of faith towards even the third stratum of the parochial organism, by an attempt to encourage natural religion as a preparatory step to the sub-Christian stage and thence to the fullness of life in the Body of Christ. This is to be attempted not by intellectual teaching or exhortation, but by inducing that state of the first form of contemplation; that is, simply "feeling at home" in the parish, "being in harmony with environment"—the state of natural religion not infrequently attained instinctively by vocational farm-workers, artists, craftsmen, and lovers. Conversion is the prerogative of the Holy Spirit, the gap between natural religion and Christianity is as the germination of the seed. We can narrow the gap between scattering the seed haphazardly and hoping for the best, on the one hand, and careful seed-bed preparation and immediate after-tillage on the other. As St John of the Cross says repeatedly, "The whole progress of the [Contemplative] soul consists in its being moved by God"; but our own part remains in placing it "in a state to receive this motion". These operations, it should be remembered, are performed in the main by the vicarious Prayer of the Remnant, but any kind of natural ascetic may be a valuable corollary. Thus the first form of contemplation is of double importance to us: it is both the *possible* first step from natural religion to Christianity, and the *essential* first step from the "individual Christian"—so called—to the corporate creative power of the *vicarious* Remnant.

(2) The first form of contemplation is the first manifestation of conscious volitional religious experience, and religion we have agreed from the beginning is the antecedent of theology.

But so long as men are endowed with reason, theology is both needful and helpful, and the only theology adapted to such experience is Incarnational. We are not concerned with apologetic, but the champions of "natural religion"—as such —might well realize that any link between the senses and the spirit, between the world of men and God, demands and leads to an essential, perfect, complete, and harmonious intercourse between phenomenal and noumenal, or sense and spirit, or man and God. This in its ultimate degree means a man-God. If theism talks of world-God *rapport*, we are still faced with a dualism albeit veiled and narrowed, until God looks on the world with human eyes and touches things—or arranges furniture—with human hands. We claim therefore, that although it is sub-Christian as compared with full spiritual health within the Rule of the Church, the first form of contemplation is as theologically Christian as the Chalcedonian Definition. Whatever happens in practice, it is only by faith in the Incarnate Son of God that we *dare* begin to find him through the senses.

(3) Our analogy suggests that as early as the second stage in our home-making process, we confront moral problems. Moral consciousness can be infused by God on his theistic first-order level of activity. But, in practice, giving way to one's mother and accepting the rule of one's father is not so easy to achieve. On however natural a level our religion, however sub-Christian or even anti-Christian it is reputed to be, we come up against the overwhelming fact of original sin. We soon find that however awkward the piano and however inconvenient the kitchen-scullery-dining room arrangements, these are as nothing to the discordances of unruly wills and vicious self-interests. So if the reasonable theology of the first form of contemplation suggests the Incarnation, then the practical, ascetical acquisition of it demands atonement. When theists speak of a primary conative longing for union with God, it means very little to many people of quite vigorous natural religion, and atonement for sin as the consummation of this longing means very little too. But if we speak of sin as the cause of disharmony with social environment we say something intelligible to all and of practical significance to all.

And this is only the same thing at a lower stage—the sub-Christian stage where most Christian souls began. Deistically to equate the problem of sin with mundane conveniences of sociology is abhorrent; to the Christian utilitarian righteousness is a contradiction in terms; adoration and love cannot be called useful. But so long as natural ethics and moral theology, natural religion and Christianity, are distinguished, then we can begin on any level and hope to work up. To begin with sin as being discordant with the first form of contemplation is no more objectionable than St Bernard's "love of self for self" as the first degree in the love of God in *De Diligendo Deo.* It is only raising "moral instruction" from a mundane ethic to a creative ascetic. Pastoral practice, as against dogmatic, must begin with souls as they are. If our average congregation is somewhere near the middle of the Book of Judges then it is no use exhorting them to come to Mass. What we can do, of course, is to suggest that sin means a whole cycle of disharmonies and that Christ's redemption is the only known method of its eradication, which might be worth, after due preparation, a venture of faith.

15

"NATURAL" AND "SUB-CHRISTIAN" ASCETICS

It is necessary at this point to clarify one or two terminological ambiguities which have arisen in our argument. We
have agreed with all the Saints from St Augustine to Lorenzo
Scupoli, from St Bernard to St Thomas, that religion is
"proper to man" and that it begins with sense-experience.
This truism would not be worth repeating were it not that
modern practice—in the teeth of so formidable a cloud of
witnesses—is ever in danger of beginning with *mind*. But
religion is antecedent to theology; conative activity and feeling are antecedent to intellection, and all the teaching in the
world is useless when phrases like "religious experience",
"love", "the presence of God", the "supernatural" and so
on, are not known by direct experience. The question is, can
we, with St John of the Cross, help to direct souls into a "state
to receive this motion"?

It is within the pastoral setting that certain ambiguities in
the use of terms tend to arise. First, it should never be forgotten that of our three-strata parochial organism, the direction of the first, fully Christian, or Remnant, stratum is all that
really matters; for this is the vicarious Body of Christ in place
which is efficacious in all that concerns cure of souls. It is
the third stratum which contains those of "natural" religion,
and pastoral contacts with some of these may be comparatively
close; especially under the influence of Remnant spirituality.
These have real religious experience because they are really
and naturally religious, but they cannot or will not accept
Incarnational religion. It is to these that natural ascetics
pertain, but two things must be presupposed: first, that these

souls, as religious, are possessed of goodwill and desire for growth—without that no direct pastoral contact is possible or even desirable; and the Remnant makes it unnecessary. Secondly, the priest-consultant is also equipped with sincerity and goodwill toward the soul as it is, and is not preparing any surreptitious underhand tricks for the purpose of "conversion". We must never pretend to be other than Christian priests, and all Christians, by nature, desire to share their joy with others. That is all acceptable; but can we apply a progressive natural ascetic, bluntly hoping for God's final conversion but in utter surrender to this his prerogative, with complete reliance on his vicarious Remnant, for all things ultimate to parochial wellbeing? More souls have been lost to our Lord by being "argued at" than is pleasant to contemplate. So it is this odd soul or two within the third stratum to whom the term "natural" ascetic applies.

The phrase "sub-Christian" offers more difficulty, since it applies to the second parochial stratum which includes a less numerous but much more varied group of souls. Under this heading we include those who would tend to synonymize "God" with "Christ" if only by convention, social tradition, or family ties. It would include most of the unconfirmed of all ages and generally most of our average congregation. But the second stratum might also include those who are progressing towards the fullness of the Church's Rule, the prospective Remnant. These are St Paul's "babes in Christ" who are immature but truly "in Christ", and who cannot therefore be called sub-Christian even if they have yet to attain the fullness of ascetical health. With this group—perhaps a large proportion of our initial congregation, our catechism and confirmation candidates—we will deal in the next chapter. But let it be clearly understood that we are, throughout, attempting to make a constructive attempt at facing facts, and these various distinctions and classifications *are* facts. Words like "natural" and "sub-Christian" and "babes-in-Christ" have no derogatory implication;[1] the approach to these, together with Jews, Mohammedans, agnostics, and atheists is one of humanism and love. And this approach is

---

[1] See above, p. 139.

only made possible by the existence and rigorist discipline of the vicarious Remnant. It is only with the assumption of a multitudinist background that these terms tend to become abusive and proud.

The only positive distinction between the soul of "natural" and "sub-Christian" spirituality is that the former is definitely *not* Christian while the latter is, in the precise meaning of the term, agnostic.[1] So we can take them together under our heading of natural or sub-Christian ascetic with two provisos. In the latter case we need not hesitate to use Christian terminology such as the Holy Trinity when this may be useful, while in the former case—without any hypocritical pretence —we can try to avoid such terms out of a sincere sympathy. In the latter case again, contact with the worshipping Church —going to church as a spectator—would play an important part in direction if very carefully applied in particular cases. In the former case such going to church would be generally undesired and undesirable. It should surely not be encouraged unless or until the second stage is reached by God's election. This whole aspect of our subject has, of course, a vital bearing on the problem of the Church's ministry to children; who— though it is extremely dangerous to make the mistake of assuming natural and spiritual age to be identical—are generally in a state of natural, and/or sub-Christian religion.

How then are we to prepare the soil, to help place the soul "in a position to receive this motion" of God, which we call ordinary contemplation or the first conative awareness of the supernatural world or even the first encounter with God? Christian tradition is unanimous upon two fundamental stages, which it calls recollection and purgation. These we may validly "sub-Christianize" so long as we realize exactly what we are doing. This is but the ascetical equivalent of

[1] I am of course speaking in pastoral terms. All the baptized are incorporated into the humanity of Christ: they are Christians as ontological fact, although they may be very bad ones! Pastorally these may need to be tended and cared for as if their religion was natural. I do not think it is contradictory to regard a baptized child as fully incorporated into Christ's Body and yet to assume that his religion is undeveloped. See note to Second Edition, p. x above.

12

talking about a theistic "God" before going on to his Incarnation, and of preaching Jesus Christ before we come to the wholeness of the Holy Trinity.[1]

Recollection and purgation are closely related. Bearing this connection in mind, the words indicate two lines of approach to a sub-Christian ascetic. Recollection implies a psychological unification of self which is the first step to contemplative union with things or places. Purgation suggests the second stage in the process, whereby such "at homeness" is achieved by a disciplined exercise of the moral consciousness. All are agreed that the end of such processes—the "first form of contemplation" expressed in all or any of our first set of definitions (p. 150)—is the most elementary experience of religion. This is what St John of the Cross would mean by "placing the soul in a state to receive this motion [of God]".

"Harmony with environment", if it be true harmony, is a mutual *rapport* between the soul and things. Where some pseudo-harmony is established by subjective tyranny or objective yielding the first task is to instil a sense of dissatisfaction with such a state. Recollection then implies the unification of self by a loving empathy—an objective going out to the world of *things*. This is the exercise embodied in Ward's *theory of attention*.[2] Quite simply, if God is manifested in his creation, if religious experience is but sense-experience plus religiousness, our obvious first step in our search for God is to *look*. As St Teresa says: "I am not asking you now to think of him, or to form numerous conceptions of him, or to make long and subtle meditations with your understanding. I am asking you only to look at him."[3] That of course is Christian recollection, but its natural counterpart is simply to substitute "at" in place of "for" and "it" in place of "him". It implies the discipline of the will, the refusal to be drawn away from the object of contemplation—which can be,

---

[1] It is the policy of Pope Gregory, who ordered St Augustine to begin on the level of early English natural religion, and so to adapt Druidical cult and temple to Christian use. Our word "Easter" comes direct from Eostre the dawn-goddess, and its popular association with eggs is as pure a pagan cult as one could find!

[2] *Psychological Principles*, pp. 60–74.

[3] *Way of Perfection*, Cap. xxvi.

as Evelyn Underhill puts it, "anything from an ant to an alp". This conative "pushing out" towards the world is but the courtship of George and Mary in cosmic terms, it is summed up in such well-known ascetical phrases as "loving regard", it is that love which is, in Elmer More's words, "the outstretching power of the imagination by which we grasp and make real to ourselves the being of others". It implies the discipline of self-giving, of "detachment", of mortification which loves rather than wants, and it is bound up with purgation, which is the volitional conquest of self. Now all this is fundamental to traditional ascetic, coupled as it must be with moral theology.

But on a sub-Christian level all this devotional theory becomes practical ascetic as soon as we couple it with Ward's "attention" and plant it in everyday experience. Union with environment may just happen, as in the case of a happy home, but failing such a circumstance it cannot be directly or immediately achieved. This is because we cannot pay attention to an environment but only to a *thing*. But if we do so discipline our senses and intellect that we attend to a single thing—even for a brief period—then our environment tends to become recapitulated in that thing and we are on our purposeful way to "contemplative harmony in place". And by the reciprocal action of this state our personality tends to become unified or "recollected"; which may be the beginning of religion.[1]

Leaving aside the subtleties of temperament, most of us would find it very hard to burst into a strange furnished room, sit down and write a book, or listen to music or read poetry. We would automatically indulge in a little rearranging of chairs, pictures, and so on in order to be comfortable; after which the introduction of a personal familiar object would assist the process. A photograph or keepsake on the mantelshelf and the room begins to be ours; this little object becomes the focus of attention; consciously or subconsciously it recapitulates the wider environment and through it we begin to feel "at home".

This is the beginning, and here the purposeful beginning, of all those common but curious everyday experiences which

[1] See E. L. Mascall, *He Who Is*, pp. 80–1.

are associated with contemplation, if we would only recognize it. After the long walk through a thunderstorm or an air raid, what a relief it is to "get home"—though in fact we are no safer there. The athlete *does* play better on his home ground, we *do* find prayer easier in a familiar church, the well-known land-mark spurs us on the last lap of our journey whatever the map shows, and a really familiar picture works wonders in the dentist's surgery. All these things lend harmony and instil Recollection.

In parenthesis it is worth mentioning what must be examined more fully later, namely the significance to all Prayer activity of Recollection-by-focus. Especially to Incarnational religion, the central crucifix is no mere bit of ecclesiastical aesthetics, and we would have far less difficulty with distractions if souls were taught—as the first elementary exercise without words, images, thoughts, or feelings—to open their eyes and look at it; attend to it.

Practical Mysticism for Normal People is the curious title of a rather curious book by Miss Evelyn Underhill which was published in 1914. It is very "early Underhill", and yet it is valuable for two reasons. First, it does sum up the general consensus of the Saints on all these topics and secondly, perhaps strangely, it is completely devoid of *Christian* terms. Any lengthy résumé would here be unnecessary and out of place, but the following points are pertinent.

In pastoral practice we meet a host of those in whom natural religion is extremely active and extremely uncreative. It has the strength of an untamed stallion and is just as useless. To these vigorous souls the cultured discipline of the Church would be as yet unattractive—even were they Christian; credal formulae are as helpful to them as they would be to the wild stallion. Their need obviously is not for teaching but harnessing. Can we help them? Given goodwill and sincerity, the discipline of attention suggests a natural starting point: attention to one thing only, anything to which natural *attrait* directs—"ant or alp"—for so many minutes a day. Empathetic love, which is only disciplined volition, a union with something, leads to a purification of will and sense, a *push* towards something—and then, at least, the technique of adoration is beginning. After such exercise in objective attention we may begin, with St Augustine, to look back into self; and here begins what is the mainspring of purgation—the sight of self which spells attrition. It is quite impossible to speak of moral virtues in any but a superficial sense until some idea of attrition is gained. This is only what the Victorines and others call self-knowledge, and it begins by looking at something *other* than self. This is firstly because self in isolation is non-existent; the "psychologists' fallacy" is just as fallacious in reverse—"psychology without a subject" is as impossible as "psychology without an object". But secondly it is because in their comparative way, things are more *consistent* in giving glory to God than men are. Despite the possibility of original sin pervading creation, buttercups are nearer to fulfilling God's plan for them than are most men and women. Now we can begin to think, now we can begin what might be called "sacramental" prayer, because invariably the contemplated world of things will begin to speak, to love back, and we can realize, in Dr Tennant's terms if need be, that the contemplated things of phenomena are not only objects (o) but Objects (O), and even objects (ω).[1]

All this means is that to George, Mary starts as an object of sense only, then she becomes Objective, and finally objective (ontologically). We are introduced to a real world of more than phenomenal significance and—here is the vital next step—this is bewildering and unlovable until it is recapitulated in an object of love. We might so recapitulate, or concentrate, the spiritual world in a hazel-nut like St Julian of Norwich, or in Ars like its Curé, or in the crucifix like both. But until we have broken through phenomena, with "the sharp dart of longing love", and this by a disciplined focus of attention on something like Mary or a hazel-nut, the idea of the Church's sacramental acts will not make experiential sense.

Apart from the rather unfortunate word "contemplation", all this, moreover, is the experience of anyone who has really loved anything, who has really looked through anything, who has any notion at all of what we mean when we speak of the

[1] See p. 152 above.

omnipresence of God. And this first form of, or "ordinary" contemplation is so truly natural, that it is instinctive to most of us on occasion. What concerns us here is that it is the first-step to a progressing spiritual life. Yet the present-day emphasis on teaching kills the experience when it develops naturally. Our children would progress far more rapidly and far more truly towards confirmation if only we said, with St Teresa, not "listen to me" but "look!"; not "pay attention" to me but to *it*, alp, crucifix, or hazel-nut; not "try to understand" but "*love*"—doll, ball, or daffodil. Sometimes one sees a child gazing at a primrose or a beetle or a frog; all of which may be objects, Objects, and (ontological) objects. Leave her alone and she will get somewhere near to heaven, explain what these things really are and we might have snatched her away from God.

But this "attention" can be helped, naturally and voluntarily, by normal educative processes which in Christian tradition are ascetical rather than moral. Anti-Pelagians have always been slightly bothered by the undisputed fact that the Church has always urged moral training of her children—of all ages. Is not this putting works before faith? The difficulty only solves itself when we ask what sort of moral training, and what is it for? If our Sunday schools and Catechism aim, as is often bluntly admitted, at producing good citizens or good neighbours or even good children[1] then plainly we are immersed in heresy; we are teaching or instilling a mundane conventional ethic against Christian moral theology. And one only has to compare the capital sins with the scandals in a popular newspaper to see how utterly incompatible these are. Moral training, in the Christian sense, is that discipline called purgation which follows so naturally and obviously upon any attempt at Recollection. "Honesty pays" and "politeness wins respect" and such precepts have no place at all in Christian morals, which are concerned with humility, self-surrender, sacrifice, purity, and all those uncomfortable and temporarily useless qualities which go to make up love, whether it be love for primroses, dolls, hazel-nuts, or God.

[1] Strictly, a good child is one who fulfils the purpose of his creation by giving glory to his Creator—but that is not usually what is meant!

We would be much nearer a sub-Christian ascetic were some competent theologian to work out a series of Sunday-school lessons aimed at Recollection and purgation, and based on the capital sins.

The Christian ethic is very largely concerned with motives, and once our motive for moral instruction is purgation of soul and so the glory of God, then we have solved both the Pelagian difficulty and that of the validity of an admitted sub-Christian pastoral starting point, mentioned earlier in connection with sin as immediately social (pp. 160 f. above). Moral instruction—especially of children—becomes but St John of the Cross's "placing the soul in a state to receive the motion of God".

Sin is defined by Dr Kirk as "that which is detrimental to spiritual progress"[1]—an admirably practical definition—which can be interpreted to mean sub-Christian ascetic as that which prevents the initial recognition of God in the soul and in the world. "For practical purposes"—a phrase used by Dr Kirk—we can say that in a Christian context sin prevents or hinders spiritual progress, and that in a sub-Christian context it stops real religion from beginning at all. And it is patently obvious that the cardinal virtues, for example, have far more to do with "environmental harmony" than with utilitarian sociology. Nevertheless prudence, justice, temperance, and fortitude do bear on the harmonies of everyday life; the practice of these virtues by members of a family does contribute to the making of a happy home. As moral instruction to the well-disposed this fact may be pointed out quite clearly, but the happy home is *not* the ultimate motive for such training. Rather is it the incidental result of purgation and Recollection and the only first step to religious progress and creativity.

The same may be said of the educative value of team-games or the public school system. When these things instil only sportsmanship, or integrity, or what is ambiguously called character, then they are ascetically negative; but they could be the basis of recollection, purgation, harmony in place, and all the elements of religion. However alike they may look at this stage, the essential difference between the ethicist and the

[1] *Some Principles of Moral Theology*, pp. 222 ff.

director of souls is that the one rests content with utilitarianism while the other dares not stop short of the ultimate Vision of God.

In this scheme of things a special word is due to the ascetical implications of craftsmanship and the arts. These are the obvious examples of the practice of the "first form of contemplation" in a sense of natural religion. Dr Kirsopp Lake has said that "one of the most common forms of mysticism is often not recognized, it is the feeling that a man and his work are one". Sculptor and stone, artist and canvas, ploughman and land, carpenter and wood; these relations clearly imply experience as "subject-object unity", "recollected attention", a "loving embrace", the "first form of contemplation" and all the rest. Thus would we recommend the use of such activity as part of a sub-Christian ascetic. But let us beware of the ambiguities with which sentiment has surrounded the arts and crafts. Craftsmanship may be the sacramental expression of Christian faith—as it is so often held to be, but it may also be the mere means to the very first stirrings of natural religion; and these are—literally—poles apart. Unless we are dealing with a Leonardo or a Michelangelo it is safer to look upon the arts as useful ascetical exercises which are as intrinsically religious as athletics or cooking—safer because religious activity issues in adoration in common long before it issues in stone and paint. Modern sentiment tends to confuse the two poles by omitting everything in between.

We are still dealing with educative ascetic, that which might help to "place the soul in a state to receive the motion of God". Let us then sum up by analogy. Take a glance at the fond father who once played cricket for England, and his infant son for whom he has like ambitions, and set them in a home pervaded by the game; there are photographs and trophies and interesting caps and blazers. Now what does the father do? At the earliest opportunity he will give his son a ball to play with; to attend to, look at, experiment with, so that the boy may discover its interesting attributes. His father knows that if the boy lacks inherent gifts he will not become a good player. Therefore he must take care to do all he can to develop what *is* in the boy or what God might implant.

So later he will indulge in a few exercises of "recollection", he will bowl gently to the boy, until eye, feet, arms, bat, body, are simplified, unified, co-ordinated.[1] Then he might show him one or two fundamental strokes, and next take him along to *watch* the game; and hope earnestly—for this is a critical stage—that he will find some fundamental interest or *attrait*. And if the boy does not the father must be very patient. Later he might suggest a proper game with other small boys, before which—and not until this point is reached—he will explain the more elementary rules, and possibly inculcate a moral tenet or two about the umpire's decision, obedience to the captain, and those points of etiquette which are necessary for the dignity and order of the game. But there is no undue stress on these things because a respect for them will all be acquired naturally by playing. Finally, the boy can really be coached. He begins to progress, plays for his school, surrounds himself by friends of like interest and so on and so on.

What happens when we translate this analogy is rather terrifying. More often than not we discover that the boy is at "confirmation age", we teach him all the laws of the game and all the moral tenets; with no net practice and no coaching we thrust him into the game as a player; and wonder why he lapses. How much better it would be if we gave him a ball to play with, or an ant or an alp or a hazel-nut, if we let him come to church and watch—occasionally and at carefully calculated times and intervals. Let the boy learn seriously to love—mother, father, or the little girl next door, white mice, railway engines, or anything to which he can really "attend", give himself, or become absorbed in. Let him experiment and discover the world beyond these things. Let him use his senses and *look* for the revealing power of God, for his Saints and angels and the fairies at the bottom of the garden. All this is religion, it will lead to joys unknown as well as tears and tension. He will know little of immorality,

[1] May I here suggest that the need of recollection gives validity (at the right stage of development) to liturgical drill? "Now boys, kneel, sit, stand, adore" may not sound very devotional but it can be a real exercise of spiritual worth. If the beautiful off-drive of the master batsman was first learned by numbers, so might participation in the flowing liturgical action of the Church. Cf. p. 219, on Eucharistic Worship.

and discover sin: then he can perhaps be introduced to the way, the only known way, of reconciliation.

But guidance of this kind demands its environment, the vicarious intercession, the corporate love of the Remnant in place, whether domestic or parochial. Not only is love by Recollection and purgation the first step to any individual religious advance, it is the first step in Remnant practice. Within the framework of Christianity this presents little difficulty. Recollection and purgation are an integral part of the Rule of the Church, and this part strengthens and consolidates the union of Remnant, priest, and parochial organism. Nevertheless we need not scoff at St Julian of Norwich and her hazel-nut which is the universe that God made, keeps, and loves. We can recollect the presence of Christ and in him, *push, strive, love* any epitome of our parochial organism we care to choose. As Christians, we can, by discipline, purgation, and grace, unite with our parochial environment and be at home in it: thence we can try to carry the whole to the altar as our Lord took the world onto the Cross.

The sight of a priest gazing intently at a buttercup on the village green, loving it, giving himself to it, recollecting the God who made, keeps, and loves it; the sight of this priest wandering around the streets with Christ before his eyes, in his heart and in his hands—this might cause comment at the ruri-decanal chapter, and it is best to be unostentatious. But such activity might well be a thousand times more creative than all the more usual parish work.[1]

Perhaps it is not without ascetical significance that the traditional Christian settlement, town, or village, clusters around its church; for this is a central focus, a thing recapitulating the whole before human eyes. Here is God's house, which is not fulfilling its function until it is our home and we are truly at home with it and in it.

[1] Supplementary Note 6.

16

THE DEVELOPMENT OF CHRISTIAN
ASCETICS

WE HAVE argued that religion begins with some sense of feeling or cognition or striving towards a harmonious union with environment; a balance between natural sense-experience and its supernatural counterpart. When such experience is qualified by some sense, or recognition, of a fundamental unity of all things, then this religion becomes theistic. We have developed the notion of the unifying and creative principle "which most men call God". When this experience is expressed as a recapitulation of a God-world or God-man encounter within the Person of God Incarnate, then we have travelled from theism to Christianity. Union with the universe is summed up as union with God in Christ and the fundamental encounter between the self and God is now a personal encounter with Christ. To be in harmony with the universe is to be "in Christ".

This progression may be illustrated by such an initially disharmonious encounter as that between a man and a sudden phenomenal upheaval—a thunderstorm, for example. Caught in a thunderstorm the naturally religious man will simply run to shelter. He will behave subjectively and, while willing the storm to cease, attempt to overcome his own discomfort by flight. The theist may simply yield to an act of God outside his control, keep calm, get miserably drenched, yet accept the inevitable fatalistically; it is the will of God and thus in some partial sense acceptable. To a Christian Saint like St Francis of Assisi, this fatalism will be transformed into a love for all things sanctified in Christ. His essential simplicity and unification will be summed in the harmony between God whose will and work the storm is and Christ whose Humanity can be cold and wet. The soul of St Francis will go out in love to wind and rain, cold and storm; his body will be so mortified, his self so recollected that he can love them in subjective-objective equilibrium as well as George can love Mary. "Brother wind and sister water" is no Franciscan sentimentality, no pantheism, no nature worship, but experiential fact. The fundamental prayers of natural-religious, theist, and Christian are "God make environment conformable to me", "God make me conformable to environment", and "Benedicite omnia opera . . .". And this is true Christian "otherworldliness" because it rides above circumstances by love for the world.

Now we have, at this early pastoral stage, one who is aware of the unifying principle which is Christ, he who is very God and very Man—which implies "very environment". All Godhead and all the world is recapitulated in Christ as ultimate God-world focal point. Here we are dealing not with a St Francis but a veritable babe in Christ. Such a soul is Christian and not sub-Christian, but it is nevertheless undeveloped, immature, an infant. It is as a newborn child, who cannot be called sub-human, but who is nevertheless *immature* because he has not reached the fullness of adult manhood. This is probably the stage of most of our parochial second stratum, those of our congregation who have at least left the Book of Judges behind. Although we are still at the stage when progress both in scale and value tend to coincide, or when we must be concerned with both growth and health, we are yet concerned with spirituality as vicariously creative rather than soteriological. Any objection to this trend of thinking vanishes when we recognize the existence of good babies and bad men[1]; nevertheless, the duty of ascetical practice is to turn the babes into men without bothering overmuch about the adjectives. So our concern in this chapter is to find out how spiritual babes develop into full grown men-in-Christ; what kind of exercise and diet to give them, in what proportions and at what stages of their development.

For this inquiry there are two sources, the traditional

[1] See p. 189 above.

ascetic of the Church and, if religion begins with sense-experience, psychological doctrine of a religious kind. For the first we will take the systematized formulae of St Ignatius Loyola, for the second the genetic psychological school of Professor James Ward and Dr F. R. Tennant. There is no point in concealing the fact that these will be found to coincide exactly. If it is objected that this is but an arbitrary selection from amongst a vast number of divergent writers on both sides, and that in so wide a field some coincidence is sure to occur, then we answer in the following terms.

As with St Thomas, it is not derogatory to St Ignatius to say that his special value lies in his classification of a more general orthodoxy rather than in his original thought. The over-systematization of St Ignatius is misunderstood by critics who regard his formulae and exercises as stereotyped methods. To say that the simpler teachings of St François de Sales, or the Oratorians or the Franciscans, are more directly practicable, is probably true; but the unique value of St Ignatius is his systematization of the whole Prayer life. He is so valuable *because* his schemes are so complex, and therefore so comprehensive and, if not directly usable to any soul, then generally applicable to every soul. The Ignatian summary, moreover, embodied in the third method of meditation commonly called the Ignatian method,[1] is not so much a method of meditation as a summary of the whole development of a Prayer-life. As a method to be used for the next half-hour it is overwhelmingly complicated, but as an ascetic guide to the next few years—which is what it really is—a masterpiece of concise exposition. Any scheme which begins with *remote* preparation and ends with resolutions must surely be more than *a* prayer. As we see it this third method is more like an ascetical creed: the briefest possible summary of all the essentials of spiritual growth from infancy to manhood. As such we must use it, for there is no comparable alternative.

As to the empirical psychology of Professor Ward, we choose this because, whatever the developments and divergencies

[1] This in fact is "prayer by the three powers of the Soul", or the third item in the *First* (of three) "methods", but it is what is usually implied by "Ignatian". See Longridge, pp. 159–65.

among contemporary psychologists, it is generally conceded to be pure psychology at its purest. It has no axe to grind and its fundamentals are accepted in general, however much we advance upon its details; and only with its elements are we concerned. Furthermore, this psychology is closely allied with epistemology and is at least reputable, and the Ward-Tennant school, within its era, is the last to have any use for what they would dismiss as "the mystics". (In a footnote to the chapter on "religious experience" in *Philosophical Theology*, Dr Tennant admits that he has not read the Christian Saints.) If, despite this, we find a fundamental agreement here with St Ignatius; if we find the Ignatian method foreshadowing in ascetical practice what Ward and Tennant discover epistemologically three centuries later, then we feel more than justified in accepting this synthesis as the basis of a venture of faith. Such synthesis is a "coincidence" far too great for reasonable man to swallow. In ascetic the wheel has turned full circle, Ward and Tennant would be puzzled, if not horrified to find themselves in support of a mystic like Loyola. Loyola would be highly amused—and probably is—to find this scientific explanation for his own experience. These are strange bedfellows; but when two such divergent streams of thought meet we feel justified in claiming validity for their common conclusions.

Let us therefore examine the Ignatian system in detail, comparing each point with the corresponding stage in Ward's psychology of experience.

(*a*) *Remote preparation* to St Ignatius is simply his insistence that Prayer depends upon one's life in environment. As Fr Harton says, "what one is in one's life one is in one's prayer . . . the life of Prayer consists in the union of prayer and life". And this "Remote preparation . . . is simply the constant effort to keep one's life habitually in harmony with one's prayer". This is suggested by the three Ignatian subheadings—mortification, recollection, humility—the exercise of looking at the world in love. Mortification here is but attentive discipline of the senses, thus recollection is simply "seeing things in God and looking for God in things". Humility is that self-surrender and self-giving, pushing out in love towards the universe as sacramental sign of God's immanence. Ascetical terminology is notoriously ambiguous, and St Ignatius is more notorious than anyone. It is not stretching things very far to call mortification plus humility simply purgation, which with recollection gives us the starting point of all purposeful religion. This we have already discussed at some length, and it is in complete agreement with Ward's premise that all experience and all knowledge, whether merely of phenomena in natural man, or the ontal behind it in religious man, begins in the world with sense-experience. And the unification or simplification of experience issuing in unified subject-object *rapport* (loving encounter with God) is voluntarily achieved by Recollection and purgation evolving out of the discipline of attention. This whole process is contained in the psychological progression from mere cognitive acquaintance, through feeling to awareness, to conative attention and its subsequent activity. Both bear witness to the teaching of St Thomas: the body and its senses, or our sensing of our own bodies, lead to self-consciousness; this introduces us to consciousness of other bodies, and thence to other (spiritual) selves. This is why St Thomas can say that the study of nature is the first step to the Vision of God. What Ward and St Ignatius are saying is that George as soul knows Mary as soul through the medium of bodily contact and in no other way. Therefore theists know God through the medium of the phenomenal world as Christians know God through the medium of his Incarnate Son, and in no other way.[1] Both Ward and St Ignatius are agreed that religious development can only begin, ascetically, with sense-life in the world and not simply with "teaching". It begins, that is to say, with the experience of, or striving towards, "the first form of contemplation": "seeing God mirrored in his works".

(b) *Proximate preparation* is the practical step of narrowing down this discipline as we approach the set time of prayer. This is but the quickening of the discipline of attention, and

---

[1] I do not mean to deny the possibility of an immediate knowledge of God in mystical experience, which is outside the scope of this book; "we", here, means devout souls in parishes who are *not* mystics or Contemplatives.

in life it forms the spiritual analogy to the principle whereby an athlete intensifies the discipline of his training a day or so before the actual contest. The first two Ignatian sub-headings, interpreted in practice by considering the subject for meditation the night before it is to be made and recalling this on waking—the schoolboy's examination trick—is a startling acknowledgement by St Ignatius of what Ward now calls the sub-conscious (or what Spinoza used to call *conatus*). The third sub-heading—"consecration"—is the final consolidation of this proximate preparation as this latter consolidates remote preparation; it is the concentrated thrust, push, volitional effort towards God—or in other words conative-faith-venture.

(c) With the *immediate preparation* we become aware of the specifically Christian. Whether St Ignatius intended to or not, he has moved steadily from a wide religiousness to a trinitarian formula. And this is common to all the Saints in their particular ways[1]; all Christian experience bears witness to the Holy Trinity—it is in fact the prior experience of developing religion which gave rise to this doctrine, it is the sum of that progressive ascetic, even of a natural kind, which creates the idea of the Holy Trinity as a necessary, obvious, and usable fact rather than obscure theological metaphysic. It is the progressive Old Testament experience of creator—Messiah—wisdom, it is implied by Dr Tennant's favourite word *rapport* and it is contained in Ward's unity of subject-subjective, object-objective by experiential activity which mediates their *rapport*. And it is the doctrine of the Holy Trinity which, we shall see presently, is the ascetical key to spiritual health. This *rapport* as concentration of attention, as conative activity expressed by volitional loving thrusts towards God, is traced by Ward through a disciplined psychological sequence—sense-impression, after-sensation, recurrent-sensation, sense-bound-image, retention. To put it bluntly, the first momentary *rapport*—soul-senses: thing-God—is "held in an embrace" by discipline.

(d) Now begins *the exercise* proper, which is what is popularly known as the three-point meditation. In a pictorial meditation

[1] See below, p. 201.

such as a Gospel narrative, composition of place is simply
the scene of the action imagined, the petition is the sanctification of this imagined scene by the continuing recollection of
the presence of God. This is the natural prelude to the recollection of the story upon which we are meditating. (It is
unfortunate that St Ignatius here uses in a popular sense the
highly technical term "recollection", but all it means is that
to *remember* the story—to act it, or imagine the action as if we
were to make a film of it.)[1]

This process, again, follows in logical sequence from Ward,
who traces memory from the imaginal and the imaginal from
the retention of the sense-bound image.

A word must be said here about the intellectual—that is non-
pictorial—type of meditation, where the subject of our prayer
is abstract and invisible. "Intellectual", of course, is a very
misleading term, and so is "non-pictorial"; and if it means
something akin to pure thought then it is an impossible one.
Here St Ignatius is often accused of ambiguity, since the
portions of the spiritual exercises that deal with this question
(first prelude, first exercise, first week; and directory xiv.
4–7)[2] fail to make any adequate distinction between meditations upon narratives and abstractives. But this is surely
more than pertinent—because St Ignatius does not admit that
there is any clear distinction; he will have nothing to do with
pure thought, and he assumes, as all commentators bear
witness, that meditation on abstract and invisible truths
demands the use of symbol or imaginal representation.[3] Thus
again, St Ignatius repudiates what Ward and Tennant, following William James, call "the psychologists' fallacy"—or
psychology without a subject. He is insisting, with St Thomas,
that the subject of Prayer is an embodied soul, and rejecting
what we might call the "asceticists' fallacy", which regards
man as angelic—all head and no body.

Thus Ward and St Ignatius agree that so long as souls live
in environment, they must accept their embodied status. Few
of us have attained, or will attain in this world, the spiritual

[1] See below, Chapter 20, pp. 244 f.
[2] W. H. Longridge (4th Ed.), pp. 53–4; 304–5.
[3] Ibid., p. 54.

heights of a Julian of Norwich; and she never attempted to
contemplate pure God—only a hazel-nut, a symbol and more
than a symbol for him who "made it, keeps it and loves it".

(e) St Ignatius would have no hard and fast distinction
between the three points of the traditional meditation. Here
the use of the intellect follows naturally upon composition of
place and yet the two are interdependent. This simple and
accepted arrangement contains what is perhaps the most
remarkable of all Loyola's psychological prophecy. And it is
also one of the staunchest bulwarks of our position against
modern pastoral gnosticism. The psychological sequence of
Ward continues from memory-image (imagination) to ideation,
thence pure conception. This completes the chain from sense-
experience to intellection, and thus from religious-sense-
experience—the first form of contemplation—to religious
knowledge or doctrine: religion as prior to theology. As Dr
Tennant words it, "sense and understanding have a common
root—sense is from the first possessed of the promise and
potency of thought, sense and thought are not disparate, or
issuing from distinct sources"[1]; or later, "thinking is a con-
tinuation of the same process as that in which the free image
emerges out of the sense-bound image or the perception".[2]

The implications are far-reaching indeed. For in this
Loyola-Ward–medieval-modern synthesis we have a complete
vindication of the Curé d'Ars "who learned all his theology on
his knees", and a complete vindication—if such was ever
necessary—of St Bernard's specific order of illiterates. It
means that if theology is to have any possible alliance with
religion, it can only be learned as living truth, through meditative prayer in its widest sense. If theology is to have any
place in pastoral practice, if it is to be religious, then it cannot
merely be taught; it can only be acquired and used by ascetical direction in the art of mental prayer. Now if we put these
last two points together, as St Ignatius insists we must, we
find a religious synthesis of knowledge dependent on the
imaginal, in turn dependent on St Thomas's "sense-life" in
the world, or St Ignatius's remote preparation, or Ward's
duality-unity experience. This is because we cannot "image

[1] *Philosophical Theology*, Vol. I, pp. 37, 39.   [2] Ibid., p. 184.

THE DEVELOPMENT OF CHRISTIAN ASCETICS 185

anything which we have not previously sensed ". The imaginal
thus maintains a key position in religious psychology, and,
significantly, "the ontological status of the imaginal, metaphysics has scarcely deigned to discuss ".[1] But the Christian
meditative tradition, culminating in St Ignatius and
supported here by Ward, strongly suggests that "imagination"
—far from being the synonym for falsity of popular misuse—is epistemologically reputable.[2] Theology cannot be
divorced from prayer, meditation is the source, not only of
devotion but of knowledge. This is what St Teresa was always
insisting upon: that her meditation was real, call it what you
will. To put it into Dr Tennant's own words "psychologically,
the imaginal is a source of the real and can be a source of
ideas ", "the impressional and the imaginal are different orders
of the objective "—thence Objective, thence (ontologically)
objective. Christians, of course, have always accepted this in
faith-venture and on authority: and backed by the doctrines
of divine inspiration and of the Holy Spirit, such faith-venture
is eminently reasonable. But to modern minds epistemology
is important, and if it can be made to support traditional
practice it is very worth while—however well certain kinds of
faith can do without it. To this matter we must return later
(Chapter 20).

(f) The Ignatian *colloquies* may be described as vocal
prayer governed by affective volition[3]; bluntly as saying our
prayers creatively and honestly. This again coincides with
Ward's psychological process wherein volition depends upon,
and follows after, ideation and intellection. Volition plus
affection, moreover, simply means active love. This is Prayer
according to the definition of St Thomas: "Loving God in act
so that the divine life may communicate itself to us, and
through us to the world."[4] And love has been defined by Elmer
More as "that outstretching power of the imagination by
which we grasp and make real to ourselves the being of

---

[1] Ibid., p. 53.

[2] See below, Chapter 20, (3), pp. 232 ff.

[3] *Spiritual Exercises*, 1st Week, 3rd Week on The Last Supper:
Longridge, 4th Ed., p. 58, p. 139, etc.

[4] Fahey, *Mental Prayer according to the Teaching of St Thomas Aquinas.*

others ".[1] If we put this medieval-modern mixture together, we have further striking confirmation of the soundness of the Ignatian psychology and also the creative value of the imaginal, which is now seen not only as the parent of knowledge but the grandparent of love. But the most pertinent pastoral fact is that only at this stage does St Ignatius take any serious note of vocal prayer at all. This colloquy is nevertheless *the prayer*, towards which all the preceding exercise has been leading.

(*g*) The *resolution* is the conative aspect of volition which returns us to the world, to the *remote preparation* for our next meditation, whenever that may be. So we begin and end with religion as conative activity; and this disciplined *resolution* is the counterpart of the last phrase of St Thomas's definition just quoted: ". . . and through us to the world". Together with (*h*) the *conclusion* this transition from colloquy or private vocal prayer to life in the world is a transition from individual to corporate spirituality. In modern terms, initial experience is a unity of subject and object, but as this object of meditation becomes, in Tennant's terms, Objective, it infers a corporate society of subjects. And such an Objective is a stage towards the ontal object (ω).

Now the Objective, in pastoral practice, can be anything from a hazel-nut to a gospel narrative, but meditation by individual members of a group (Remnant) upon one single Object tends to bind those members into a corporate whole. And if the ontal objective reality (ω) is recapitulated in the Incarnate Son of God, then the ultimate stage in this spiritual progression is a "corporate colloquy" between related subjects and God in Christ. And this is the liturgical worship of the Church. This last stage is important because the ascetical goal is very frequently assumed to be Contemplation of an individual kind. It is true that in most, traditional ascetical schemes, Contemplation is assumed to grow out of meditative exercise, and therefore Contemplation is the highest grade to which we can attain. But the great ascetical Saints have always presupposed corporate order as the setting for all spirituality; monastic Order is the parent of an ascetic which

[1] *Christ of the New Testament*, p. 123.

came to replace it, and although this same corporate Order may be changed, it cannot be abolished. St Ignatius, St François de Sales, and the Spanish Carmelites all gave full expression to the Contemplative life, but it was still corporate, whether set within the discipline of the Society of Jesus, the Order of the Visitation, or the Carmelite Rule.

In short, we must guard against the old hierarchical heresy, and distinguish between grade and value. The fundamental advance in value is from the individual to the corporate, the rise from meditation to Contemplation is but a hierarchical grade. Thus corporate mental prayer or corporate vocal prayer—as in the Office—is a greater value than individual Contemplation. As Dr Kirk explains so clearly, the Vision of God, as our ultimate goal, is always a corporate one in New Testament thought and onwards.[1] It is necessary to emphasize that Christianity is social, and that all revolves around the Church as the Body of Christ. So much ascetic, even Ignatian, is nowadays regarded as entirely a matter of private prayer. The considerable numbers of modern souls who are seeking spiritual progress by piously living through *The Exercises*, are missing the whole point of them if they are not becoming more and more engrafted into their parochial Body. The Ignatian background of the Society of Jesus must be replaced by the parochial Remnant unless the whole scheme is to become negative and abstractive.

Now in our Ward-Loyola, modern-medieval synthesis, we have not an isolable and personal method of meditation, but a whole scheme of spiritual growth from Christian infancy (or possibly religious infancy) to the fullness of maturity in the Body of Christ. And we can discover four related yet well defined stages of this growth, which are as follows:

(i) The whole Ignatian *preparation* is the initial conative awareness of God which, disciplined and directed by recollection and purgation, becomes the first form of contemplation. This is the search for God in his world, the sacramental acquaintance with the ontologically Real through phenomena, and to the Christian, the sense of the Presence of the living Christ. This experience may be largely intellectual, active or

[1] *The Vision of God*, p. 108 ff.

moral, or a sense of spiritual feeling; but it will contain all of these elements in some degree.

(ii) The Ignatian *preludes* and the first two points of the *exercise* comprise what is more generally known as mental prayer or meditation. This is a spiritual exercise, strictly so called; that which may constitute real prayer but which more often serves as a disciplined prolegomena to real prayer. To the Christian it is this disciplined exercise of recollection and attention to the gospel narratives which leads to, and creates, the fundamental encounter with the living and glorified Christ. It is the second point of the exercise which gives us knowledge of Christ and thence, by reflection, theology.

(iii) The encounter having thus been established, we can now, and only now, hold *colloquy* with Christ—or as St Ignatius insists, with God the Father, God the Holy Spirit, or even the Saints who appear before us in the gospel narrative. In plain language, we can "say our prayers". So we call this stage simply colloquy.[1]

(iv) The Ignatian *resolutions* and *conclusion* take us back into the workaday world which is a world of society in environment. Our private colloquy with Christ can only lead us into the worshipping fellowship of his Body. This then, is the stage of *corporate liturgical worship,* which is the hall-mark of Christian maturity. And this fourfold order of growth is surely, apart from anything else, a matter of common sense. If religion is fundamental and if conversion is the prerogative of God, then it is quite useless to *talk* about religion, God, prayer, or worship to those to whom such words are meaningless. Moreover, you cannot talk to, or hold colloquy with, those whom you do not know. Only meditation can introduce us to Christ. And one cannot usually act in unison with others until one has mastered an art by one's self—net-practice comes before playing in a corporate team; five-finger exercises come before the solo part of a concerto.

---

[1] Ancient writers frequently use the words "vocal prayer" to qualify all prayer where words are used—including the liturgical Office. To avoid ambiguity I keep to the word "colloquy" for private petition, intercession etc., as distinguished from the use, privately or corporately, of "set prayers".

If we elaborate the Pauline analogy of balanced ascetical dietetics we can think of four stages: milk, gravy, vegetables, beefsteak in infant to manhood diet. There is no need to linger over the arrangement of these in any hierarchy of value, since all are needed equally by the mature adult. Nevertheless, there is a hierarchy of grade by way of digestibility. We cannot, that is to say, call beefsteak better than milk, but beefsteak *is* only usable and digestible by adults. We are, then, faced with something rather frightening. We have a full synthesis of agreement between such seemingly diverse schools of religious thought as St Ignatius Loyola and Professor James Ward; the one medieval, ascetic—even in the idiomatic sense—and Catholic; the other modern, ethical-humanist and Protestant. These agree, but their agreed conclusion is categorically opposed to the general consensus of pastoral practice.

This synthesis gives us a clear-cut order of development stage by stage: (i) the "first form of contemplation", or "natural" contemplation, then (ii) meditative prayer, then (iii) vocal prayer, then (iv) corporate worship. Yet at the first stirrings of religion in the modern soul, the religious birth of a babe in Christ, at the very first stirring of spiritual consciousness, such a soul—irrespective of physical age, which might be anything from 4 to 90—is told brusquely to go to church. This implies corporate worship (iv), raw beefsteak to the new-born child. After which the child-soul is told to say his prayers (iii)—boiled potatoes; and all the time meditation (ii) is fit only for the very advanced—light gruel for the adult stevedore; and admitting the ambiguity of the term contemplation, words like Recollection, purgation, humility, and consecration are the very last thing in advanced technique. The whole order, by some Satanic twist, is exactly reversed.

The position is alleviated to some extent when we consider, as we must, the Christian social tradition of our age, wherein no one is asked to begin with Moses and work slowly through the Old Testament to Caesarea Philippi. We do in fact begin in a general environment where "Christ" and "God" are synonymized. Even the babe-in-Christ is helped by immersion in the Christ-charged environment of a consecrated church where Mass is continually offered—even perhaps where his sacramental Presence lives locally. But this is a return to the parable of the paralytic, where four strong men may carry the weak to our Lord. There is still no point in two fairly strong men struggling with a paralysed multitude. It is also a return to our analogy of the player and spectators; even the babe may benefit if he is allowed to watch corporate worship, occasionally and from a safe distance. Corporate worship is seen as a kind of fulcrum balancing infancy–maturity on one side and maturity–progress on the other. The worship of the Church is thus the end of one spiritual journey and the beginning of another: the end of one's basic education and the beginning of one's life work. It is essential to distinguish—as did the early Church—between what is worship and what is merely instruction: "going to Mass", "going to Sunday school", "going to hear a sermon" are straightforward statements, but "going to church" is really meaningless. It points to the basic problem of a lack of pattern, shape, and form.

But we have now reached Christian maturity. We have all the ingredients for mature adult spirituality, we have finished basic education and we are to begin our life work. We have learned to digest milk, gravy, vegetables, and beefsteak, gradually and in that order; because we have recognized a sense of the Presence of God and because we have ruminated meditatively on this, we are capable of colloquy; and because of this we are fit to take our place "in church". Now we are to combine all these together in an ascetically balanced diet. Having reached this stage the matter becomes simpler, because we need no longer concern ourselves with growth or progress directly. We can give all our attention to the maintenance of spiritual health and leave progress to God in faith.

Religious health springs directly from the soul's experiential conception of God and the Christian experience of God is a synthesis of the transcendent Father objectively adored, the immanent Spirit subjectively experienced, and what has been called a personal "I–thou" encounter with Christ in love. This synthesis is ultimately expressed by the worship of the Trinity in the Body of Christ; in more familiar language worship of the Father, in the Spirit, through Jesus Christ Our Lord. Ascetical theology we have defined as applied dogmatic, thus the maintenance of adult spiritual health, the formation of an ascetical balanced diet, depends upon the pastoral application of the doctrine of the Trinity, to which we must now turn. And this, we would mention in anticipation, finds traditional expression in the Rule of the Church when, and only when, its items are interpreted ascetically.[1]

[1] See below, Chapters 18, 19, 20.

17

SPIRITUAL HEALTH:
THE HOLY TRINITY[1]

THE HEALTH of the soul depends upon the health of its Prayer, which in turn depends upon the adequacy of its conception of God. This conception of God is rooted in religious experience comprising cognitive, conative, and feeling elements. Thus Prayer-venture, or religion-as-activity, gives rise to a theological conception of God, and here as always, corporate Prayer-venture is a much more dependable guide than individual interpretation. The Christian doctrine of God the Holy Trinity is the result of progressive corporate experience, which is inherent in both Old and New Testaments. The transcendent personal God of Deutero-Isaiah, the Messianic concept, and the indwelling Holy Wisdom of the "wisdom" writings is the foreshadowing of Father, Son, and Spirit. This is the result of fundamental religious experience in different souls or the same soul at different times; cognition and intellection must eventually lead to monotheism of a transcendental kind, feeling implies an indwelling divine spirit, and theistic sacramentalism must finally demand a mediator between these two types of experience. If the soul, psychologically, is a trinity-in-unity—cognition, feeling, conation—then its experience of God must also be trinity-in-unity, transcendent, immanent, mediatorial.

If the first constructive religious progress in the soul is towards self-simplification or unification, then only perfect simplicity or unification can express itself in the worship of the Trinity perfectly unified. Here theology is generally in

[1] For the basis of this chapter I am greatly indebted to a series of lectures by Professor H. H. Farmer at Cambridge.

advance of religion since it sets an ideal, dogmatically, which takes a lifetime of struggle to achieve ascetically. In other words the soul's successive experiences of Father, Son, and Spirit precede the unified experience of the undivided Trinity. Accepting Christian dogmatic we have to face the fact that however loyal we are to our creeds, we are ascetically inclined to tritheism throughout this life. All Christian souls (with the possible exception of pure Contemplatives) will stress one person of the Holy Trinity when suddenly confronted with the word "God". Our first psychic reaction to this word is either a cognition of the transcendent Father, or an image of our Lord Jesus Christ, or a spiritual feeling for the immanent Spirit. And this, incidentally, gives us our first ascetical classification; a grouping much more fundamental than James's "once-born" and "twice-born", meditative and Contemplative, or even the classical "three ways". Whether a soul's religion is mainly transcendental and intellectual, emotional and moral, or "mystical" is the first thing to ascertain in direction, and the ascetical application of Trinitarian dogmatic gives us our clue.

This ascetical scheme must now be expanded. But first it is important to face these ascetical facts in case we are accused of accepting tritheism. In dealing with the three Persons of the Trinity separately and in seeming isolation, we are only accepting the fact of human frailty, which pastoral theology is bound to do. We are only saying that unless we are Contemplative saints, our Prayer *is inclined* to tritheism—however fervently we recite the creed. The fact of living in temporal conditions and reciting each clause of the Creed or *Gloria Patri* in succession does not help to conceive an integrated Trinity. Because of finity, in other words, we are inclined to lay emphasis on one single Person of the Holy Trinity and divorce him from the other Persons; this we gladly agree should not be, but it is so, and pastoral theology must face facts. We intend therefore, to divide the Trinity in most blatant fashion. This course may be justified in two ways. Firstly, because in a temporal-spatial world it is necessary for any sort of constructive analysis. Secondly, because it is more convenient to deal with ascetical health negatively; it is simpler to work creatively towards spiritual health by finding out as much as we can about spiritual disease. By dividing the Trinity we are going to discover prevalent spiritual diseases—which should satisfy dogmatics—and by watching the Holy Trinity reintegrated in the Rule of the Church we are, in the next chapter, attempting to suggest cures for these diseases.[1]

The basic religious tendency associated with the idea of the first person of the Trinity is one of transcendence, majesty, or awe. If, in a particular soul, the single word "God" immediately suggests the notion of the Father as omnipotent Creator and supreme Being, then that soul's religion will find its natural expression in a sense of absolute dependence. Such a soul will know the fear of God in one sense or another, its approach to God will be generally objective, its religion may well contain a considerable intellectual element, it might achieve adoration or it might sink to a legalistic moralism.

If God is immediately apprehended as the Incarnate Son, a sense of communion, *rapport*, and finally love will be to the forefront of the soul's experience. Such a soul is likely to be widely sacramental, probably imaginative and meditative rather than intellectual, and possessed of instinctive understanding of sin and redemption. It might be suggested that dependence on a supreme Being suggests original sin, and redemption by the Incarnate Son, actual sin.

The Holy Ghost is immanent in the world and within the soul and he is spontaneously known as the Paraclete: he is the Comforter spiritually experienced, he is God indwelling, and gives feeling to religious experience.

In a particular soul, therefore, the omission of all notion of the transcendent Father to be feared and adored produces errors similar to those which result from an over-emphasis upon the Paraclete immanently indwelling. The mutual result

---

[1] "We can never attain to a completely synthetic view of what God has revealed Himself to be. For that would involve a level of unified knowledge which can belong to none but to God Himself. Such a simple and simultaneous knowledge of what God is must exist in God Himself. But we on our part must be content to approach the sanctuary from the outside and from a number of different points of view." L. S. Thornton, "The Christian Conception of God": *Essays Catholic and Critical*, p. 126.

is some form of spiritual eudemonism; false mysticism,
subjectivism, introversion, sentimentality, pantheism, over-
stress on feeling and the like.

Conversely, the religion of a soul which eliminates the
immanence of the Spirit and over-stresses the transcendence
of the Father, tends to become over-intellectual, deistic,
formal, legalistic and generally "transcendental" in the
Barthian sense. If the moral factor is prominent in these
two hypothetical souls, the former would probably be wholly
intuitive, laying great stress on "conscience" perhaps even
to the extent of antinomianism. The latter would veer towards
the imperative and objective, laying stress on the laws of God;
cold, uncharitable, and Pharisaic.

It is obvious that neither of these tendencies, in whatever
combination, can produce full Christian health without the
focal mediation of the love of God manifested in Christ. It is
also significant that in any context, love is the synthesis of
awe and comfort, or fear and joy; the three forming themselves
into a kind of Hegelian triad.

But an over-emphasis, or a wrong emphasis, upon the
second Person of the Holy Trinity leads to a false Christo-
centrism which tends to one or other of the fundamental
errors already outlined. If the Incarnation is rightly conceived,
the Father and the Spirit are indivisible from the Son, for he
is Incarnate God and God is the Trinity. But if our concept is
but vaguely Arian then we are again moving towards mundane, immanental subjectivism: we have lost sight of Almighty
God, and Jesus is a semi-divine "friend". If our notion is
Apollinarian we are back to an unknowable spirit; awesome
but cold, over-intellectual, and finally Puritan. In short, without the Son we have Deism, and with the Incarnation according
to orthodoxy we have a full sacramental Theism. It is plain
that this scheme of health and ill-health in a living religious
experience tallies with the threefold make-up of the elemental
self: Father, Son, Spirit; Cognition, Conation, Feeling.

The pastoral application of this properly belongs to the
following chapter, but it may be mentioned here that the Rule
of the Church *in full* provides for a complete Trinitarian
concept of God, and that fragments of such Rule without

balance and proportion provide for every conceivable kind of chaos. All prayer, ideally, is to the Father, through the Son, in the Spirit; but ascetically and analytically the Office tends to emphasize the first objectively, the Mass is the mutual loving embrace of Christ, and prayer in private depends upon the Paraclete's indwelling. In practice it is not quite so simple, since some satisfaction of feeling may be legitimate to the Office and meditation might constitute objective worship; nevertheless these emphases and tendencies are of considerable ascetical value, since eudemonism, subjectivism, false mysticism, and the like invariably occur where the Office is neglected or misused; and legalism, formalism, and intellec-tualized deism are symptomatic of the absence of mental prayer.

We must also be warned that ascetical balance does not mean a rigid mathematical formula applicable to an hypo-thetical balanced self. In unique souls, cognition, conation, and feeling; intellect, moral consciousness, "spiritual" emotion and fervour; will be found in an infinite variety of proportions. The religion of a philosopher will rightly be more intellectual than that of an artist or a bank-clerk. In general, however, the dour metaphysician may do well to contemplate a gruesome painting of the gruesome scene on Calvary; while the eudemonist might be well advised to sit down quietly for half an hour and do a little hard thinking about Almighty God.

Many of our well-attended ritualistic churches would do well to guard against formalism by stressing the emotional content of private meditation, while a great deal of subjective sentimentality and quasi-mysticism would disappear were the Office recited more regularly with objective boredom. Even the Mass, dissociated from meditation and the Office, may lead either to legalism or to an unhealthy Christo-centrism.

By this simplest possible summary, the first Person of the Trinity inspires the objective approach, the second Person inspires the mediatorial and redemptive, and the third Person, the subjective element in religious experience. And by the necessary balancing of their traditional expressions—Office, Mass, and private prayer—we have an ascetical framework of greater practical value than its simplicity might suggest.

But we may usefully elaborate a little by expanding the Trinitarian formula into five elements[1] necessary to the full Christian apprehension of God.

(1) *God the Father as ontological other* is, in general, an intellectual and metaphysical concept. It is the element which comes through the discursive reflection upon the being of God, and such reasoning, we must always remember, is truly a religious experience according to Dr Temple's definition. This is the factor which inspires the religious man's concern for the mysteries of creation, providence, eternity, and so on, and which suggests the classical attributes of God, such as omnipotence and omniscience. It is from this source that Schleiermacher finds his notion of "absolute dependence", and the philosopher his genuine humility and need for a sacramental approach to God through his creation. This might be called the ascetic aspect of the cosmological argument. If there were any over-emphasis upon this element it would be difficult to avoid the substitution of religion by metaphysics, and there would be a tendency towards Deism in philosophy and a cringing fatalism in life. God is "wholly other"—wholly transcendent, unknown, and unknowable, and hence a blind impersonal power. If prayer exists at all in relation to this trend—as it undoubtedly does in Islam and extreme Calvinism—it is largely, if not wholly, Quietistic.

But if we omit this element altogether, we fail to do justice to the necessary part played by reason in all Christian spirituality, upon which such as Professor Farmer and Dr Matthews so rightly insist. We end, inevitably, in superstition, obscurantism, or naïve credulity. If this element is omitted within the Christian concept of divine Fatherhood, and divine Personality, we lay bare all the errors which spring from anthropomorphism. Without this Personality-Father element, of course, we are reduced to mere metaphysic; a conception against which Professor Farmer's writings are rightly renowned. But here we assume divine Personality to be inherent in all Christian doctrine, and its omission to be no mere

---

[1] Professor Farmer adds a sixth, that of "*sui generis* awe", but ascetically this is so near to (2) below, God as "axiological other", that it seems needless to treat it separately.

erroneous tendency within Christian spirituality but something outside it altogether.

(2) *God the Father as axiological other.* Here we turn from metaphysic to, in its widest sense, ethic; and if Professor Farmer subtitles his second element the "Platonic strand" of religion, we might distinguish by calling the first the "Aristotelian strand". Etymologically we are concerned with God's otherness or transcendence in terms of value or worth rather than power, and this covers both moral and aesthetic elements. Thus we pass from philosophical fact to religious awe, or from knowledge to worship; a cringing, or even stoical fatalism becomes Adoration. This element, needless to say, cannot be overstressed,[1] while its omission leaves us with no real religion at all. We need therefore spend little time upon its analysis, except to mention the obvious dangers of exaggerating either ethics or aesthetics into synonyms for real religion. And, though on the outer perimeter of our subject, we are warned against the danger of slipping into a vague impersonal numinous as a substitute for God the All-Father. Platonic "higher values" and "universals" tend to a God who is but the "concrete universal of the good"; who is universal goodness, truth, and beauty without Personality.

(3) *God the Son offers perfect succour.* This conception gives us the subjective side of love and is the factor which gives rise to Christian Joy; the rightly subjective desire of the Christian soul to be loved by the Incarnate Son, to accept this love of God poured down upon him with surrender and joy. Without it we not only dissociate ourselves from objective redemption but become immersed in some or all of the large variety of errors which come under the general heading of Puritanism. And with an over-emphasis—regrettably so common—we sink into a sentimental eudemonism; we are overwhelmed by the divine mercy to the exclusion of divine justice; we seek love without wrath, comfort without fear, forgiveness without penitence, and reward without endeavour. But, even allowing any of these (strictly indivisible) divisions for the

[1] Except possibly by the Stoic, but this is really misinterpretation rather than overstress.

purpose of analysis, this element cannot even be discussed without its essential correlation with:

(4) *God the Son makes absolute demand.* Here joy, love, and freedom are balanced by duty, discipline, and sacrifice. The omission of this fourth element is obviously similar to an over-stress upon the third, and the most pertinent result is the virtual elimination of any creative ascetic and any real spiritual progress. If we place total reliance upon this element we are back at Puritanism, with particular emphasis on legalism of a Pharisaic kind, whether in moral rules, conventions, or religious duties.

These factors together create the ultimate and largely inexplicable synthesis which is the Christian's true joy and true glory. The paradox of succour and demand is the very essence of all love, and here it occurs in its most sublime form. These two factors give us the paradox of humanism and rigorism combined in a new creative whole—which makes it impossible to see Jesus Christ as one or the other. And here we cut short our analysis because we are approaching the common, mutual loving embrace of Christ and the soul actively surrendered; and there is no more to be said. If we were to speak of practical pastoral ascetic, we are at the very moment of communion, in the centre of the Mass, in the centre of the Church; and no saint, philosopher, poet, or theologian has ever tried to define exactly that state. We have arrived at the point where—as Otto has pointed out—the Bach B minor Mass finds its most adequate expression in complete silence.

But it is, perhaps, relevant here to mention that the attempt to divide these two indivisible elements brings us to the very root of the Catholic-Puritan, High Church-Low Church, controversy in its modern setting. The Puritan demands a dour moral discipline, the Catholic an ascetical discipline; the one an endless training of individual conscience, the other a sacrificial corporate loyalty; the former claims a grim liberty while the latter is joyfully bound to corporate authority. And the bewildered masses, whom no one can blame, cry for the superficial best of both worlds. We might offer some slight alleviation to them by demonstrating the impossibility of any

14

compromise, and clearly showing the alternative: on the one hand, no ascetical obligation and no corporate loyalty, with no beer, no skittles, Puritan Sundays and black clothes; on the other, ascetical struggle, the Lenten fast, sacrifice, suffering and penance—but also colour, gaiety, and Joy. There can be no love between persons without tension or "value-resistance".[1] Even on the level of human marital love both of these elements are demanded in synthesis, each partner not only gives himself or herself wholly to the other but demands so to receive the other; there is no love unless partners not only give all but are willing to take all. (And, as already noted, this surely is the real basis of Christian mono-gamy, a basis far deeper and firmer than social convenience, family nurture or ethics. We might even be bold enough to claim, against the Puritan, that if ethics is the science of behaviour then ascetics is the science of love.)

(5) *God the Holy Ghost as Indwelling Spirit* is the immanen-tal and subjective element in religion which is necessary to spiritual health, and the absence of which leads us to rational-ism, Deism, and a revolt against all feeling. Here it is enough to warn against the obvious tendencies involved in its over-emphasis; a general religious introversion, false pantheistic mysticism, weakening of moral judgement and lack of objective corporate discipline—intense individualism of all types and a general egocentricity. The whole unhealthy tendency appears in to-day's world with existential philoso-phy and an exaggerated preoccupation with psychology—generally misinterpreted and misapplied.

It would be arduous but not particularly difficult to elaborate such an analytical scheme by examining minutely detailed trends, tendencies, and sub-divisions within the general headings which we have now reached—and they are still very general. But this would be to exaggerate ascetical science at the expense of art; and art—that is, the personal application of rules and decisions to particular souls—there must surely be. Christian spirituality cannot be reduced to mathematical tables; creative direction cannot be achieved by

[1] *The World and God*, pp. 19 ff., 60, 79.

the completion of an elaborate questionnaire, reduced to a schedule, and answered by post. But if we need some art we also need some science, and the current pastoral tendency is either a refusal to face the issue at all or a complete reliance on art at the expense of science. So there need be no further elaboration, but by way of a general summary, three points might profitably be made.

Firstly, it cannot be stressed too often that this scheme is *analytical* because the Most Holy Trinity is undivided and indivisible; so also is the human soul. We can profitably examine the points of a pedigree pig; length, head, shoulders, legs, back, markings, and so on; but as soon as we think in terms of life we have simply one live pig, and the expert judge is he who both knows all the detailed points and gains a very accurate opinion by a total examination of this whole integrated pig. What we have said about the essential correlation of final succour and absolute demand applies to all the elements in the Christian concept of God. A saint is one whose living religion contains all these elements in the right proportions *for him*, and within sanctity these five elements are synthetic; the whole is something very much more than the sum of its parts. But in spatial-temporal life, such synthesis is only attained by analysis; we might, by divine fiat, vocation, or election, suddenly find ourselves in a loving embrace with Christ, but without this it is possible to learn to love. Only possible, however, if we first accept his succour and then surrender to his demand: the loving embrace of the soul with Christ only comes by first purging and unifying the subjective self in the Holy Ghost and then offering an objective adoration to the Father.

This basic Trinitarian scheme underlies all the ascetical writings of Christian spirituality, though it is presented in various ways and with different emphases. St Bonaventure bids us recollect the presence of God as (1) above, (2) around, (3) within. St Julian finds eternal truth and value in her hazelnut because God (1) made it, (2) loves it, (3) keeps it. A modern Christian writer like A. E. Taylor seeks God (1) simply as God, almost metaphysically, (2) in ethics, (3) in nature. The Oratorians' famous prayer form is based on the apprehension of Jesus (1) before the eyes, (2) in the heart, (3) in the hands, and this by common consent follows the opening petitions of the paternoster: (1) "Our Father" (transcendent in heaven), "hallowed be thy name" (in adoration), (2) "thy kingdom come" (in Christ and with Christ), (3) "thy will be done" (in the world, by the Spirit's immanence). I have not presumed to add anything to these or any other champions of ascetical orthodoxy, only to clarify their common acceptance of dogmatic theology and to reduce their art to some workable semblance of scientific order.

Secondly, in all this the Incarnate Son is the essential fulcrum or focus, the unifying principle of subjective and objective, immanent and transcendent, cognition and affective feeling. And this fulcrum, focus, or unifying principle is supplied ascetically by the Mass. This agrees with our "George-Mary" analogy of ascetical courtship and also with the principle of parochial microcosm. The first form of contemplation demands a focus, be it ant or alp. Christian purgation and unification need the focus of Christ who, as mediator between transcendent creator and immanent comforter, is the recapitulation of all ants and all alps and all things besides.

I would claim, therefore, that the only *pastoral* outlook which does justice to the Trinitarian concept of God ascetically, is the Remnant concept, because only here do we find the Body of Christ, parochial and microcosmic, as focus or fulcrum between the whole multitudinous creation and the Spirit indwelling all things. Multitudinism, with its stress on numbers of "church people", narrow ecclesiasticism, and preoccupation with the soteriological element simply does not do justice to God the Father as ontological and axiological other. It fails to realize that God is greater than his Church. And this is why multitudinists can advance no further than the ideal of a "good congregation". The exclusive sects similarly do injustice to the Fatherhood of God, while their emphasis on the Spirit's indwelling can only spell a kind of ascetical polytheism, however much they deny it in doctrine. Finally, the all-pervading individualism of both manages to overstress and underrate the *complete* immanence of the Holy Ghost at the same time; it exaggerates his personal indwelling and forgets his all-pervading omnipresence.

Thirdly, there is an interconnection of our scheme with moral theology. The theological virtues bear ascetical resemblance to the Trinity: *faith*, as faith-venture, is activity towards God the Father, transcendent and unseen; *hope* is the result of the indwelling Paraclete—hope is *comfort*, and ἀγάπη ἐν χρίστῳ is the focus and synthesis of both. In very general terms the pessimist knows not the Spirit, the faithless forgets the Father, and love is impossible except in Christ. From there we deduce that the cardinal virtues are attained by the Demand-Succour synthesis given us in the Incarnate Son, that the first six "gifts of the Spirit" depend upon our ascetical notion of the Father's ontological and axiological otherness, while Ghostly strength—the seventh—implies a Prayer life in the Holy Spirit.[1]

Negatively, the ascetical attack upon the capital sins may be safely sustained by the application of the Rule of the Church as it corresponds with Trinitarian doctrine. To reduce the capital sins to their threefold division, pride of life seems to be associated with an over-rational preoccupation with God's ontological otherness and a failure to perceive his axiological otherness. Spiritual pride means over-subjective mystical feeling in an isolated Spirit; even a personal polytheistic Spirit. Lust of the flesh results from all eudemonistic tendencies which we have unearthed, and Lust of the eyes, ascetically, might be combated by purgation and recollection with Christ as focus.

This correlation of ascetic and moral theology is obviously important, for if moral theology is the applicable *test* for spiritual progress, then the pastoral answer to sin must surely be ascetical rather than ethical. Spiritual health is obviously coupled with moral health, but invariably sins—even root sins like pride, envy, anger, etc.—are often not distinguished from spiritual diseases—eudemonism, Puritanism, quietism, legalism etc.—which are even more radical. All we wish to make clear is that sins are the particular symptoms of spiritual ill-health, and here ascetic presents itself as the combatant of

[1] Cf. St John of the Cross, *Ascent of Mount Carmel*, Book 2, Cap. 6.

Sin. It is true that the existence of human free-will implies a direct fight against sin, but this without ascetic is not only Pelagian but notoriously inadequate. The position here stated is set out by Dr Kirk:

". . . among the principal rules of life advocated by Christian ethics are some which have no place in other systems— *rules directed towards obtaining, preserving and developing that grace without which the normal rules of conduct cannot be observed.* It is true no doubt that this grace can be gained by no mere human effort; it is something wholly from without; but man can so rule and order his life as to open it out to divine influence, and to give that influence the fullest possible scope when once it has been received. It is in the supreme emphasis laid upon this principle that Christian ethics differs from every other system."[1]

The principle to which Dr Kirk is paying tribute is that although we are to make volitional battle against sins, our most potent weapon is the Rule of the Church.

[1] *Some Principles of Moral Theology*, pp. 18–19.

18

THE RULE OF THE CHURCH:
(i) THE OFFICE

IF WE reduce the Rule of the Church to its simplest terms, we have a scheme which presupposes the soul's encounter with God as a Wardian duality-in-unity experience; the "subject-object—George-Mary" analogy. And this agrees with the simplest interpretation of the Trinitarian formula. The psychological attitude implied by the recitation of the Office is a self-sacrificing, objective offering to God the transcendent Father. In private prayer—meditation, recollection, self-examination and so on—we are receiving the love of God by way of surrender to the power of the Paraclete immanently indwelling. In the centre of the Mass we aspire to communicate with the Christ in a mutual loving embrace. But these emphases vary, and as only the Saints perfected in the Church triumphant can live in an eternal, mutual, loving adoration, the best we can do is to try to retain a balance throughout temporal life. Even with the Saints of the militant Church, a perfect union with God is only attained in momentary fragments of time, and even here it will degenerate into either a subjective mysticism or a mechanical transcendentalism without the balancing discipline of Rule.

The Rule of the Anglican Church can be summarized as consisting of (1) *the Office*, which is the corporate worship of the Body of Christ to the Father, or, as Richard Meux Benson puts it, "The prayer of Jesus to His Father through His Body". And this is a twofold Office "daily throughout the year". (2) *The Mass* is the loving embrace of Christ in joy, attained by the synthesis of his complete succour offered and his absolute demand accepted. And it is stipulated on some seventy-five days of the year (the Red Letter days) when a special collect, epistle, and gospel are supplied. (3) *Private prayer* concerns the sanctification of the individual soul by the indwelling spirit, to the glory of God.

Before we consider these three items from the ascetical viewpoint, two small points are to be noted. Firstly, that in terms of time or quantity (1) is, strictly speaking, invariable; (2) the Mass is variable by addition, and possibly by a slight subtraction—this will be discussed below; and (3) private prayer is infinitely variable according to the needs and gifts of different souls. Thence secondly, we have not only a subjective-objective, or immanent-transcendent, balance, but also an individual-corporate balance. The same warning about analysis applies in that all Christians are unique souls at all times, and also that it is impossible to be an "individual" Christian at any time. But in short, and for analytical purposes, we may say that (1) emphasizes the corporate aspect almost to the point of individual abnegation; (3) emphasizes the glorious uniqueness of each individual soul; and (2) synthesizes these in being not only essentially *corporate* but also essentially *social*. Here is an ascetical expression of the Catholic ideal of Order without uniformity; "Variety in unity is the principle of Christendom", wrote St Peter of Cluny.

This conception of Rule as a threefold system, an interconnected framework, might be illustrated by the idea of a fence. We are constructing a fence—to keep the devil out of the garden of the soul—for the disciples of St Thérèse who like such pictures. This carefully constructed fence of the spiritual life is built around a series of big strong posts, firmly embedded in the ground, and placed at regular intervals; these represent the Mass, which acts as the central support of all else. A more numerous series of smaller stakes, embedded in the ground and placed at more frequent intervals between the main posts are the Offices. Finally there are a number[1] of horizontal, parallel cross-pieces which may vary in number, size, strength, or material, which link up the verticals and which are dependent upon them; this is private prayer.

[1] Essentially four horizontal strands: see Chapter 21.

Now we may say that the ground into which the vertical posts and stakes sink directly is the solid corporate whole—the very "ground", the "common ground" of humanity—the solidarity of the race, and so these are of *direct* corporate significance. The cross-pieces are parallel and individual; they vary in infinite ways, materials, strengths, etc., but nevertheless attain indirect corporate significance in being supported by Mass and Office. In other words, private prayer may be as varied as the soul requires. But it (here literally) falls to the ground without the support of the corporate liturgy. Conversely, once all this variable prayer of varying souls does become supported by the corporate liturgy of the Church it reaches the ground indirectly through this liturgy, and so becomes of corporate and social significance.[1]

This analogy offers a useful illustration of the correlations between these three elements of the Rule of the Church. The Mass stands firm enough, but alone it is not a fence at all. It might be suggested that these posts could be placed so close together that an impenetrable wall would result: daily Mass by itself. But such a wall would be less strong than one comprising a scientific network of strains and stresses both vertical and horizontal. Each Mass, moreover, would be isolated from the whole life—a series of pools against a flowing stream. The Office alone would be open to the same objections, and prone to a general weakness. And private prayer alone, as we have seen, "falls to the ground". This analogy may also be used to tell us a little about *proportions*, that is the interrelated frequencies here suggested by the wisdom of the Church. In such a context mathematics is apt to become a little ridiculous,

[1] "The Church's whole life is thus, as it were, a contemplation by her of the Father through the eyes of her glorified Head, and her Liturgy, her social action and the prayers of her members—whether they individually ascend to the mystical heights or remain on the lower levels of ascetical prayer—are the various modes in which it is manifested and the various components that go to make it up. What belongs to one belongs to all, and the peculiar graces of the mystic—his illuminations, and his sufferings as well—are given to him not merely for his own sake but for the sake of all his brethren. And he in his turn is aided by every act that they perform in faith, hope and love." E. L. Mascall, *Christ, the Christian and the Church*, p. 219.

but it is just worth noting that the mind of the Church infers a yearly Rule of 75 communions and 730 Offices, or, very roughly, ten acts of objective offering as preparation for the Mass: in terms of time, two hours of objective giving in preparation for the loving embrace of Christ in communion. Without actually sinking into the absurdity of treating souls as mathematical theorems, we may usefully remind ourselves that the Church has something to say about the distance between the main fence posts and the number of smaller stakes between them. The Mass alone possesses within itself an inherent subjective-objective balance—therefore it may be varied by addition according to the state, type, and *attrait* of individual souls. But, geometry aside, we can safely deduce from the experience of the Church that daily Mass with no Office at all, or with only a minute or two's objective recollection of the Transcendent Father is liable to end in a sentimental Christ-mysticism. And daily Offices with thrice-yearly communion and no prayer can only spell legalism. Private prayer may well be used as an individual balancer; a fence of a single horizontal strand may be quite adequate and efficient in some cases, while others will need many closely spaced strands. All souls will vary as to objective and subjective needs according to temperament and emphasis; but the Rule of the Church suggests a basic mean which we disregard at our peril.

For the faithful the obligatory Rule of the universal Church is entirely acceptable in its own right. Here is joy in simple obedience, without an intricate system of ascetical reasons. But it is worth remarking on the wisdom which dictates three or four consecutive communions at Christmas, Easter, and Whitsuntide: the corners of our fence which need extra strengthening by three or four big posts in close proximity. By the Red Letter Saints' Days rigid mathematics is rightly over-ruled by the real humanity of the Body of the Lord. Here is the sublime ascetical counterpart of the Christian principle of order without uniformity. In short, frequency of communion or other liturgical prayer cannot be a purely personal choice because the Church at least has something to say about it. But the very Rule of the Church is in opposition to formalism. And this incidentally pays homage to the fact of human "periodicity" and shows up the inadequacy of a "Sunday" rule without observation of the "Red Letter Days".

It is hoped that this simple analogy, in conjunction with the subject-object, or "George-Mary" analogy will help to bring some sort of pattern to our spiritual activity. It might serve as the outline of a spiritual map to guide our journey. The irrefragable fact remains that our religion is healthy and our direction is safe when we keep comfortably near to the Rule of the Church. But—and this qualification is vital—*the tripartite Rule must be interpreted ascetically.* Maintaining all the reserve about the processes of analysis, we must now give some consideration to each of its aspects in turn.

The Office is *opus Dei* of St Benedict, the objective prayer of the Church of Christ to the Father, and it is the foundation of corporate religion; the ascetic mediator between private devotion and the Mass and between the Mass and devotion recollected in life. In essence it is corporate, and its volitional emphasis is objective. Throughout the whole Christian tradition, excepting only the odd century of Puritanism and Deism, the be all and end all of the Church's Office is *praise.* The Church's experience and example regarding the Office is perhaps best summarized by that interesting seventeenth-century Benedictine, Fr Augustine Baker. He describes three clear-cut stages in the art of reciting the Office, and these are worth quoting at some length. For the sake of exposition, and clarification of my own position in this context, I have taken the liberty of using italics freely.

In the "*first degree*", which we may call the subjective or elementary stage, "there is an attention of express reflection on the words and sense of the sentence pronounced by the tongue or revolved in the mind. Now this attention being, in vocal prayer, necessarily to vary and change according as sentences in the Psalms, etc., do succeed one another, cannot so powerfully and efficaciously fix the mind and affections on God, because they are presently to be recalled to new considerations or succeeding affections. . . ." That is, we are engrossed in subjective ruminations on the meaning of the words. "*This is the lowest and most imperfect degree of attention,* of which all souls are in some measure capable, and the more

imperfect they are the less difficulty there is in yielding it. . . ."
The italics are mine, but the meaning surely is that the author
regards this "think what you are saying" idea as a definite
temptation and *fault*. "For souls that have good and established
affections to God can hardly quit a good affection by which
they are united to God, and which they find gustful and
profitable for them, to exchange it for a new one succeeding
in the Office; and if they should, it would be to their
prejudice."[1]

It is to be noted that Fr Baker does not hesitate to refer to
the "gustful profit" (of the next degree). This, it might be
argued, is a subjective element. It is inevitably so, since we
cannot avoid some subjective element in all (duality-in-
unity) experience, nor can we give Godwards without his
divine love giving back a thousandfold. But this, as we shall
see presently, is the joy of objective offering attained by
objective emphasis of will. It is obviously not a subjective
search for consolation in words by discursive sentiments.

"*The second degree* is that of souls *indifferently well practised
in internal prayer*,[2] who, coming to the reciting of the Office,

[1] *Holy Wisdom*: The Third Treatise, Sec. 1, Cap. ii, para. 12 (ed. Abbot
Sweeny, 1950, p. 347).

[2] A word of explanation is needed here. Like most of his contemporaries, Fr Baker is very vague in his use of terms; to him religious
"extroversion" is an almost unqualified evil (op. cit.), "introversion"
is an unqualified good and is the "internal prayer" of the Contemplative religious Orders. There is a strong emphasis upon solitude of a
rather egotistical kind (op. cit., pp. 135, 152, and *passim*), and a pane-
gyric of the Egyptian Fathers (op. cit., pp. 166 ff.); which seems
strange from a Benedictine. On the other hand, this "internal prayer"
is denied to no state within the world. Even "simple women" are
capable of it (op. cit., pp. 135 ff.), and secular ecclesiastics certainly are!
(Pp. 137 ff.) In short, all Fr Baker is really guilty of is an ambiguity
tending to active-Contemplative and religious-secular duality. In other
places this "internal prayer" is simply that dependent on grace and
controlled by the Holy Spirit; and discursive meditation and "vocal
prayer", though elementary stages, seem to be part of it. In any case,
what we are calling objective worship is the true end and is not contrary
to "internal prayer". Fr Baker is certainly no religious introvert in the
popular modern sense. The result of internal or Contemplative prayer is
simplicity of soul, constant recollectedness, and hence the Contemplation
—objectively—of God. The only conclusion I wish to draw here is that

and either *bringing with them* or by occasion of such reciting
raising in themselves an efficacious affection to God, do desire
without variation to continue it with as profound a recollectedness as they may, not at all heeding whether it be suitable
to the sense of the present passage which they pronounce.
This is an attention to God, though not to the words, and is
far more beneficial than the former. And therefore to oblige
any souls to quit such an attention for the former would be
both prejudicial and unreasonable. For since all vocal prayers,
in Scripture or otherwise, were ordained only to this end, to
supply and furnish the soul that needs with good matter of
affection, by which it may be united to God, a soul that hath
already attained to that end, which is union as long as it
lasts, ought not to be separated therefrom, and be obliged to
seek a new means till the virtue of the former be spent."[1]

Fr Baker's third degree is a synthesis of these two: "the
most sublime degree of attention", and "happy are those souls
(of which God knows the number is very small) that have
attained to this third degree, the which may be ascended to
*by a careful practice of the two former in their order, especially of
the second degree!*"

In our pastoral-parochial context we need hardly quote
more, but some further examination of this second or ordinary
degree is necessary. Three points now arise for consideration:
(1) This third degree is simply contemplative adoration. The
second is an attempt at objective worship; the apparent stress
on interior or subjective feeling is countered by the aim of
recollected "attention *to* God". Fr Baker, like all Contemplatives tends to sound subjective, but we must always realize
that Contemplatives do rightly feel a good deal as the result
of affective states won by rigorous discipline in purgation and
recollection. Much ambiguity vanishes, here and in other
writers, when we remember that Contemplation is objective
although attained through "internal prayer"—*self*-discipline,
self-examination,   *self*-purgation,   *self*-surrender—again   an

to be "*indifferently well practised in internal prayer*", even in the
context of *Sancta Sophia*, is not too great an ambition. It might fairly
be interpreted as "having had some practice in the art of Recollection".

[1] Op. cit., p. 348; see also ibid. for "third degree".

active spiritual battle. And "union" here means obviously a union of subject and object—that is, some volitional *rapport* with God, and not necessarily the close integrated union of an "embrace". What Fr Baker attacks is the reducing of the Office to a series of discursive meditations; he is the last person in the world to find the twenty-third psalm, as part of an Office, "so comforting".

(2) ". . . bringing with them . . .". Recollection tends to simplify the soul, whereby we come to the Office "bringing with us" an attitude of attention. This implies an emphasis on will, not on feeling. Thus the discipline of private prayer acts as training in what we can call both the art and science of the Office. We can therefore contemplate, meditate, yield to, read about, and generally think about, just God, and "bring with us", to the Office, as worthy a conception as possible of just God—which if it is in any possible sense worthy will be largely negative and wholly incomprehensible; and this supplies the first of our five elements—ontological otherness. And "at these times, therefore, let us give praise to our creator for His just judgements".[1] Here worth and personality—in a word, value—supply our second elemental need, axiological otherness.

(3) We are to attain to the third degree—perfect Contemplation—whether in this life or the next "*by a careful practice of the two former in their order, especially of the second degree!*" The inference here is that we are to practise the first degree until we have gained a familiarity with it, until we know the Office and the psalms by heart; that is the obvious first step without which the second is meaningless. This is of great practical importance, since it means that our Office must be familiar and invariable, there must be a real sense of the mechanical, even of boredom, if the second or normal stage is to be attempted. Thus, ascetically speaking, all such experiments with permitted deviations and variations such as those proposed by the 1928 Prayer Book are insupportable; they are either reducing the Office to a nondescript "church service" or they are making its objective recitation impossible. I would finally add that having attained such familiarity, we are in a

[1] *Rule of St Benedict*, Cap. xvi.

position to try to achieve Fr Baker's "second-degree"—and the Church's norm. Fr Baker makes it sound difficult; it *is* difficult; but it is a little more creative to begin by doing the right thing badly than by doing the wrong thing well.

But supposing we—even the Remnant—are quite familiar with, and healthily bored by, the Office; can we then translate Fr Baker's ideal from these rather high-sounding affective terms into something the parochial Remnant can at least approach? The answer may be suggested by the following analogy.

A very small girl has a father who is incomprehensible to her inasmuch as his work, interests, and processes of thought are quite beyond her understanding; she regards him with a sense of ontological otherness. But he has also worth and value; whatever his work he is clever, whatever his interests he is kind, and the child is dependent upon him. He is possessed of an axiological otherness. From these a love evolves, and this is a matter of cognition, feeling, and, more immediately, conation. In other words, the little girl's love goes out to her father actively; and the more cognition and feeling for him, or the greater the experience of him, the greater the love. This love is conatively translated into a desire to be with him, a desire to love, know, and serve, and here especially a desire to *give*. In terms of a sacramentalism which is inevitable, this aspect of giving must be expressed in a practical way. The girl wishes to give her father a present, and she faces two difficulties. First of all she has nothing to give, she has no money to buy a gift, and if she had it would have come from her father in the first place—which seems unsatisfactory to her. Secondly, the child's father is so incomprehensible, so perfect, so self-sufficient that she has not the slightest idea what kind of present would please him, although she has a strong notion that the general intention would meet with his approval. Now the girl's only solution to these problems is to consult someone whom she can trust, someone who is richer and more knowledgeable than herself, someone a little nearer to her father yet also a little nearer to her; a mediator between them. So she goes to the only person fulfilling these qualifications, who is her mother.

Her mother is helpful and understanding, and in due time she gives the father's present to her daughter to pass on to him. This will be a real act of giving, it is a practical conative action springing from the depths of a loving and obedient heart. The Puritan would say that this thought, this affective emotion is in itself enough, that father does not really mind about the gift at all, that it is the inner love, dutiful obedience, and so on which really count. But this would only break the child's heart, for she is a sacramental being and the giving of a solid, visible, tangible *thing* is of the first importance to her. Suppose the gift which the mother has produced is an ounce of tobacco, at sight of which the child is dubious and disappointed. It does not seem to be very useful or attractive, it feels nasty, smells nasty, and looks nasty; one cannot wear it, play with it, or make anything with it, and it is positively horrible to eat. What on earth can father *do* with it? Does he really want it? Will he really enjoy or even accept it? Would not a puppy or some pretty ribbons or a nice lollipop have been much more suitable? Presumably not—because the father is an incomprehensible, transcendent sort of a person and without doubt her mother knows best. So the gift is given objectively and selflessly and received with love; there is *rapport* and there is joy on both sides. It may well be that father *can* enjoy this stuff in some celestial way; possibly the child's little brother has given him a pipe and her baby sister a box of matches—all from the same source—but how are we to know that? Let us not bother to know unless we find such metaphysical speculation interesting, but in any case and in all cases, *trust mother*.

The inference here is plain; we are very small, weak, penniless, and ignorant children, but we can give good gifts to the Father in heaven when, and only when, we trust our Mother the Church.

At this point we cannot avoid certain domestic difficulties ensuing from Anglican liberty and prevailing custom; and much as the former may be upheld in general, the Office is the one part of Rule which demands rigidity.

The first and most fundamental difficulty is that the recitation of the Office—particularly in common—is in itself by far the most difficult ascetical feat demanded by the Church. Even as private rule, the Office needs much practice in recollection and attention, some training in the technique of objective *giving* in worship, and a grasp of the principle of obedience which is not easily learned. Such devices as Professor Emmet's "open space" notion are to be known and used if justice is to be done to the ontological and axiological otherness of the transcendent Father.[1] Above all, the office must be familiar and it cannot be too familiar; recitation must contain the mechanical element, rightly interpreted, because our whole attention and our whole will are firmly to be fixed on *God*. This mechanical element is essential because the Office is to be said rhythmically to counter distraction, and fairly fast to help maintain a tiring volitional effort. The ideal of "efficacious affection", of "union in the loving embrace", remains the ultimate goal of all prayer. Yet on the parochial level we can safely say that the less we feel the better; the Office is intrinsically unemotional. The less inspiring the words, the less exciting the discovery of the thick bushes, the very stupidity of the shoes over Philistia and the dullness of the Moabites and Hagarenes are all real aids to objectivity at this elementary stage. It is important that our little daughter dislikes the smell of the tobacco. The incomprehensible glory is that the more we can surrender to the Father and *give*, the more we submit to our mother and *push* Godward, *push* out the responses, *push* out the psalms and *push, push, push* at the colon pauses, then we come to love the Office so much—even the Moabites and Hagarenes. But it is the objective love of giving to the glory of God, the peace of surrender, and the freedom of service. If a priest is ever allowed a little despair, it is surely permissible when faced with the attitude: "Such a *helpful* service, Vicar, I must come to Evensong again."

[1] The Cambridge Stanton Lectures, 1951, on *Religious Language*. The point here is that if God is conceived as ontologically and axiologically transcendent, he cannot be focused in a symbol of attention. Our symbol thence becomes an "open space"—in the clouds if need be—*through* which the Office is directed; to be carried by Christ to the Father invisible and unimaginable.

15

In addition, the Office is essentially corporate, which makes it more difficult still. It demands "team-practice" drill. The plain implication, in flagrant opposition to prevailing custom, is that this, of all parts of Rule, is best left to the Remnant. The idea that Communion is for an esoteric élite, after which all are cordially invited to Matins and Evensong, is the complete reversal of tradition, ascetical science, and orthodox theology. And it might be borne in mind that although all corporate liturgy is ideally choral, the Office is so immensely difficult to say that it is—literally—the last thing to try to sing.

The second, essentially domestic, difficulty is that in the Office liturgical simplicity—and indeed loyalty—is of ascetical importance. It may well be argued that the Eucharist ought to be slightly variable with circumstance and locality; because it is sacramental it is also intensely local, whereby the expression of particular social aspirations and needs may have rightful place. The evolution of a specific group-mind may well find a worthy outlet in Eucharistic liturgy by the right sanction of local custom; at the very least, special intentions may fit local needs. But no such individualism is permissible to the Church's Office; to omit a psalm, add a collect, or alter a lesson is inexcusable. It is no less than selling father's tobacco and buying him a lollipop instead. Our personal improvement of the Office is no less than the same lollipop tied up with pretty ribbons—the gift mother knows that father does not want. In short, the Eucharist is the family meal, the Office is the parade ground.

In the Office therefore, the Church must dictate, which Anglicanism is ever loath to do. This tolerance is misguided, for the allowance of any alternatives and variations (even as in 1662, let alone the 1928 chaos) is putting an intolerable burden on loyalty rather than being lenient. The English Church is being kind to be cruel. In our analogy the little girl asks her mother for a present for her father because she does not want to be given a choice. Any such freedom undermines the essential objectivity of the Office itself. Meanwhile it is difficult for the loyal Anglican to decide what the Office is; we speak of an "introduction" and "State prayers" presumably as additions and not parts of the Office itself, while a series of alternative lectionaries intersperse it with extracts from 2 Chronicles (or 1 Kings) and Romans (or 2 Corinthians). All this demands a sequence of volitional gymnastics which the Saints would find difficult and the lay-Remnant impossible; which is unfair to those who only seek loyalty and obedience.

We can only continue to plead for an authorized, rather than merely customary, omission of confession and intercession from the Office proper—for important as these are, their place is in the more subjective portions of integrated Rule—and for a return of the invariable "short chapter". "Bible study", or, better, meditation on the Scriptures, is also of the first importance to Rule, but not in the middle of the objective Office! Meanwhile hope remains that some authority will come to the rescue, and the problem is surely not so difficult. All we ask is for an Office *from* the Church to offer *to* the Father; it does not matter so very much if it is in Greek, Latin, or Double Dutch so long as it is authoritative, definite, invariable, and objectively giveable.

This problem is of outstanding importance; of far more consequence to living religion than most of the topics at present causing so much heat and trouble. And in view of what happened in 1928, it is ironical that the English Reform aimed at simplicity in an Office which the laity could share.[1]

[1] The proposed Lectionary of 1956 is therefore a very slight improvement.

19

THE RULE OF THE CHURCH:
(ii) THE EUCHARIST

WE HAVE spent a long time on the Office because it is the most neglected element in the Church's Rule, and also because it is the most difficult to achieve. Whether the Office is neglected because in these days we are all inclined to subjectivism in religion, or whether this subjectivism reigns because the Office is neglected, it is difficult to say. The practical, pastoral, ascetical *answer* is plain enough anyway. The ascetical approach to the Eucharist is very much easier. And this is so for two related reasons: first, because doctrinally, metaphysically, and psychologically it is a glorious and finally incomprehensible mystery, thus we can think and will about it as much or as little as we like; and secondly, which is virtually the same thing from a different angle, because we can approach it in more than one way according to gifts and *attrait*. The Office is difficult because it is simple, direct, and demands a rigid order and single approach. The Mass is easier because it is more complex, and therefore more elastic. The Office demands a tremendous amount of disciplined effort while the sublime glory of the Eucharist is that, although it is the supreme mystery of the Church, men, women, children, and infants, priests, religious, professors, and illiterates—all these may here worship corporately, socially and differently. We may rightly speak of reciting the Office well or badly. Applied to Eucharistic worship these adverbs do not seem to fit. For this reason the Mass is and must be the ascetical centre of parochial Christianity, quite apart from theology, tradition, ethics, or anything else, however important.

Our Lord Jesus Christ said "Do this in remembrance of

me", which is almost the only direct imperative order he ever gave; and many simple (in the best sense of naturally Recollected, unified, and "once-born") souls are joyfully glad to obey. For these well-favoured ones, riding transcendently above the mundane clashes of intellectual and ecclesiastical conflict, there is no more to be said. Less happy souls, albeit still happier than most, are able to summon up acts of surrender at the time of the Mass and obey in a spirit of simple faith-venture. Liturgists may lose themselves in the eternal rhythm of the rite, and metaphysicians can worship here with something truly describable as the "intellectual soul"—faith-venture can be closely akin to intellectual venture. Some souls can pray the prayers of the Mass minutely, continually, and creatively; while children and aesthetes gape at colour, rhythm, and ceremony, doubtless seeing much more than most of us see. All these approaches, attitudes, volitions, thoughts, experiences, and even fancies, can be legitimate and worthy; this is the glory of the Mass, its supreme pastoral and parochial significance, its manifestation of the Glory and Goodness of God.

But ultimately the Mass is a direct act of God upon which the Church's very existence depends, and souls may well be content simply and faithfully to let him act. The one sure method of advancing in Eucharistic worship is to take part in it—and go on taking part in it.

Throughout this study I have tried to avoid a shallow anti-intellectualism. Pastoral ascetic is very much more than mere teaching, but that does not banish mind from the full religion of an integrated soul. There seems little point in burdening a soul with the metaphysics of the Chalcedonian Definition or the doctrine of the Trinity when it can grow in Christ and in the Trinity without such effort. But the Mass is unique in that a knowledge of its theology and liturgical history is of direct ascetical value. By such knowledge and recognition our living status within the Mystical Body is expressed and used.

This points to the important pastoral fact that if ascetic needs an intellectual balance within itself—if, according to Ward, cognition issues in intellection and is correlated to conation and feeling—then Eucharistic doctrine is the pre-eminent subject to teach. It is the most directly practical of all dogma, and if studied by the intellectually gifted, it can embrace the whole faith. I still insist, however, that true worship at the altar cannot ultimately depend upon such gifts; true discernment of the Lord's Body, and the soul's status within it, does not depend on mind. Indeed some very elementary ascetic may still be extremely useful.

The Mass is centred upon the Second Person of the Holy Trinity. That is obvious enough. We will also see that it is concerned with the basic elements of *complete succour* and *absolute demand*; and these synthesize in love. In other words, the Mass, as the extension of the Incarnation and Atonement of Jesus Christ, supplies our central ascetical focus or fulcrum just as Christ himself is our focus as mediator between the Father's transcendence and the Spirit's indwelling. God is both invisible other and omnipotent spirit, yet in Christ or by focusing our whole being on Christ, we see God, and grasp God.

The early tradition of the Church divides the Mass into two distinct portions, *missa catechumenorum*, which is the proclamation of the gospel in prayer, Scripture, and homily, and *missa fidelium* which is the consecration, oblation, and worship of the faithful: all of which leads to, and is consummated by, communion. The first portion, the proclamation of the Good News to hearers is largely (not wholly) concerned with our Lord's offer of Redemption and *succour*. And this leads on inevitably to an examination of the cost of such redemption and succour, which is the Cross. It is the Cross which makes upon us absolute *demand*. If such demand is conatively and volitionally accepted, if, that is, it is accepted in faith (*missa fidelium*), the result is thanksgiving and adoration. These we have seen become synthesized into joy and love: Holy Communion is our loving embrace with and in Christ, for in communion we are both giving and receiving *all* in an identical moment. This agrees with the rather more prosaic analysis of modern teaching, which divides the Mass into (i) preparation, (ii) consecration and communion, and (iii) thanksgiving. We can say, therefore, that if anyone needs a rough ascetical guide, we begin subjectively—rightly and with a clear conscience—by preparing ourselves for the joyous succour now to be offered. And this we may do by praying the prayers, listening to the Epistle and Gospel, or getting on by ourselves if we can. We may make little meditations on a particular verse or hold a private colloquy with the Holy Ghost. In any case we have infinitely more freedom than is permissible anywhere in the Office.

And then we make all the spiritual effort we can to pay the price—which is abject surrender; always a conative or volitionally *active* process. We empty ourselves to receive all, we give all to be full with God. Communion is as indescribable as love itself.

And the only end is objective thanksgiving, and—greater still—objective adoration: push, push, push.

If necessary, we can elaborate a stage further by preparing for an objective thrust, outward and Godward, at the moment of consecration—rather obviously at the elevations; and by allowing ourselves the luxury of inward colloquies and acts of love—even personal petitions of the right kind, immediately after communion.[1]

This kind of ascetical scheme—it is not the only kind—can now be summarized into six simple points:

(1) Preparation. (*a*) Remote, which is religious life in the Holy Trinity according to the Rule of the Church (of which this is the central focus). (*b*) Immediate: *missa catechumenorum*, acceptance of complete succour offered in Scripture (epistle and gospel and summed up in the Creed), thence offertory confession, absolution, self-surrender, or oblation.

(2) A single, volitional, active thrust of adoration at consecration and elevations.

(3) Communion.

(4) Post-communion colloquy.

(5) Objective thanksgiving, after the manner of the Office: thus the prayer of *thanksgiving, gloria in excelsis*, etc., should be made especially familiar (possibly in private prayer) and *given* rather than meditated upon.

(6) A resolve to return to (1) (*a*) in the power of Christ's indwelling.

---

[1] For what is possibly the best *ascetical* exposition of this, see Jeremy Taylor, *Holy Living*, Cap. iv, Sec. 10

This is little more than the briefest synopsis of Jeremy Taylor's exposition.

We have been reminded again, in the first and last of these points, that the Mass stands not alone but in the centre of a wider Rule. Yet these six points are seen to contain in themselves all the elements elucidated by Professor Farmer (Chapter 17). The Mass, in other words, is not Christocentric but Trinitarian; it begins with "Our Father" and ends with "the Peace of God", it is a balanced spiritual Rule in its own right.

So simple a scheme is of course inadequate for very long. It might almost be seen as practice for the future fuller development of integrated worship. Such analysis is like learning to dance by halting steps and numbers which in time issue in a connected rhythmic whole. Ascetical drill of this kind may be useful or even indispensable at the early stages, but we must always realize that the Mass is essentially one transcendent act; not a series of edifying prayers or psychological sensations. Ascetical or liturgical analysis is only allowable as a means to an end, and may be dangerous if the objective unity of the Eucharist is forgotten.[1]

But it may further be asked why, if the Mass is itself a balanced Rule, should we need to bother with Offices and meditations? Or what is the necessary relation between these three? Communion is our focus or fulcrum of balance, and if we take this idea of balance quite literally, the question is answered quite simply. Those entertainers who ride bicycles across tight-ropes maintain their balance by means of a pole—and it has to be a long pole. The Mass alone sends us off along the high wire armed with something the size of a cricket stump. If they had to rely on something so inadequate even experienced acrobats would *lose their balance*. The devout (and they assuredly are) who go to Mass daily, bother little about prayer, and never say an Office, are in precisely this danger; they are liable to become either formal and cold or eudemonistic. It is only when we continue the Mass in both directions, towards subjective meditation and prayer on the

[1] Since writing this an excellent, simple ascetical approach to the Mass has appeared in R. A. Knox, *A Retreat for Lay People*, pp. 168-73.

one hand and the objective Office on the other, that we equip ourselves with a long pole. That makes balancing much easier, and our spiritual journey much safer.

In the most general possible terms we have seen that the mediation of the Incarnate Christ is necessary if we are to avoid a transcendental deism or an immanental mystical mundaneness. If religion is to be progressive and creative, then it must—quite literally—have some point, it is plain that our whole spiritual life must revolve around a sacramental *focus*, which is the act of communion. If we seriously consider the *ascetical* necessity of a focal point, we at once see the need for a central crucifix on an altar in the centre of a building of basilican form; things fundamental to religion rather than "Churchmanship" or architecture.[1]

Similarly we can explain what are so often regarded as but the petty minutiae of liturgical tradition. Nothing should ever be placed with its back to the central cross: the missal is closed with its spine *outward*. The only exception is the priest himself on the occasions when he faces the people; this in turn gives ascetical value to the chasuble—which should be the same on both sides. Thus all the worshippers may be focused—visually and conatively—on either the altar cross or the intersection of the orphreys on the chasuble, whichever happens to be centrally visible at any particular time. And significantly indeed, this is but paying due regard to the first form of contemplation, the ascetical act of Recollection by "attention", which we have seen is the very starting point of disciplined religious activity. This in turn explains why the Mass is so suitable for the veriest babe in Christ and at the same time beyond the capacity of the Saints fully to achieve. We could go further to suggest that when, as here, the object of attention is the central cross or crucifix of an altar, the symbolic association can hardly fail to be purgation-succour-demand.

---

[1] This principle is illustrated by the traditional instructions to the would-be architects of the new cathedral at Coventry, who were advised to conceive an altar and put a church round it rather than build a church and put an altar in it; this, too, is basically religious rather than ecclesiological.

This fundamental ascetical emphasis on focus—and it is fundamental whether our focal object is a crucifix on an altar or a lily on a lawn—is the obvious root distinction between the Eucharist and a "service", between a church and an oratory. We might even say that the Mass is focused upon a point and the Office is offered up through an open space, an open space through which, infinitely far off, is God the Father. The one is focused upon God Incarnate—himself the supreme focal point, the other is offered by and through him to the Father transcendently other; to the Father unseen and unfocusable. Ultimately the open space is just a spiritual vacuum unless we place an altar in it, yet an intangible and unfocusable God is required by any worthy conception. Indeed, this is the God who became Incarnate and still becomes Incarnate on the altar. If this is forgotten, as it is bound to be if we neglect or mutilate the Office, then we are half way to Arianism, anthropomorphism, or worse.

One further point emerges. Obviously the focal point of the focal Mass is in all conceivable senses *central* to Christian spirituality at whatever stage of progress or maturity. This is neither theology, ethic, nor High Church propaganda, but ascetical common sense: the only possible conclusion when religion is treated as an active faith-venture rather than static complacence. But if our religious life is to be healthy, balanced, and creative, it must fill all of life, and be dominated by a rhythmic style, or series of cycles. And this has some bearing upon the frequency of communion or the frequencies of the focal points. The Mass is to be prepared for by both remote and immediate preparation, and the former is but the rest of the Rule of the Church. Also, the Mass is to be continued, or carried out into the world until the next Mass is celebrated. The distance between communions, therefore, is important because upon it depends the whole tempo of our spiritual rhythm, which rightly varies with individual souls. We cannot be mathematical, but the need for meditative prayer and the Office would naturally tend to vary in proportion to frequency of communion. In other words, if any aspect of Rule is emphasized or neglected, the whole spiritual tone is involved. If the Mass by itself is a little dangerous, then the Mass out of all proportion to private prayer and the objective Office is something to be guarded against, if our Eucharistic worship is really to be in the centre of *life*; if we are to be, in Dr Mascall's phrase "liturgical men". In no other way can our everyday psychological experience become the experience of religious men: become, that is, "religious experience". All we are here saying, in terms of ascetical direction, is that daily communion is no necessary or inevitable ideal for all souls at all times. And conversely a rule of thrice-yearly communion is hardly defensible, since one cannot begin seriously to make preparation for Christmas communion on Whit Monday. It is interesting to see how even Jeremy Taylor, presupposing some such scheme, is forced into a dangerously subjective, ethical view of the communicant's "worthiness". St Paul's emphasis in 1 Corinthians 11 is surely on faith—the "discernment" of the Lord's Body—rather than ethics or psychology; and both depend upon the ascetical discipline within the rhythmic Rule of the Church. So the Church's framework of weekly communion, with an all-round quickening of tempo at the three great festivals and some score of Red Letter Days, suggests a greater wisdom than is sometimes admitted.

THE RULE OF THE CHURCH:
(iii) PRIVATE PRAYER

IN ONE particular sense there is clearly no such thing as private prayer. Here I refer to that important part of the spiritual life which the soul pursues in private, and, in the purely physical sense, alone. This, we have noticed, is the infinitely variable portion of the Rule of the Church, and although discipline and order are vital here as elsewhere, such discipline and order may rightly vary from soul to soul according to individual *attrait*, gifts, temperament, and material circumstances. This freedom of individuality is legitimate so long as the primary truth is not forgotten: that every prayer, however subjective in form, every self-examination, confession, personal petition, and intercession is only of value in that it adds to the prayer of the Mystical Body, and so is part of the total prayer of the Church.

This aspect of the Rule of the Church begins with a recognition of the uniqueness of all human souls, and thus it is that part of the ascetical ethos where the art of direction may take precedence over its science. It is a contradiction in terms to speak of a scientific system pertaining to the unique, because what is unique cannot be systematized. I therefore accept the living tradition of the Church which is embodied in the writings of her Saints and which is to be discovered empirically, whether by priest or layman, only in a disciplined life of prayer within this living tradition; that is, by the practice of the Rule of the Church, together with devout experiment.

Nevertheless there is the necessity for further inquiry, and our immediate task can be set down under four heads: (1)

Private prayer must be placed within the framework of the Church's Rule; it must be specifically correlated with the Office and the Mass. (2) Whether or not private prayer includes what is sometimes called spiritual reading, it is based upon the spiritual experience of the Saints, and although, as Archbishop Goodier says, "the diversity of the Saints baffles analysis", they are normally studied in various schools according to some pronounced outlook or emphasis. Even in private prayer therefore we can look for the aid of some modicum of ascetical science. (3) If meditation is to take its rightful place in the centre of *modern* private prayer, it must be raised from either authoritative credulity or mere piety to some sort of epistemological status in its own right. (4) Prayer must be carried out into the life of the world, or even carried out *in* the life of the world. We must accordingly make some study of the ascetical possibilities of modern life, work, and environment. We do not believe that these are wholly adverse. We will take these four points in order.

(1) *Correlation with the Rule of the Church*

Although it would be against the spirit of Christian spirituality to reduce Rule to meticulous detail; it is nevertheless worth pointing out that Office-Mass-"private" prayer is the tripartite Rule in its ideal order. Five minutes' preparation by way of Recollection before the morning Office, followed by Mass and meditation; recollection throughout the day, and the evening Office followed by the other necessary parts of private prayer such as self-examination, thanksgiving, petition and so on—this constitutes an ideal scheme according to the experience of the Church, psychological emphases, and ascetical theory. Most souls find such a succession one in which not only do the various aspects of Rule follow on naturally, but also volitional energy is demanded in decreasing scale; which is only the common-sense arrangement of doing the most difficult jobs first and leaving the easier ones until the end of the day. But in pastoral practice much will depend upon practical circumstances. On the other hand, it should be noticed that here is an example of the equally fundamental principle that Rule, rather than being a pious burden, is largely advocated because it makes everything easier. And here two small points are worth a little extra emphasis. First, that whatever the circumstances, any period of private prayer should begin with prayer of "Office type": that is with a collect, canticle, or psalm objectively given to the transcendent Father. A paternoster objectively given, "Office-wise", followed by another paternoster subjectively prayed, would constitute a repetition, but the very antithesis of a vain one. Not only does such a simple rule maintain balance, but the majority of souls find the Office naturally preparatory to private prayer—that is, it makes private prayer easier. If the Office has not been recited in full and in common by a particular soul, some part of the Office for the day—collect, psalm, etc.—forges some real link with the Church corporate. Secondly, it must be made quite clear that any corporate parochial scheme whereby Mass precedes the Office is ascetically indefensible.

The corollary to this private prayer-Rule relation is the modern pastoral implication of Fr Augustine Baker's "first degree" method of reciting the Office, in which "there is an attention or express reflection on the words and sense of the sentence pronounced by the tongue or revolved in the mind". Now this "first degree" is a prolegomena to, or elementary practice for, proficiency in the "second" or "normal degree". In other words, we cannot recite the Office correctly until it is wholly familiar, and this process, in modern secular life, is likely to take a very long time—two or three years of daily recitation is not too long for "first degree" preparation. It seems sensible, therefore, to shorten this period—with anything less than daily recitation the time factor would become hopelessly unwieldy—by bringing portions of the Office right over into "private" prayer. As in our simple example of the two paternosters, each portion of the Office might be used both as preparatory "Office-type" prayer, before private prayer, and it might also be prayed within private prayer. Such practice could reduce Fr Baker's preliminary "first degree" to a few months and would help to attain the fullness of his "second degree" method.

For this, collects, canticles, responses, and psalms should be familiar enough to suggest a specific gift to God without discursive thinking about the words themselves. Within the context of private prayer such portions of the Office may be subjected to discursive consideration as much as need be; and the Offices contain wonderful material for such prayer. Correlation in the converse direction, from Office to private prayer, also occurs when the Holy Ghost insists on breaking through some particular part of a psalm or lesson. This is always happening, and such verses or stories are obvious subjects for our private meditations; but *not* during the Office! Such inspirations, when ideas seem almost to jump out of the Scriptures into our hearts, are to be accepted with thanksgiving, and firmly shelved until the Office is over and we have opportunity to turn them into private, meditative prayer.

The same principle applies, and more easily applies, to the Eucharist. The prayers of oblation, thanksgiving, and the Gloria in excelsis are objective, Office-type prayers; while the rest, notably the prayer for the Church, the prayer of humble access, and the consecration prayer may most worthily be prayed privately. And this is as good a place as any to state the all too obvious yet frequently forgotten fact that any liturgical confession presupposes a methodical self-examination prior to the rite. Such self-examination therefore forms an item in any daily rule of private prayer.

Finally under this head, the whole Rule—Office, Mass, private prayer—is welded together by the principle of periodic or actual recollection. This is the disciplined attempt at actual recollection of the Presence of God throughout the day. Although but a momentary experience, it both links and has an obvious link with, the Office, the Mass, and the resolution which concludes meditation. We need not discuss the matter in detail: so long as recollection is practised it does not matter very much how; recollection by means of the Jesus Prayer of Eastern Orthodoxy, by daily successes and failures, by clock-time or the divisions of occupation, or by grace at meals—all these are variously useful to different souls. But if this last means is used it should be recollection within Rule rather than an outmoded convention of Victorian piety.

(2) *"Private" prayer and ascetical science*

Direction in private prayer is an intensely individual thing, which presupposes an accentuation upon art over science. But a modicum of scientific background is desirable as a fundamental framework, and this is supplied by the Church's tripartite Rule. This Rule itself is the prime safeguard to spiritual health, and yet private prayer, with its intrinsic freedom and variability, may be usefully employed as a subsidiary balance. Even where the Rule is kept with sincerity and obedience, each part of it will be more or less difficult to achieve according to *attrait* and temperament. The conventional and formally minded will accept an ordered recitation of the Office with easy pleasure, the more emotionally inclined will spend happy hours in meditation and recollection while the Office may be burdensome. This is the roughest possible illustration, yet clearly private prayer can help to save *attrait* from too great a freedom, and obedience from too much formality; it could be a useful subsidiary balance wherein individual faults may be corrected.

The scientific groundwork here implied is that already deduced from our examination of Trinitarian doctrine, and it will be sufficient to concentrate upon the five elements necessary to the Christian conception of God discussed above. The omission, under emphasis, or difficulty regarding any of these is countered by stressing the relevant aspect of the Rule; thus, for example, the first step needed by the inherent subjectivist is frequent recitation of the Office, and direction in Office-type prayer—Fr Baker's "second degree". But it should be clearly understood that despite our persistent argument against over-intellectual teaching, there has been no animadversion on the right use of reason as inherent in direction; one can think ascetically as well as one can think dogmatically. Thus, in the example given above, the recitation of the Office may be raised from a mere formal obedience to a creative offering, implying joy. By such prayer form, meditations and even reading—even teaching—may bring out a religious awareness of the ontological and axiological otherness of God.

This brings us to the question of some working classification, not of the Saints, who are unclassifiable, but at least of the main schools within Christian spirituality. The Saints themselves are unclassifiable under any such scheme as this simply because they *are* Saints; because, that is, we can find in them no flagrant omissions from the full Christian conception of God. The classification of spiritual schools thus depends not upon under- or over-emphasis of any necessary element, but upon *attrait* within balance. This distinction brings us to a point of overriding importance. We may safely say that the first axiom in ascetical direction is that souls are individually unique. In other words, although Christian spiritual health demands all five necessary elements and their many corollaries in a worthy idea of God, balance does not imply a uniform mathematical proportion: 20 per cent on each! We may truly say therefore that all the Contemplative Saints, such as the Spanish Carmelites or the modern Trappists, are "subjective" or "internal" or "interior" in *attrait*, yet none of them suffers from the disease we have called subjectivism. In similar vein, we may speak truly of the early Cistercian emphasis on, or *attrait* towards, the divine Humanity of Jesus (succour and demand), on Jesus the perfect worshipper (adoration) in the seventeenth-century French Oratorians; on the humanism of the Salesian school and the Rigorism of the Carmelites (succour and demand); of Thomist sacramentalism (immanence and transcendence) and the intellectual Order of the Victorines. But in all these we are not speaking of *over-*emphasis, even less of *omission*, but of the progressive development of "*attrait-within-balance*".

In short, we cannot speak abstractively of a balanced diet without reference to the health and constitution of the person concerned. In such a sense may corporate schools of prayer be classified roughly for purposes of direction. Such classification, however, is one of spirituality and can only be spiritually determined.

The issue here is that in parochial life undisciplined *attrait*— God-given indeed—is bound to issue in disease unless it is carefully nurtured by the Church corporate. And somewhere within the Church's historical tradition there are Saints and schools of similar *attrait* perfectly developed. There are also

16

Saints and schools of opposite *attrait* perfectly developed, which may well be employed when even a God-given emphasis has gone astray by undisciplined indulgence. The correct relation between the development of *attrait* and disciplined attention to its opposite elements provides what is perhaps the most difficult item in the art of pastoral direction. Taking an extreme example, we might suggest that the self-absorbed quasi-mystic might well concern himself with Karl Barth's commentary on Romans, and it would not harm Barth himself to pray with St Thérèse of Lisieux! But we would not suggest that the Little Flower should waste her time on Barth's *Romans*, because beneath her sugar-coated crust of apparent sentimentality, she sees God more transcendently other, more awesome, fearful, and rigorously just, than most of her transcendentalist critics will ever understand.

(3) *Private prayer and epistemology*

The ground and cornerstone of private prayer, even of the whole spiritual development, according to our Ward-Loyola synthesis, is meditation. This is a very wide term containing a great variety of types, methods, and techniques. The selection of the right form for a particular soul in a particular need is another example of directorial art which can never be wholly reduced to systematic science. But if meditation is the ground of private prayer, then the disciplined use of the imaginal is the ground of meditation. The imaginal is the first and most creative of the common "three points" of discursive methods, and the centre of most affective methods as well. Now within the Rule of the Church meditative prayer has a rightly, though not necessarily, subjective emphasis. Meditative prayer, therefore, is qualified by two things: subjective feeling—"religious experience"—and the imaginal, both of which are slightly suspect to the modern mind. Despite the prevalence of a shallow and often sentimental subjectivism, due, we repeat, to the neglect of the Office, any religious emotion is regarded by many people with open dread. This recoil is not wholly unhealthy, but it can be exaggerated to the point of rationalism, and also to superficiality—words like penitence, contrition, and humility, although primarily concerned with volition, usually imply some *feeling*. The right sort of penitence implies emotion just as surely as joy does, and our religion is incomplete without either.

And although in Ward, for example, the imaginal mediates between sense-experience and ideation in a fundamental psychological chain,[1] popular misuse continues to equate the imaginal with the false. The claim to have seen a ghost, or to have a headache, or to have left a non-existent hat on the 'bus is countered by the inference that we "have imagined it"; these things are but "figments of the imagination". Whether this suspicion is a throwback from rationalistic deism, or whether due to the advances of the mechanistic sciences, or simply to the religious reticence of the phlegmatic English, it is hard to tell. The fact remains that any discourse, instruction, or guidance in meditative prayer is apt to create an atmosphere of the false. With whatever sincerity or faith-venture we begin, the modern cultural ethos breaks in to suggest that we are indulging a little pious make-believe: it is "auto-suggestive", something from fairyland, rather "fishy".

This point of view is a perfectly reasonable one. From whatever source it springs, and whatever the philosophical ramifications in particular cases, the advance in the concept of reason can be nothing but healthy. It is certainly an improvement on the medieval conception of directorial authority and blind obedience. So if meditative prayer—albeit of forms culled from the Saints—is to have its proper place in the centre of modern devotion, it is the first duty of ascetical theology to present it as reasonable. This task we will attempt under three headings. First, we will have to take one more look at "religious experience" within the context of mental prayer. Secondly, we consider the epistemological status of the experience we call, and frequently miscall, imagination. Thirdly, if the subject matter of most of our meditative prayer consists of odd extracts from literature nineteen centuries old, then the reasonableness of such an exercise depends largely upon a philosophy of history. The only proviso I wish to make

---

[1] "From the senses to the imagination and from this to the intellect —such is the order of life and of nature", *Psychological Principles*, p. 178.

is that our subject is still ascetical theology and not metaphysics; moreover it is *pastoral* ascetic. Our aim, in other words, is to help the modern mind—in parity with the modern soul—to see the traditional process of meditative prayer as not only orthodox but intellectually reputable. There is no particular reason why we should not place our inquiries in a theological setting which the pure metaphysician could hardly allow. If we help the modern Christian to be more comfortable about mental prayer, we have fulfilled our purpose. We are still concerned with the parochial Remnant, not with the agnostic philosopher.

(a) *"Religious experience"*

Archbishop Temple's definition "that religious experience is but the ordinary experience of religious men", is not only valuable in itself but it also points to the principle of recollection; an important item in any rule of private prayer. To the Saint the whole experiential continuum of his life is "religious experience"; and the degree with which specifically religious feelings such as contrition, praise, dependence, thanksgiving and so on, attach themselves to our everyday experience is the degree of sanctity which we have attained. As the beloved is constantly in the heart of the lover, so is God in the heart of his Saints, whether they are reciting Offices, peeling potatoes, ploughing, eating, or washing-up. And this is achieved by disciplined recollection. Recollection of self and recollection of God at thrice-daily or more frequent intervals is simply the quest for religious experience or the quest for God in ordinary experience. Such recollection, practised methodically within the framework of Rule, tends in time both to connect Mass, Office, and private prayer, and also to expand into continuous recollection: God becomes firstly "in the back of our minds" and in our hearts, all through each day.

Let us now examine a piece of fairly simple visual sense-experience: what Ward calls "subject-object", "duality-in-unity experience", or Tennant the "sensum-sensatio" relation, or what we may call simply "seeing a tulip"—a rather exotic one if need be, yellow with crimson edges flecked with white. If the subjects of this experience are a botanist, an artist, and St Francis of Assisi, we may say that these three experiences are identical in one sense and quite different in another. They are, in Dr Temple's definition, quite ordinary experiences, and in Ward's teaching they are unified experiences because all experience is unified; we can only divorce subject from object by analysis. But these three experiences infer different emotional reactions, which can be roughly distinguished as "How interesting", "How beautiful", and "Glory be to God". The last is both ordinary experience and also religious experience. The whole difference between St Francis and ourselves is that to him all experience is religious whether it begins with hearing, smelling, tasting, feeling, or seeing; whether the sensible object is an exotic tulip or a decaying cabbage, an alp, an ant, or a lump of wood: each manifests the glory of God. But to us such "religiousness" enters into everyday experience only rarely, and then by a disciplined, volitional act of recollection.

What may be called the religious reality, or rather the outward sign, or hallmark of the religious reality, of such experience, consists not in the subjective emotion, or in the tulip, but in the spontaneous outburst of praise. This is the certain fruit of such religious experience, and it matters little just how it is inspired. If it were the result of intellectual or moral experience, or the volitional urge and strength to some moral or social good, then the modern mind would be happy enough. But the source of all these states of feeling is in some way the imagination; and even if it is wholly of the imagination, the test of the validity of such religious experience is still the outburst of praise. Ascetically this only means that a three-point meditation, or even a momentary act of recollection, consists of a disciplined arrangement of imagination, intellect, and will; its end is the worship of God, no matter at which point such worship arises. Creative religion is that which moves towards the human perfection and end, the adoration of God. To create is as practical a verb as any modern mind could wish for, yet paradoxically the modern mind which suspects the imaginal in religion does not hesitate to praise the creative artist.[1] Why a symphony issuing from the

[1] See Matthews, *God in Christian Thought and Experience*, p. 211 ff.

imagination should have any greater epistemological value than prayer issuing from the same source is curious. We must examine this more fully.

(b) *Imagination and prayer*

It is well to remind the imaginal-suspicious modern man that all his reason has sprung from ideation, which has in turn sprung from the imaginal; also that if we cannot image what we have not previously sensed, the imagination is rooted in so practical a thing as "ordinary experience", and religion can have little to do with ordinary life without it. As Dr Tennant has written: "Metaphysics has scarcely deigned to discuss the ontological status of the imaginal."[1] This is the root of much modern difficulty, and it is to be hoped that soon some competent metaphysician will so deign.

We must place meditative prayer in its immediate setting of private prayer, then in its proximate setting of the Rule of the Church and finally in its ultimate setting of the corporate Rule of the Remnant. Then, and only then, can we really be prepared to speak of the fruits of the imaginal by which it may be fairly tested. If all members of a parochial Remnant centre their private prayer on imaginative meditation, and if the ultimate result is corporate worship of vicarious significance to a parochial organism, then we need not quibble about epistemological status. If a large audience in a concert hall is engrossed in the Eroica symphony, there is no special need to argue about the metaphysical implications of Beethoven's imagination.

This illustration is important, not only rhetorically but because it meets the modern misuse of the word half-way by suggesting degrees of imaginative worth; the work of a lesser composer might fail such a test yet he could make equal claim for its imaginal source. Meditations, like symphonies, vary in value, and some souls are more competent in the art than others. Upon what do these degrees of imaginative worth depend? Primarily upon conative-faith-venture backed by reason and experience.

Suppose we form a mental image, of, say, a desert island,

[1] *Philosophical Theology*, Vol. I, p. 57.

pear-shaped, with sand and palm trees (a particularly large one near the shore—with a monkey on it, and many yellow and blue parrots). The relation between such an image and any real island is itself non-existent, because there is unlikely to be any such place. No one would "put very much faith in it", the image bears no conative or active interest, it is uncreative. We might paint it or write a story about it, but only after hosts of other imaginal and intellectual experiences; the imagined island *gives* very little.

But an image of, say, Oxford Circus, is rather different. Here there *is* a relation between such an image and a place sensed in a single memorized experience. Not only do we grant Oxford Circus more existence than the desert island, but we "put more faith" in our image of it. Conative activity might stimulate an urge to go there for some real purpose, which is impossible in the case of the desert island. Our image, moreover, is restricted to some extent by memory and reason; we *can* place a palm tree in our Oxford Circus image, but only at the cost of moral and intellectual strains. Somehow it is not really there—even in our minds. We can do just what we like with the island.

If we substitute these images and places by sacramental *persons*, another step is taken. The image of a well-known person who is separated from us, husband, wife, son, daughter, or lover, is fraught with potential conative activity. It is an experience which is governed by all sorts of moral and emotional feelings; the relation between direct visual experience of a person and its corresponding mental image is comparatively slight, since either may make moral and conative demands upon us. The desert island might be described as a passive, and this as an active image. And what is so pertinent, conative activity, emotion, or any other experience of a person can only be mediated through sense-perception, or its later manifestation through memory to the imaginal. For a person to be so known and loved that he is "ever in our thoughts" really means "ever in our imagination"; which is why we stimulate the images of our friends by photographs or symbolic keepsakes.

If we agree that the relation of visual contact and image is fairly close in such a case, then it follows that the relation is closer still when the imaged person is in the next room; and whatever we may think of Berkeley and his followers, the relationship between two people is even closer when one stands before the other with eyes closed. In fact, whether we stand before a person with our eyes closed or our eyes open makes very little difference to our relationship, even "visual" relationship, with him. At least our imagination has taken on a far more creative status than in the case of the desert island.

Plainly the imaginal can be the source of evil emotion and activity as well as being religious—which is why it must take its place in any scheme of ascetical training. And if imagination can play us false, so can visual experience and intellection. But the one significant question here is: What is the epistemological status of a disciplined mental image of God seen in Christ? To think of a person in Australia, communicate by post with someone in Canada, speak to someone in Edinburgh by telephone—all these presuppose imagery. What is the difference if we think of, and speak to, and communicate with, Jesus Christ? If would seem that the faith-venture implied is much the same as the image of our friend present in the next room, or in the same room when our eyes are shut. Or, in different experiential circumstances, the same as communicating with a more distant friend by letter. Admittedly this is to include theology and leave out time, or rather, to take a theological view of a time-eternal sacrament. To introduce theology here may be bad metaphysics yet perfectly consistent with its ascetical branch. The time-eternal sacrament is only the theological basis of our faith in the Presence of a living and glorified Christ in his divine Humanity. To imagine this Presence is no more vain than the "imaging" of present company by a blind man, or the imaging of an absent friend. Just as sense impression precedes a deeper knowledge of persons in social relationships, so the imaged Christ is the only first step to a deeper knowledge of him in prayer. But we can go further than this rather dogmatic insistence on mere faith-venture, and this dogmatic acceptance of a time-eternal relation. To ask what are the implications of time in this context is to ask what are the implications of history. In other words, what is the real difference between our knowledge, gained through imagination, of close friends, of the Prime Minister, of St Teresa—and of our Lord Jesus Christ?

(c) *History and prayer*

"It is doubtful whether life can be significantly lived without conscious relation to some tradition. Those who do live without it live as a kind of moral proletariat, without roots and without loyalties. For to be significant life needs form, and form is the outcome of a quality of thought and feeling which shapes a tradition. The 'practical past' is history co-ordinated by a form of faith."[1] The history of a religion is the history of a group, and a religious group is an evolving, living organism; its history is its (incomplete) life-story; this is its "tradition", and this grows from its "practical past".

In one sense all history, with the possible exception of some scientific types of natural history, is the history of a group— humankind. For this reason the idea of history as a series of isolable events—"brute facts"—is now being replaced by some scheme of selection and interpretation. The question, "What really happened?", is replaced by three questions: "Did this really happen?", "Is it important?", "What does it mean?". This explains the phrase "practical past"—that which not only in fact happened but which has a meaning of practical or present importance. In other words, the "practical past" consists in events which continue to form a living tradition. If a past event continues to have practical meaning, there is a sense in which it is present. History, in truth, is something which begins *now* and forms a wedge back into the past rather than something which once began and continues to unfold. We can say, for example, that the discovery of the internal combustion engine is in one sense an event which happened in the past, but in another sense that "the internal combustion engine has been discovered" is a present statement of a present fact.

An event of importance, interpreted in or by a living organism—what is sometimes called an "interpre-fact"—belongs

[1] D. M. Emmet, *The Nature of Metaphysical Thinking*, p. 163.

to the "practical past" so long as that organism continues to live. My birth is both a past event and a present fact, and within an organic Body such as the Church, so is Calvary. Thus the Crucifixion of our Lord Jesus Christ is an historic event, it really happened on a particular date in the past; but in meditative prayer within this organic Body, it is a present fact. The Crucifixion is a part of the living tradition, the "practical past" of the living group, so we may safely say that an imaged representation of the Cross in mental prayer is concerned with present fact. It is part of the living "character" of the organism, it is here and now shaping this living tradition, in the same way as my writing these words is "solid" with my present "character" and "solid" with my learning the alphabet quite a long time ago.

History then is a wedge, or better, a living stream, going back to certain selected events in the past. And it is made up of three things: the event as historical fact—did it really happen?; the interpretation—what does it mean?; and its selection—was it important and why? This is plainly the process of a discursive three-point meditation: imagination— did it happen?; intellect—what does it mean?; and will— why is it important? or perhaps, what bearing has its importance on my activity as part of an historic organism, the Church? Meditation, therefore, is but a recapitulation of history as "practical past". And this infers some important truths. First, that meditative prayer is only valid within the living organic tradition of the Church, which is another way of saying that it is not isolable from Rule. And the historical documents, selected by the organic Church because of their "importance", are simply dead history outside the organic Church. Secondly, the historical truth of these documents (the New Testament) has some bearing upon the continuing "thought and feeling which shapes a tradition". Here again we find support for the view held in Chapter 7 of this book, that the fundamental interpretation of the Scriptures is "group-meditative". Thirdly, since we are concerned with *living* organisms and *living* traditions, the interpretation of historical events continues. Thus although doctrinal statements on the Atonement are truly part of the living tradition,

mere knowledge of them will never replace the interpretative
questioning demanded by the imaged picture of the events on
Calvary. Doctrine is no substitute for ascetic, or knowledge
for meditation. The full interpretation, meaning, and significance of the Cross is inexhaustible. The young Church—and
we mean, *vide* Bacon, the *young* Church and not the *ancient*
Church—was quite bewildered by Calvary; only after three
days did the interpretative questioning process really begin.
In meditation and worship this interpretative element continues, and only thereby does organic tradition live. And
to-day's meditation is the same process, by the same Organism,
of the same historic event, as the young Church looking on
their dying Lord. Meditation on the Cross by the modern
Remnant is not intrinsically different from the discursive
review of the Twelve on the first Holy Saturday: it is the same
event and the same organism.

We find the whole process of individual meditative experience within, and part of, the organic Church, aptly summarized in a quotation made by Professor Dorothy Emmet from
Professor Hocking: ". . . the history of any group is a corporate questioning process. . . . Now the mystic is a bearer in
his own person of the questioning out of which he was born.
When he joins his community in worship, he joins in its
questioning—for worship when it is alive contains a new
groping of the soul, not a wearing deeper of old ruts. And if he
finds an answer, he must bring it back into the context of the
questioning to which the answer applies. He must vest his
insight in that particular historical campaign."[1] The word
"mystic" is ambiguous, but obviously the statement applies
to any individual experience or interpretation of a meditative
historical scene.

In short, while the Church lives, the events of "importance"
within its tradition—Bethlehem, Calvary, the empty tomb,
Pentecost—can never be past history in the sense of dead
history; and meditative prayer within this tradition constitutes a review and reinterpretation of these events. The
Church's past is "practical past"; the meaning and importance of the meditative image is directly related to the historic

[1] *The Nature of Metaphysical Thinking*, quoted, p. 155.

event; both are re-presented—made present—by living organic tradition.

Fully admitting Christian theology, the mystical body itself transcends the temporal. Because of the Incarnation, the historical events of the Gospel story are possessed of eternal significance, and because the Christian is incorporated into the human nature of Christ by Baptism, he has his share in the eternity of that nature. So meditations by members of the Church truly re-present and re-enact the mysteries of our Lord's incarnate life. The calendar of the Church is an actualization of eternal events and not a bare memorial of historical events.

Historians may well claim present validity and importance for their meditations on the fall of Jericho or the battle of Hastings. Christian devotion is doubly secure. Whatever the epistemological status of the imaginal, meditative prayer within the Church transcends time and such encounter with Christ is in all senses "real".[1]

(4) *Private prayer in the twentieth-century Order*

It is frequently held that the Middle Ages were steeped in a spirituality which we have lost; that progressive prayer and the modern world simply do not mix, and it is useless to be anything but regretful in retrospect. But were the Middle Ages in fact quite so prayerful as is sometimes supposed? Is the modern cultural ethos so completely inconsistent with progressive spirituality? Is there no hope of a new creative adaptation? The answer, as always, is that there are tenable arguments on both sides. What is required here is an emphasis on one or two twentieth-century advantages as a stimulus to the modern soul's faith-venture. Ascetical adaptation of first principles is ultimately made by devout experiment. Let us therefore count some of our blessings.

In the eighteenth century Jethro Tull invented a seed drill which made it possible to sow turnips in rows. The Middle Ages had few root crops and all seed was sown broadcast. The point about rows of roots is that they can first be horse-hoed

[1] See further E. L. Mascall, *Christ, the Christian and the Church*, pp. 115–18.

and then quickly cleaned by hand; the latter work demanding a particular psychological technique. If we watch an experienced farm worker at this job, we find that this psychological technique is remarkably similar to that arising out of monastic prayer process.

The first thing to be noticed is the experienced hand's sense of timelessness; his psychological reaction to a thirty-acre field with quarter-mile rows is no different from his reaction to a square half-acre. He does not, like the novice, keep wondering how long the work will take—except possibly for professional calculations; he does not bother about meal-times, he just works until an almost instinctive sense tells him that it is time to stop. He is continually concerned with "attention to a focal object"—a rather high-sounding name for a turnip perhaps, but it is a turnip not so very different from Dame Julian's hazel-nut or Miss Underhill's ants and alps. These things together add up to a "state of recollection"; we have a soul unified and simplified in attention to an object. And this is borne out by the fact that an experienced farm worker seldom feels tired, and is seldom worried by summer heat, winter cold, or by such extreme physical discomfort as comes from barley awns down his neck or thistle spines in his boots. His senses, however surprised he would be to learn it, are mortified.

This kind of psychological state precedes creative mental prayer. It is little different from the state at which monastic Order purposefully aimed, and the experienced farm-hand has at least this in common with the Saints—that their efficiency will never allow them to hurry. There is no question of nostalgic sentiment about rural craftsmanship here; arts and crafts such as thatching, hedge-layering, horsemanship or for that matter sculpture and painting, are values of spiritual significance because they unify and absorb the whole personality. Hoeing turnips does *not*, it sets the mental processes free by a focus of bodily and sensual attention. A painting may be a meditation in itself, a field of turnips can constitute an effective training ground for meditation.

This agricultural process is necessarily associated with semi-skilled routine work like hoeing, rolling, or harrowing.

The significant work in this respect is the work of disciplined humdrum, in fact, the dull monotony of modern work. And if this applies to turnips and tractors why should it not apply to conveyor-belt work in the factory or painting the Forth Bridge? It would appear that such aspects of modern life possess far more meditative potentiality than anything available to the medieval peasant outside the monastic gate; we have, in fact, a discipline of attention and timeless mortification which had to be artificially created within the monastery. We do indeed need a modicum of religion! We do need volition and conative-faith-venture. But we are still concerned with the Remnant, not the multitude, and we are only interested in showing that the adverse secular circumstances of twentieth-century life are often exaggerated.[1]

The evil influence of the cinema has been proclaimed far and wide—often with more considered vehemence than is directed against the root sins of moral theology. No doubt films, like books and paintings, can be good or bad, and some certainly are immoral. But what of the present fact of the cinema itself? Is not this overwhelmingly favourable to the technique of mental prayer? Meditation was largely invented as a technique for the medieval illiterates who were not sufficiently advanced to say their prayers adequately. The imagination precedes intellection, which accounts for the vivid reality of fairies, cowboys, and Indians in a child's game. We can imagine St Bernard telling his twelfth-century *conversi* to imagine a *picture* of the Cross, or of the stable, or the tomb or of Gethsemane. Such representations were familiar enough—the parish church was probably full of them—but in meditative prayer visual imagery is not enough; the Biblical narratives have got to live and move and speak. Had St Bernard referred to pictures that moved and talked he would have filled his

[1] There is an interesting sidelight here upon the main thesis of this book. The farm worker would be very bewildered were he told that this ascetic-psychological analysis is what happens to him as he "just hoes turnips". He would be equally dumbfounded by all our other ascetical-theological schemes, analyses and so on. But if he *can*—not "understand" it all—but just hoe turnips, there seems no reason why he cannot equally "just pray in the Trinity". And this is only demanding ascetical direction in practice against theological teaching of theory.

audience with utter bewilderment. Whatever the superstitious
credulity of this age, pictures simply did *not* move or talk in
those days; the very idea was the wildest fantasy. To-day the
simple existence of such entertainment can only be valuable,
for the first point of ordinary discursive meditation is but the
direction of a film of a Gospel narrative with the Holy Ghost
as Producer. How many times is this simile used in direction?
And how difficult would direction be without it? The cinema,
whatever its value compared to other forms of dramatic
representation, has the quality of the vivid; if anything it
exaggerates tension, which is all to the good in an age which
is so scared of the divine humanity. Our "I-Thou" encounter
with Christ is so apt to be, in Professor Farmer's phrase,
"unbearably refined". But the humiliation, public flogging,
and sadistic execution of God, are things which cannot come
within such a definition. Whatever the modern demand for
spectacular brutality, a detailed depiction of Julian of
Norwich's fourth revelation, in technicolour, would doubtless
receive an "X" certificate, and it would teach more about
sin than a thousand sermons. And our meditations are to be
true and blunt; we have to face facts.

Again, we are told that prayer is difficult in these days
because of *noise*: that it must have been easy before the
industrial revolution, when everything was so "natural". Was
it, in truth, so easy? Any Londoner who spends a night in a
really isolated farm-house knows very well that if nature
abhors a vacuum, she also hates silence. The Londoner cannot
sleep because of so many little, inconstant, and unpredictable
noises; he prefers the solid roar of the Edgware Road. The
discipline of attention is applicable to sound as well as to
sight. To many, if not to most, prayer is easier when the eyes
are fixed in attention on an object—ant, alp, or hazel-nut—
than when they are closed. That is the principle of hoeing
turnips, and the distractions caused by noise can be avoided
in aural attention to one loud continuing noise. The constant
drone of a tractor in a forty-acre field—row-crop work—is
if anything less distracting than turnips plus the multifarious
little sounds of nature. An eccentric flight of fancy might
visualize a retreat beginning not with "let us now be quiet",

but "turn on the turbine": it would come to very much the same thing—with the latter course possibly more effective. Do we not exaggerate our modern difficulties to the point of pessimistic excuse, even to the sin of despondency?

In general, modern life is highly organized to a fairly rigid pattern. It may be monotonous, but we should remember that it was against the uncreative freedom and muddle of medieval existence that monastic *Order* arose. Like the old orders, we live fairly efficiently to time-tables and we have the unparalleled ascetical advantage of clock-time; it must have been very tiresome to "get up at the eighth hour of the night by reasonable calculation",[1] and highly exacting to decide daily precisely when "daybreak" and "a little after midnight" occurred. Nowadays praying by the clock is everywhere recommended as one of the elements of a constructive prayer-Rule; and this is the kind of true Rule which carries with it immense freedom. To make a self-examination before confession of twenty, thirty, or forty minutes on the advice of our director implies a job efficiently and validly done; the alternative is a timeless conscientious struggle as to whether we have or have not achieved a sufficient self-examination: an intolerable burden. In meditation and all other such things, the conscientious medieval man had always to strain heart, mind, and spirit in more and more monotonous duty, while his less energetic brother was thrown back on the fickle inadequacy of feeling. And here is another example of why monastic *Order*, or detailed minutiae throughout the whole year, was so necessary to the Middle Ages as compared with the present time. If we take ascetical Rule at all seriously, what a wonderful friend a clock can be!

Surely what was the greatest medieval advantage is become the greatest modern curse—not the cinema or amenities for pleasure, or humdrum routine, or mechanization, but *instability*. This is obviously of vital importance to Remnant theology; in the Middle Ages "contemplative harmony in place" was an inevitable corollary to any spirituality. Monastic Order nurtured it to the full, but now it is one more thing dependent on ascetical science rather than practical

[1] *Benedictine Rule*, Chap. viii.

organization. That is an inevitable and by no means unhealthy result of the succession of ages and techniques in a living stream of tradition. So long as people marry and live together in houses ascetical stability is possible; and trends like organized societies, garden-cities, and compact satellite towns point in a direction which justifies restrained optimism.

17

21

THE RULE OF THE REMNANT

THE REMNANT acts as the Body of Christ recapitulated in place; or the local microcosm of the Body of Christ. And the Church militant is the Body of all faithful parishes; immediately of all faithful Remnants. Only by taking such a view can we maintain the corporate relations of individuals which ultimately make up the Body of Christ, *in pastoral practice*. Only such a view can solve the apparent paradox wherein individuals, in relation with other individuals, can add up to a Church which is both theologically and practically—in a word, ascetically—*one* Church. The pastoral solution of the paradox is common Rule, which comprises not only balanced spiritual health, but also a balance between corporate worship and truly private prayer development. The genius of the Christian tradition has developed a Rule which includes all these elements; which gives pastoral expression to the theological fact that the Church is one. In its Anglican form this Rule is as follows:

(i) Mass—on Sundays and Red Letter Days, or more;
(ii) Office—twice daily;
(iii) private prayer—infinitely variable.

But despite the essential variability and freedom of private prayer, there are three fundamental subdivisions:

(*a*) Meditation—in its widest possible sense, which leads into colloquy;
(*b*) self-examination and confession—as the only yardstick of progress;
(*c*) actual recollection.

Such a Rule we claim, is as traditional and orthodox as the

creeds themselves, if only because it is the ascetical equivalent of these creeds and is based on the dogmas contained in them; the Holy Trinity, the Incarnation, the Atonement, and the organic Church; Catholic and Apostolic. This is the essential Rule of the Church, monastic and secular, throughout the ages, however much proportions, methods, systems, orders, and techniques may have varied. The Remnant concept of modern parochial practice demands but one additional sub-section to (iii) above; this is

(*d*) Recollection in *place* and in *community*,

which is the substitute for the "contemplative harmony with environment" inevitable in medieval stability. Again, what was automatically, even unconsciously, gained by rigid monastic Order is now to be achieved by conscious ascetical discipline.

The inference here is that if the Remnant is to be the Remnant and not merely an exclusive élite, it must function in sacramental contact with the parochial organism. The central principle of the Remnant as vicarious must be fact as well as theory; it anticipates ascetical effort rather than a comfortable complacence. It is well to state that any stability of life such as is still implied by, say, the work and obligations of the farmer, farm worker, schoolmaster, postman, policeman, shop-keeper, or housewife in a village or small town community (those, that is, whose home life and work are carried on within the parochial boundary) will attain such sacramental contact as inevitably and naturally as people in the Middle Ages did. But much that is operative in modern life divorces home from work and recreation. This cannot be wholly condemned, for although the necessarily broadening influence of travel is a fallacy, the rigid secular stability of a manor organized on the feudal system created anything but an ideal community. Even St Benedict legislated for "monks going on a journey"—which, presumably, did not do them or their Orders any great harm. But if these modern circumstances are not wholly to be condemned, they create a problem which demands a purposive, clear-cut ascetical answer. This answer is contained in the first form of contemplation, or prolonged acts of the recollection of the presence of God in *place*, as integrated parts of a daily prayer Rule. The contemplation of hazel-nut, ant, or alp, in Christ, can be of vicarious and pastoral significance in proportion as these things are in parochial place and can be experienced as microcosmic of parochial organism. As Julian's hazel-nut recapitulated the world of God's creation, so not only the altar cross but the main street, green, churchyard or central buttercup may recapitulate an organic parochial whole. Strange as it may seem to many, a soul of the Remnant in recollection of the presence of Christ, wandering "aimlessly" down the street or over a meadow, is attaining a vicarious sacramentalism, expressible at the altar, which may be far more creative than it appears.

As St Thérèse of Lisieux said, "To pick up a pin for love can save a soul "—but the environmental circumstances of the pin are of some significance.

The whole principle of recollection is the link between liturgical worship and secular life—though as progress is made the distinction implied in this word diminishes and in the Saints adoration pervades all. Therefore such recollection, however rigidly set within Rule, may very well become expressible in the context of local society: playing cricket for the village or parochial team rather than in the nearby town is of ascetical importance. And it is no contradiction of earlier arguments in this book to suggest that the growing faith of the Remnant will find more and more expression in moral good works. It would be a pity if these were not parochial. It matters little whether we comfort the aged, mind the children, run the tennis club, or mow the churchyard, provided that these activities are the fruits of faith and give glory to God. It is only when such works are pervaded with grim "evangelistic" motives that there is failure.

Furthermore, as the Remnant progresses, so its members, inevitably and unselfconsciously, love one another: that, again, is a fact as irrefragable as the creeds, and if two people —as the result of angry words at the previous night's meeting of the Parochial Church Council—deny this, we must ask them to live to the Rule of the Church under the direction of their priest for twelve months before we argue with them about it. It would also be a pity were this corporate sacramental whole to be enjoying its love wholly outside the parochial boundary. The creativity of the whole Remnant enjoying a quiet, or if need be noisy, session in the local pub is a picture which makes the average youth fellowship look a little pale; and what depths of meaning the word "local" here takes on. Were this preceded by a winning last-wicket partnership by two Remnant members, in the annual blood-match, then indeed the angels would rejoice at Mass to-morrow.

The individual members of the Remnant are called, elected, predestined, by God; it is his choice alone. But we are to make use of circumstances when favourable, and ascetically to conquer them when otherwise. Yet it is worth noticing the good fortune of a parish with a Remnant of a farmer, farm worker, the resident schoolmaster, and the postmistress—perhaps with the publican also, which would make things easier still. And how vitally important is the housewife —not because of her maternal influence, nor her educative or moral powers, but simply in virtue of her ascetically creative *stability*.

Let us now tabulate our completed Rule once more, and consider its practical implications:

(i) Mass—Sundays and Red Letter Days, or more;
(ii) Office—twice daily;
(iii) private prayer—infinitely variable, but including:

    (*a*) meditation (leading to, and including, all colloquy —petition, intercession, etc.),
    (*b*) self-examination and confession,
    (*c*) actual recollection,
    (*d*) recollection in place and community.

At first sight this looks rather formidable; nevertheless it is the standard Rule of the English Church, and if loyalty, obedience, and ascetical doctrine have any meaning at all, then no personal alternative can be substituted for it. This Rule, moreover, is the Church's ascetical interpretation of Christ's absolute demand; which at least supplies worthy incentive to zeal against a convention which makes no demand at all and offers no reward. That this Rule could apply to any but the parish Remnant is preposterous, but can it even apply to them? Christianity, whatever its ideals, is ever reasonable.

The greatest practical difficulty remains with the daily Office, which may well prove too heavy a burden, and is probably out of all proportion to the private prayer of the laity. Our Offices are very long; twenty minutes at Matins followed by ten in meditation and colloquy would be most disproportionate, as would fourteen Offices to one Communion in a ferial week. If the worthy Reformation ideal of a common basis for priestly and lay Rule is to be maintained, both Offices could be—and should be—considerably shortened; the plea already made for "short chapters" would go some way to meet the need.

But in the regrettable absence of serious consideration of the whole subject by authority, some workable compromise between loyalty and practicability becomes possible as soon as the Remnant is accepted as a corporate organism with vicarious inter-relations. A Remnant of six, sharing twelve ferial Offices in terms of one day a week each, would be far more creative than any six individual souls keeping six self-constructed sets of rules. The Book of Common Prayer seems to presuppose private recitation for all but the parish priest, although the injunction that the Office is to be preceded by the tolling of a bell infers the ideal of corporate recitation. This should not be impossible if the Office is given its rightful priority over any other parish business. Once this rather startling fact is accepted, the Rule itself looks less imposing and difficult than it at first appears. In time, the whole Rule requires between five and six hours a week, which is considerably less than the willing laity are wont to give to the multifarious practical activities of the parish. It is not unusual for double this time to be given to clubs, organizations, choir-practice, parish magazines, and so on, while daily Evensong —twelve minutes—is looked on as an impossible burden. It is ideal when the Remnant can participate in these activities, but if personal duties do not permit, we must keep a rigid sense of proportion. The Rule of the Church is the *work* of the

Church; other things, however good, can be left to the second parochial stratum.

The rest of the Rule is as ascetically sound as it is compatible with modern living, so long as we never lose sight of the basic principles of Rule itself; it is always and necessarily the means to an end, but never an end in itself. Rule forms a pattern of spiritual life to be embraced rather than promised, and although any of the capital sins may breach it, the breaking of Rule is not sin in itself. Rule embraced and occasionally broken—even through pride or sloth—is very different from a most Prayerful life without Rule at all. And as soon as we introduce corporate vicariousness, we allow for a variability which should cover almost any particular parochial circumstances.

Whatever parochial variations are allowed, we have here the basic Rule of our Church, which is an authoritative, creative, and definite ascetical composition; that it makes a real demand on the faithful is neither surprising nor discouraging. Any worthwhile endeavour demands discipline; but compare, for example, the following, picked at random from a hundred such:

Some rules for Lent

(1) Attend church at least once every Sunday.
(2) Attend the Holy Communion service more often.
(3) Attend a weekday service regularly.
(4) Spend longer at daily prayers than usual.
(5) Forgo some pleasure and give what you save for the work of the Church.
(6) Perform acts of thoughtfulness and kindness which cost something in time and trouble.

Comment in detail would be superfluous. Such rules are entirely unbalanced, vague, poisonously personal, generally negative, and possibly dangerous. It would be possible to keep such a set of rules for ten years without moving an inch Godward, without having the slightest Christian influence on anyone or anything, and with little chance of avoiding pride, legalism, and Pelagianism. And the burden would be more onerous than the Rule of the Church pastorally applied.

The tragedy is complete when we realize that with little more than alternative wording, these rules could become:

Rule

(1), (2) Mass on Sundays and Red Letter Days.

(3) Regular Offices.

(4) Private prayer under direction:

    (a) mortification, purgation, and recollection;

    (b) self-examination by moral theology.

And this is not so very far from the full Rule of the Church.

22

SYNOPSIS AND CONCLUSION

THIS INQUIRY began by insisting that the pastoral function is concerned with *religion*, which, although crystallizing into theology, remains a *sui generis*, and therefore an indefinable, term. But we describe religion as verbal, i.e., as a fundamental activity, and the strange verb "actively-to-religion" may be translated "to Pray". The science of Prayer we call ascetic, which evolves from dogmatic theology—thus ascetic may be defined as "applied" dogmatic. But Prayer is of both individual and corporate significance; ascetic applies both to personal Prayer-process and to relations within Christian society (parochial theology). And the whole Christian process is tested by moral theology. (Chapter 1.)

The central function of pastoral priesthood concerns religion rather than theology, or in personal terms, faith ("conative-faith-venture") against belief. So the core of pastoral practice is not teaching or even evangelism, but ascetical direction—correctly interpretated. (Chapter 2.)

We have been forced to criticize a one-sided individualism in much modern ascetical thought. Christianity is social, and its traditional ascetic is rooted in corporate order. We must therefore bring some form or pattern into parochial relationships, to provide a setting for individual prayer-process. To achieve this we need first to understand the meaning of the term "cure of souls". (Chapter 3.)

Having considered three possible interpretations of the term, we conclude that it is only valid to look upon a parish as a sacramental *organism* embracing both the *function*, "cure of souls", and the *place*, parish. (Chapter 4.)

Our first need, before we consider the questions of pastoral ascetic, is to formulate a systematic parochial theology in which to set it. We introduce the *Remnant concept*, which we claim passes the tests of practicability, orthodoxy in theology, and historical tradition. Part One of this work is concerned with substantiating these claims. The Remnant concept is concerned with the real religion, progressive and creative, of those souls within the parish (it makes no difference if there are two or two thousand) who are vocationally elected by God to his Church. But the notion of organism will have nothing to do with an exclusive élite, we can be concerned with nothing less than the whole parish and the complete cure of souls. The concepts of vicarious spirituality, of the parish as the Catholic Church in microcosm, and of the "sacramental contagion" of adoration in "contemplative harmony with place" are deduced from the key doctrine of the Church as the Body of Christ. (Chapter 5.)

This parochial pattern is suggested, illustrated, and confirmed by our Lord's example (Chapter 6), and by the New Testament interpreted as a devotional manual: that is, group-meditatively (Chapter 7). The history and theology of the Apostolic Church suggests the parochial Remnant as its pastoral norm. What is glibly called missionary work in its popular sense is a true part of the Church's work; but this may be regarded as a divinely sanctioned deviation from the norm rather than the norm itself. (Chapter 8.)

But the most potent missionary force remains the adoration of God by the Remnant in place. The truth of this is best demonstrated by monasticism, which is by far the greatest historical example of the Remnant concept. Is it so impressive as to be the only answer to modern religion? Contrary to popular misconception, the monastic ideal presupposes the closest possible relation with the secular world consonant with its separate existence, and this is precisely the same ideal as that expressed in Remnant parochialism. But there remains one important distinction in the initial ventures of the two concepts: traditional monachism begins with an heroic flight from the world, thence a gradual return towards secular life. The Remnant begins with secular life in an attempt to lift it above irreligious secularism. (Monastic history supplies one example of the latter (Remnant) process in St Gilbert of Sempringham.) Two points are given special emphasis in this portion of our inquiry: first, the essential medievalism of monastic Order in its traditional form, i.e., the vast *secular* distinction between the life of the thirteenth and twentieth centuries, for example. And secondly, the theological difficulties involved in the monastic flight—the gradual slackening of ideals and the practical difficulty of arresting this process before complete secularity is reached. (Chapter 9.)

If monasticism is the specific form of the Remnant during the Middle Ages, the seeds of a progressive move away from it are discernible long before the sixteenth-century Reformation; and this movement became the orders of friars. Parallel to this process, the whole conception of ascetic was changing; from its roots in the practical minutiae of monastic *Order* it was evolving into a modern ascetical *science*. This points to the conclusion, startling to modern minds, that ascetic, embracing such things as mental prayer, Rule, discipline, purgation, mortification, etc., is not peculiar to monachism but rather constitutes its true successor. Ascetic is the modern secular alternative to monastic Order. This evolution is traceable from St Bernard to St Ignatius Loyola; and by an unfortunate historical accident the English Reformation came in between. (Chapter 10.)

Disastrous results followed when, of two evolving strands of tradition, English religion followed, or subconsciously clung to, that leading to rationalism, deism, and the form of evangelism which is interpreted as mere recruitment. The eighteenth and nineteenth centuries form the only period in Christian history when Multitudinism abounded and the Remnant concept was completely thrown over; and this era saw English religion at its lowest ebb. Nevertheless, the seeds of true religion remained buried and fertile; and a gradual improvement is discernible from the start of the Oxford Movement until to-day. By another regrettable accident of history, this doctrinal revival was followed by an immediate interest in liturgy rather than by the rediscovery of ascetic. In spite of this, much modern pastoral custom is traceable to the eighteenth and nineteenth centuries and to no other source. (Chapter 11.)

We conclude our study of the Remnant concept with reference to the increasing reputation of natural theology rightly interpreted. (Chapter 12.)

Central to our thesis is the tenet that an "individual" Christian is a contradiction in terms, or at least an abstraction. Ascetics, as the science of the prayer process of single souls, therefore demands a consideration of parochial theology (Part One) as its essential prolegomena. Only thereafter are we justified in dealing with such a prayer process; this is the subject matter of Part Two. As an introduction to this subject we confine ourselves to *pastoral* ascetic, i.e., to its most elementary principles consonant with normal pastoral practice. The traditional ascetical ethos of the Catholic tradition is accepted. But fundamental questions remain, such as the relations between spiritual progress and spiritual health, between art and science, or perhaps risk and safety, in direction, and the ambiguities contained in the classical spiritual "hierarchies". (Chapter 13.)

We are also confronted with the great problem of "religious experience", but a large measure of practical clarity is attained when pure psychology is applied. (Chapter 14.)

This approach also helps to create an elementary natural, and so a sub-Christian, ascetic which is demanded by pastoral theology. (Chapter 15.)

We continue to trace progress from the initial stirrings of real religion—the first form of contemplation—to Christian maturity, by examining both the traditional ascetic of St Ignatius Loyola and the modern religious psychology of the school of Professor James Ward. This results in the conclusion that these attitudes are in complete agreement. Four distinct stages of development then appear from this synthesis. The order of these four stages is generally reversed in modern pastoral practice. (Chapter 16.)

We have now reached Christian maturity in the sense of truly Christian as distinct from sub-Christian spirituality; but if this is the end of a journey from natural religion to Christianity, it is only the beginning of the journey towards sanctity in Christ. From now on things are simplified, because pastoral direction need concern itself only with maintaining spiritual health; God alone gives the increase. The simplest ascetical scheme is based on the application of the Church's central dogma—God the Holy Trinity. If need be this can be elaborated into the five or six elements contained in a worthy conception of God as analysed by Professor Farmer. By studying various combinations of emphasis and omission within this analysis, certain fundamental spiritual diseases are diagnosed. (Chapter 17.)

The cure for all these diseases—or the general safeguard of spiritual health—is now seen to be contained in *the* (orthodox and traditional) *Rule of the Church*. But only when the three parts of this Rule *are used and interpreted ascetically*. These three parts are (1) the Office (Chapter 18), (2) the Eucharist (Chapter 19), and (3) private prayer (Chapter 20).

Pastoral practice is frequently found *not* to interpret this Rule either in its integral wholeness or as ascetically creative.

When this traditional ascetical Rule—on the surface orthodox to the point of dullness—is set within Remnant parochialism it emerges as the Rule of the Remnant, with but one small additional sub-section to (iii)—"private" prayer. And this addition is necessary as an ascetical solution to the modern religious problem of instability. (Chapter 21.)

SUPPLEMENTARY NOTES

SUPPLEMENTARY NOTES

1. PERSONAL RELATIONS IN PASTORAL PRACTICE

The Remnant concept raises a series of questions of relationship to which modern Anglicanism seems to have no adequate answer. We must be content, for the present, to pose some of these queries and hope that continuing thought and experience will eventually solve them.

Much is said and written about the priest-penitent or director-directed relation, but—like the generality of modern ascetic—it tends to assume "advanced" souls seeking out "specialist" directors: both presupposing extreme individualism.

I have argued in favour of a right priestly professionalism, a sane other-worldliness and detachment from vocational and other personal interests, but as soon as direction is accepted as the normal, everyday pastoral activity on an elementary, even sub-Christian level, within *local* organism, we must ask if the prevailing convention of cold, impersonal, austere respectability, does not need a certain modification. In view of our Lord's example at Cana, his relation with the beloved disciple, the family of Bethany and above all with Magdalene, I must be bold to ask whether our modern convention is not a little over-refined. The Church has always insisted upon her children's right of free choice of confessor and-or director, which alone suggests that—with all warning against the horrors of a wrong personal attachment—it admits to the existence of a right personal relation. Even St Teresa not only admits the pastoral fact, but writes of this relation in terms which seem, at first sight, strangely out of character.[1] The point is that however well the prevailing convention suits the advanced soul, the would-be penitent and the potential

[1] *Way of Perfection*, Chapter IV.

18

Remnant soul need a little more warmth and a little full-bodied Love. And fearful as we seem to be of this misused word, it remains, in this context, the only adequate one.

It is plain therefore that a Christian's confessor, director, and parochial incumbent may be one, two, or three priests. When all these are embodied in a single man the position is straightforward, but this may not, and need not, be the case. So soon as we admit both ascetical and parochial *pattern*, we confront an intricate series of relations and loyalties comparatively new to Anglicanism. A director may suggest Holy Communion twice weekly as part of balanced Rule, while the circumstances of a parish may demand it once or three times. Or a soul may embrace a Lenten Rule which strains its capacity to the safest possible limit, only to hear on Quinquagesima that Fr X is giving a series of meditative addresses which all the faithful are requested to attend. By my favourite analogy, a cricket coach may rightly advise a boy to concentrate on defence rather than scoring strokes, while the circumstances of an actual match may cause his captain, equally rightly, to give opposite instructions. A young fast bowler may be advised by both coach and doctor to bowl no more than ten overs at a time, but his captain may not unfairly make a greater demand at a critical stage of a match.

In current practice, either the laity please themselves or the problems are solved by a series of gentlemen's agreements. But if parochial theology is taken at all seriously, this and kindred problems could be very real ones, and some authoritative statement would be welcome.

2. PASTORAL REORGANIZATION

We very frequently hear that the parochial system is breaking down. If this were so, any pastoral approach that centres around parochial theology, local organism, and "harmony with place" would be futile. But the statement is misleading; what is usually meant is that a particular parochial system with which we are familiar is giving way to a new one. If the Diocesan Bishop is fundamental to Christian doctrine and practice—*ubi episcopus, ibi ecclesia*—it can hardly mean anything else. However, the position raises new pastoral problems which accentuate rather than lessen the need for the Remnant system.

In rural districts the old ideal of one priest to one (secular) parish or village has broken down. The problems of plurality are with us, but this also is an ambiguous term. The real problem and the real danger, I suggest, is not plurality but duality; and that the latter is slowly giving way to the (literal) former is helpful to this thesis. For when two villages are held in plurality (i.e., in duality) the parochial-theological position is an impossible one; it implies not only the complete Rule of the Church duplicated daily by the incumbent, but also the ascetical achievement of a vicarious "harmony" with two, possibly quite different, parochial organisms at once: all of which is equivalent to being married to two wives with two families and two households. But as soon as the plurality, or duality, becomes a single united benefice the position is saved; theologically we are but re-drawing the boundaries of one parish. Practical difficulties doubtless remain, but my insistence is that plurality, united benefices, conventional districts, and chapels of ease are not matters of mere practical convenience but of the deepest theological import. So, in practice, a literal plurality, that is a union of six or eight small villages, makes the Remnant concept more workable than any other system: two villages will ever remain, in practice, two villages, whereas eight become one area or district, or, theologically, one parish.

If such an area is served by a clerical staff concentrated in the central church, we are returning to something like the Cistercian abbey-grange system.

The urban problem is that the ascetical unit of contemplative harmony is the town rather than the parish; it is simpler to achieve a vicarious relation with, and pray *for*, say, "London" than for "the conventional district of St Mark in the parish of St Luke, Hampstead North". The latter only exists as an ecclesiastical unit of convenience and has no being as a social, political, or commercial unit. It is possible to "know", "love", or "feel at home in", London, Cambridge, or Liverpool, rather than a characterless group of streets. But this does not impair the Remnant concept as truly parochial;

I have never championed the cause of truly narrow parochialism; it is absurd to suggest that purposeful Recollection of Christ in place stops as soon as we reach the parish boundary. Dr E. L. Mascall makes the interesting suggestion that the fullest expression of Christian unity is not a crowded church at parish communion but rather twelve little groups around twelve priests at twelve altars in one church; all doing the same thing.[1] Thus the Remnant achieves perhaps its ultimate consummation when twenty close-knit groups worship in twenty churches in one town, and all are in a vicarious relation with that one total town.

Here it is worth noting that monachism, following St Basil, has always thought in terms of *ideal* numbers in community, as an ascetical unit; about thirty. And as soon as that number is attained, the surplus is sent to establish a daughter house. This is perhaps not unlike our policy of conventional districts in new housing estates. The important point is that Christian tradition has something to say against the view that the ideal congregation is necessarily the largest.

3. CHURCH FINANCE

It is stated with varying degrees of seriousness that if we lose our congregations we lose our parish income. If ever there were a case of the cart being put in front of the horse it is surely here. If a congregation ever really exists to save the parish bank balance, it can matter little whether either exists at all. The Remnant system has nothing at all to do with losing congregations; ultimately it claims to be the orthodox method of increasing them. But there are more serious problems which the Remnant claims to solve.

To-day so much Church money comes from extraneous sources. We are always hearing of men and women who seem quite willing to "support" the local church but who will not come to its services. When such donations are seen as justifying works—as occasionally they must be—we are not far from the pernicious associations of indulgences. All the work

[1] *Corpus Christi*, pp. 164 ff. Dr Mascall's remarks here also add a most illuminating confirmation of our theories of vicarious recapitulation and parochial microcosm.

for the bazaar, fête, or sale of work, if undertaken by any but the Remnant, is Pelagian through and through; or so it would seem. But if the parish is an organic whole we are not justified in speaking of particular men and women as isolable units at all; individuals may give alms, or raise funds in whatever way they like, when in and through the Remnant the organic parish is recapitulated. We are reminded of St Paul's hopes for the pagan wife of a Christian husband; if the twain are one flesh the husband in Christ brings the wife into Christ; the one is sanctified in the other. So with the heathen almsgiver: either such monies are "unclean" and to be rejected out of hand, or all is sanctified in the Remnant—the faithful spouse.

Any unorganic or numerical system either cannot avoid the taint of something like indulgences or it must seek to apply a kind of spiritual means test to every donor and every money-raising work. It is important that the vicarious doctrine be widely disseminated; that it should be clearly understood that the Remnant does in fact recapitulate and serve all. Only then is all money and all work acceptable, not as an indulgence or as justifying works, but in the sense in which all pay dues to support a police force which in turn serves all vicariously. Justification, if any, then applies not to the work of the donor, or helper, but to his faith or the faith of the Remnant Church. But I would suggest that in practice the idea of indulgence or buying justification is rare; the good people in question are either bewildered, conventional, or a little embarrassed by their "support" for the church. With due allowance for the pride of individualism, I feel that the vicarious idea would be acceptable, and that the appeal for a church which does and is serving the whole would be well and healthily supported. In fact it possibly *is* the vague general notion behind much almsgiving, but much could be gained if it were more clearly formulated and understood.

4. THE SHORTAGE OF CLERGY

So far as the present problems are concerned, little need be said about the obviously far-reaching implications of Remnant doctrine upon this question. Suffice it to say that as soon as we stop thinking entirely in numerical terms, whole new vistas of pastoral and parochial thought open before us. As an extreme example, the plain inference of Note 2 above is that a priest with two assistants would find a plurality of two tiny villages with no Remnant theologically impossible, whereas it would be *possible* for him to be Vicar of Greater London. Such an exaggeration at least points to the possibility of a far greater creative economy of clerical man-power by a pastoral reorganization on Remnant lines. And the prevailing system of numerical assessment appears as the most inefficient of all.

But much more pertinent is the reason for the shortage itself. Many extraneous causes are suggested—notably the financial position—but we are already committed to the view that when any profession or calling is forced to recruiting propaganda, there is something internally wrong with the job itself.

Now the young man of true vocation is not interested in popularity, adulation, or even respect. He does not worry very much if his work is unknown to the populace or misunderstood by his friends; but he might possibly wish to know precisely what it is himself. The current idea of some chaotic admixture of preaching, teaching, evangelism, visiting, study, sociology, good works, tea-parties, and youth work, just is not a job at all. I suggest that pastoral practice itself, or rather its lack of clear pattern, frustrates vocation more than any other circumstance.

Compare for example, the priest of fiction with the doctor, farmer, solicitor, or scientist of fiction; these latter, whatever their character, have *jobs*, whilst the priest is at best a professional educated gentleman. Who can recall, off-hand and between the trivialities, "parish matters", and pious clichés, a fictional priest on his knees, at the altar, or in the confessional? We must claim sufficient sense of humour and just enough humility not to mind this very much, but the argument that our Lord was mocked and so we must not mind being ridiculed has all the dangers of proud mock-modesty. And this idea does not nurture vocation.

A Christian novelist like Miss Sayers could do great service by depicting a priest who is a "professional Prayer" or even a director of souls. We do not want eulogies or heroes—nor ordained detectives like Father Brown—but the minor character of a parson who is really a priest. With all respect to one who should, and in fact does, know better, Mr Venables of Fenchurch St Paul and the country parson in *Busman's Honeymoon* are not very inspiring. We might even hope that one day the opening gambit with the Vicar is something else than "Do you get a good congregation, Sir?" One does not begin polite conversation with the doctor with, "Have you a nice lot of patients?"

I suggest that instead of vague propaganda we might define the work in terms of Prayer as a life, and direction as a skilled trade. If the hero of the school story scores the winning goal with a broken leg, Prayer can also *hurt*. Practical difficulties are not to be belittled; in all senses Priesthood demands great sacrifice, but it must be worth while and it must be definite.

5. CHRISTIAN UNITY

However great the difficulty or remote the prospect, the practical reunion of Christendom must be sought by all possible means. But there is a mystical unity of the Body of Christ which schism cannot violate nor human pride impair. In all our struggles for reunion, this tremendous fact is generally accepted as a comforting theory, made the ground of an eschatological hope, and then shelved as of little practical relevance.

The Remnant Concept offers a contribution to the problem in that it sees this mystical unity as the very heart of the matter, and seeks to give it ascetical—that is, practical—expression. The recapitulation of all within the vicarious Remnant translates the pure doctrine of unity into applied doctrine; it places a hopeful theory on the basis of practical Prayer, which may prove more creative than theological debate or sentimental tolerance. In claiming to be the Catholic Church in England, wherein *all* are vicariously served and contained by parochial Remnants, we not only state a fact, but act in a venture of faith in that fact. Certain other religions and denominations may not like this idea, but there need be no active provocation. There need be none of the bitterness aroused by direct attack nor yet the sterility of a misplaced and insincere tolerance. The Remnant can offer all charity to all and quietly get on with its job.

But we must be firm in imputing pride to any who bluntly refuse the Prayer of the Remnant on their behalf, while for my part I would freely and gladly go out to meet and accept all other Prayer as contributory to the whole spiritual ethos of God's world. The fruit of the Prayer of, for example, Mahatma Gandhi, is of irrefragable power, and I have neither wish nor reason to deny it, because I have found no conflict between first and second order Divine activity. For this reason we may give place in the whole redemptive process to the social work of the Salvation Army or the evangelism of Dr Billy Graham, without disloyalty to our own theological position. If these wish to argue with us we must stand firm on our dogma; if they do not we claim a mutual interrelation and suggest we get on quietly with our respective jobs.

I do not put forward the Remnant as panacea for all our ills, but I suggest that all *religious* problems are most likely to be solved by *religion*; that is by ascetic rather than argument. At least the Remnant offers something immediately practicable in terms of faith-venture, and within its context, unity does not necessarily mean uniformity.

6. PASTORAL VISITATION

Visiting people in their homes may be inspired by one of three motives. First, as blunt recruitment, which I must oppose; "a visiting parson makes a churchgoing people" is either luckily false or regrettably true. Secondly, it is suggested that the purpose of visiting is to show that the Church cares for people and to offer the love of Christ to all for whom he died. Admirable as this sentiment is, I must claim that the Remnant concept is a far truer method of achieving it; always realizing that Prayer must issue in works of charity, especially towards the sick and distressed. But so long as we think numerically, we must visit all or none, and, to undertake such a task as central to priesthood is to squeeze out nine-tenths of our ordination vows.

When the parish is seen as organic, a third motive presents

itself; the necessary achievement of "contemplative harmony in place". Vicariousness demands a sacramental contact with the parochial whole equal to our Lord's union with the world. Here access to people and places, and sympathy with them, takes on a new importance, but it matters little *how* it is achieved. Visiting may well play its part, so may cricket on the green, darts in the pub, or the recollection of the presence of Christ in the post office: none of these things needs pages of serious study in books on pastoral theology.

If visiting is equated with true evangelism in the missionary sense, we must first ascertain if the priest or layman concerned has the necessary direct missionary vocation. This implies the gift of direct appeal; direction of souls and the achievement of contemplative harmony demand rather a self-effacing reticence. Visiting may play a part in both of these approaches, but it is important to know precisely what we are aiming at. Plainly both are truly missionary, though different in method, and it is significant that many an African mission station is far nearer to Remnant ideals than a great deal of activity at home. For such missionary venture consists primarily not in visiting but in planting the *Church* within areas where the Faith is as yet unknown. The majority of Anglican overseas missions regard the establishment of such mission stations as the first requisite of preaching the Gospel to every creature; this is precisely the Remnant position. Christianity in England is in danger of so stressing even true evangelism that it divorces it from the adoration of the Remnant Church which is the ultimate source of spiritual power.

INDEX

Abelard, 83

Adoration, 31ff., 67, 71ff., 127, 139f., 171, 211, 231, 256

Alvarez de Paz, 5n.

Amos, 22

Andrewes, L., 104

Anthony, St, 76

Anthropomorphism, 197, 224

Apocalyptists, 35

Apollinarianism, 29f., 85, 88, 96 195

Apostolate, 59, 62–5

Arianism, 195, 224

Aristotle, 198

Ascetical theology, *passim*, 8–12, 98, 179, 223; both corporate and individual, 6ff., 133ff., 186f., 248, 255; and dogmatics, 5ff., 78, 108, 112, 131ff., 184ff., 255; and monasticism, 76, 88ff., 93f., 96, 98ff., 102ff., 142ff., 186f., 257; and moral theology, 6, 57, 110f., 160ff., 203f.; and natural religion, 165–76; in New Testament, 31ff., 43ff., 59, 86, 104; and pastoral practice, 6, 102f.; and psychology, 149ff., 177ff.; as science, 76ff., 103, 131ff., 230–2; and stability, 246–7

Attrait, 73, 95, 128, 175, 208, 218, 226, 230ff.

Augustine of Canterbury, St, 61n.

Augustine of Hippo, St, 65f., 137, 165, 171

Bach, J. S., 199

Bacon, F., 241

Baker, A., 100ff., 209–17, 228ff.

Baptismal controversy, 65

Barth, K., 195, 232

Basil, St, 78–81, 266

Basilides, 125

Beethoven, L. van, 236

Belief, 5, 9, 107f.; *see also* Faith, Tennant

Benedict, St, 10, 61, 78–81, 86ff., 96–102, 114, 209, 212n., 246ff.; *see also* Rule

Benson, R. M., 205

Berkeley, Bp, 109, 120, 238

Bernard of Clairvaux, St, 54, 73, 81–91, 96f., 165, 184, 257; and Abelard, 83; his allegory, 86, 97; and Apollinarianism, 85, 88, 96; his *De Diligendo Deo*, 85, 164; and the "double standard", 84; and meditation, 85, 96, 244

Bicknell, E. J., 9, 58

Bonaventure, St, 201

Bossuet, J. B., 110

Bouquet, A. C., 67n.

Bowman, J. W., 33–5, 38, 70f.

Box, H. S., 131n.

Bradley, F. H., 18, 109, 141

Bruno, Fr, 77

Butler, Bp, 85

Calvin, J., 65f., 197f.

Cambridge Platonists, 110

Canons regular, 92, 95

Carmelites, 6, 13, 84f., 99, 103, 114, 142, 187, 231

Carthusians, 81, 114

Cassian, 77

Cathari, 94

Celsus, 54

Cerinthus, 125

Chamoisy, Mme, 13

Christ: adoration of, 31f., 45, 54; Baptism, 30, 33ff.; boyhood, 30f.; as director of souls, 9, 31, 37ff., 43–59, *passim*; as healer,

Made in the USA
Monee, IL
09 April 2021

65284037R00164